Dancing Naked

Breaking Through the Emotional Limits that Keep You from the Job You Want

Robert C. Chope, Ph.D.

New Harbinger Publications, Inc

Publisher's Note

This publication is designed to provide accurate and authoritative information in regard to the subject matter covered. It is sold with the understanding that the publisher is not engaged in rendering psychological, financial, legal, or other professional services. If expert assistance or counseling is needed, the services of a competent professional should be sought.

Distributed in the U.S.A. by Publishers Group West; in Canada by Raincoast Books; in Great Britain by Airlift Book Company, Ltd.; in South Africa by Real Books, Ltd.; in Australia by Boobook; and in New Zealand by Tandem Press.

Copyright © 2000 by Robert C. Chope
New Harbinger Publications, Inc.
5674 Shattuck Avenue
Oakland, CA 94609

Cover design by Blue Design
Cover photos by © TSM/Torleif Svensson, 1999, and
   Novastock/Index Stock Imagery
Edited by Heather Garnos
Text design by Tracy Marie Powell

Library of Congress Catalog Card Number: 99-75280
ISBN 1-57224-184-5 Paperback

New Harbinger Publications' Web site address: www.newharbinger.com

02   01   00
10   9   8   7   6   5   4   3   2   1
First printing

To Robert and Dorothy Chope

Contents

Part 3
Handling Your Emotions during Your Career Search

Part 4
Staying on Track

Preface

This book is perhaps the most important—and unique—career book that you will read during your career search. You won't find formats for résumés, cover letters, reference letters, and portfolios. Instead, I'll show you how the change process you are going through is affected by your emotional experiences. After all, emotions color the process every step of the way—and those emotions can block you from being effective in the various stages of the job search.

Looking for a job is a lot like learning to dance. You need to know the basics, and then, as you get more proficient, you need to learn a variety of new moves. Learning new steps can be difficult, but it can also be fun.

The job search, like dancing, can expose you to all sorts of emotional baggage that can get in the way of your activities. Your history, your feelings, your barriers, and your ideas about yourself come bubbling to the surface . . . and there you are on the dance floor, feeling naked. This book will teach you how to handle your emotional issues and will show you how, at times, you can use them to your advantage.

Based on my work as a psychologist over the past twenty years, I think that the emotional aspects of the career search are the most important but still uncovered issues that remain. Yet until now, there has not been a career search book that has emotional challenge as the primary focus. Whether you're troubled by doubt, fear, anger, by real or imagined barriers, your emotional state of mind needs to be addressed during the search.

In this book, I've attempted to cover the most common career search experiences. Each chapter addresses different job-search issues and exposes the emotional challenges they bring. There is advice on what to do with particular problems, as well as a focus on how to maintain physical and psychological wellness as you put your body through the grueling dance of the career search.

The text is filled with examples from my experience as a career psychologist, with details changed in order to hide the identity of my clients. I have found that many of the issues discussed here are rarely talked about. How often, for example, do people find themselves in careers that they never really wanted, living their parents' dreams, but not their own? How many people are frozen in fear because the jobs they have held for many years may be in jeopardy due to an impending corporate takeover? How many newcomers to the job market are terrified of the prospect of a lifetime filled with job changing? How many middle-aged people, looking for work, feel panicky that the rapidly changing job market doesn't have a place for them? How often does fear of public speaking keep someone from a good job performance rating? And how many people find that their anger keeps them from advancing?

These are the kinds of issues that are addressed in this book. While they may be discussed in the privacy of a psychology office, they are rarely even mentioned in other career books. Yet they are the issues that seem to be on everyone's mind.

There are many people who have helped with the project but none have been more involved than my colleague and partner Roberta Ann Johnson, Ph.D., from the University of San Francisco. I am eternally grateful for her love and patience. She kept the project on track and relinquished large portions of her own research and publication time to read the text and listen to new ideas. My children Jeff and Luisa provided the important ingredient of enthusiasm. Edna Arbetman, who worked with me for almost twenty years at the Career and Personal Development Institute in San Francisco, suggested to Matt McKay that I write this book. Matt was my initial contact at New Harbinger, and pulled me along through the early stages. Other New Harbinger staff who worked on the project include Heather Garnos, Farrin Jacobs, Donna Latte, and Tracy Powell.

Most of all, I would like to thank my clients, whose career issues allowed me to delve into this area and my students in the Department of Counseling at San Francisco State University. They helped carry this distinctly psychological career counseling style forward, long before it was fashionable to do so.

PART 1 | Managing Your Career Change

1 | What to Expect When Making a Career Change

You know what my strong advice to you is?
Think of yourself as superior in some way!

—Jim O'Connor in *The Glass*
Menagerie by Tennessee Williams

Do You Think You Need This Book?

There are lots of books about career change, and you're undoubtedly familiar with some of them. This book has a different approach, one that will help to free you up emotionally and psychologically to be the best career searcher that you can be. Most career counselors leave emotional issues to psychiatrists, psychologists, and therapists. But, for those of you who are transitioning, the emotional area may be key, because the career search probably feels a bit emotionally chilly or even unfriendly. This book can serve as a companion text to help you deal with personal issues like nervousness, fear, frustration, and anxiety. You can use a special journal or notebook as a place to record your thoughts, as well as your responses to the exercises in this book.

The majority of job seekers need to be nudged a little— maybe even two or three times. Perhaps you don't feel so marketable right now. Or you may feel that you have yet to reach your full potential. Some of you may have summitted the career track roller coaster and feel that you're free falling down the other slope. Maybe you feel blocked by other emotional barriers. And some of you may just feel that you're unable to break loose, to dance freely. This book is for all of you.

How Can You Use This Book?

This book can guide you, but, really, change is up to you, and it will take more than a little planning. You must actively seek out and discover new directions for yourself. This book is not directly a healer or a teacher, but you might want to think of it as a consultant who will help to emotionally unblock you, motivate you, shield you a bit, and ignite your creativity. I recommend that you keep a personal journal in which to do the exercises. This can also be a place to log thoughts, feelings, and ideas as you read along.

Career Change Is Inevitable

Like it or not, you'll experience numerous career transitions in your lifetime. It's impossible to avoid. Not long ago, career counselors thought that you'd go through four or five changes in your career. The current thinking is that you'll go through seven or eight. Take Suzanne. She's only thirty-three, has an English degree from an excellent school, and already has had four different careers: print journalist, radio news announcer, business writer, and public relations specialist. Now she's considering applying to law school.

Desperately Seeking Familiarity

Career change, difficult enough on its own, happens in a marketplace that is changing at breakneck speed. Even with an expanding U.S. economy, there's more turmoil than ever in the job world. In a global, interdependent economy, institutional change and growth are rapid. Some of us are also "wired" to new, innovative job choices as our communication capabilities become "wireless." But even with all our technological advances, the average American's full-time work week is a daunting 47 hours, according to the Families and Work Institute.

In an atmosphere of constant change, it's not surprising that anxiety and fear about job security continue to increase for both blue-collar and white-collar workers. Do new, mysterious job titles make you feel like you can't get a foothold? When you see companies swallow each other up, do you feel like you won't find a workplace that will feel safe? Are you puzzled by the rise of companies manufacturing high-tech products that you don't understand? Consider all of the changes that are taking place around you and how they affect the way that you envision your career.

The bottom line is that mergers cost people jobs. Unemployment figures are down, but layoffs are certainly up. The *Baltimore Sun* reported that in 1998, U.S. companies cut nearly 575,000 jobs, the highest number since 1993. Researchers at San Francisco State University mark the figure at closer to 678,000. While corporate mergers often merely realign the wealth of top executives, other workers, caught in the middle, fear they'll lose their jobs if higher-ups perceive a duplication of effort. If you've experienced a corporate coupling then you know that it usually leads to extra work, feelings of disorientation, frustration, and even a new corporate culture.

Layoffs Abound

There is, of course, instability in all sectors. Layoff is always a palpable threat, and there is overwhelming evidence that layoffs are a common instigator of frustration and violence in the workplace. (That's been well chronicled since the Great Depression.) There is no gender discrimination here either: Women who lose their jobs are six times more likely to exhibit violent, aggressive behavior than are women who keep their jobs.

Furthermore, consulting groups have reported that new companies don't necessarily place workers in the proper roles in the first six months after a merger. At newly coupled companies, managers often don't take much time and energy to evaluate new staff. Some roles, particularly at the highest levels, are well structured and defined. But those at the median and lower levels may not be.

A Whole New World

New workplace landscapes abound. New, unfamiliar, sometimes frightening paradigms are everywhere. Physicians and other health-care professionals must face new relationships with insurance carriers and an ever increasing influx of HMOs. Tobacco farmers can't be sure whether they'll survive, because litigation has demanded that they spend millions in advertising against their own products.

Meanwhile, college professors are struggling to save time-honored tenure policies. Video store owners await their demise with the advent of Direct Television. The Internet threatens to take a stranglehold on the musical recording industry as youthful listeners download songs for free. There was more advertising money made on the Internet in 1998 than on all of the billboards in the United States. Traditional newspapers seem to be on the way out, as cities with two daily papers find themselves with only one. The list goes on.

In the meantime, your career vocabulary exemplifies fleeting changes in the workplace. How old are the terms Web master, digital marketplace, Internet consultant, Java engineer, browser, cybershopping, and cyberplumber? Even "clicking on" has a new meaning. What's a file squishing technologist or digital distributor? What kind of music is techno-underground-punk? Have you ever befriended an Internet auctioneer? Does cybersquatter sound like a naughty role? How many of you have friends who are day traders or market timers?

New words that reflect a changing work world besiege you. And there is substantial pressure on you to keep current. You probably know something about your local police force, the FBI, and the CIA. But have you ever heard of the Computer Emergency Response Team (CERT). They're probably among the most influential of our protectors, helping to apprehend the authors of computer viruses.

So What Happened to You?

Are you looking for a job? Were you hit without warning because your company was sold? Or did your company go out of business because it couldn't compete? Do you happen to be a doctor or lawyer whose work world was turned upside down by HMOs or corporate cost cutting?

Are you looking to leave your job because the unthinkable—a merger, acquisition, or buyout—is soon to take place? Are you leaving because your workforce was downsized or furloughed?

Do you feel that you're being underutilized or that your employer is not putting you in a position to garner new skills? Do you feel that your underutilization is due to any kind of employer discrimination?

With the excitement of the Internet and the high-rolling companies that end with .com, have you envisioned making your move into a new company for the millennium? Do you fear that you will be unfairly characterized by your old line of work and will not be able to easily enter the new high-tech world of young, growing Internet companies?

Was your choice to look for a job yours and yours alone? Did the company encourage you? Were you offered a severance package or a "golden handshake" to leave without a quarrel?

Are you ambitious or desperate? Have friends, spouses, partners, lovers sanctioned a change because they think you can do better or because you're miserable in your current job? Has an intimate demanded that you get a different job because your schedule takes you away from the relationship or your children?

Are you using this book because you're looking for your first job? Or have you been looking for a long time? Did you think that the work world was waiting for you to enter and now you realize that you're not so special? Or are you a career search bridesmaid, always the second choice in whatever job you apply for?

Are you a workplace adventurer, a roving migrant? Are you not completely fulfilled with what you're doing? Do you want to feel passion for what you do?

Exercise 1-1   For the Record

Whether or not you relate to the situations described above, take a few moments to record the particulars of your circumstances. This brief exercise will give you a perspective on where you are coming from and where you fit in among career changers.

Read the statements below and underline the part of the statement that pertains to you. If there is nothing in the statement that is relevant, leave it as is. Write more detailed notes in your journal if you wish.

- Are you new to the work world or old to the work world?

- Are you searching for a new position because of a merger, downsizing, firing, layoff, or your own choice?

- Are you searching because of family pressure or job dissatisfaction?

- Are you considering self-employment, or a small or large company?

- Are you a rover, picking posts to learn new skills and shortly thereafter moving on?

- Are you looking for work with passion, skill development, or stability?

- Add any further information about your circumstances below.

This simple exercise will assist you in remembering what it was that prompted this search. It will also give you a brief chance to reflect, vent, and possibly reconsider.

You may already know that searching for a job is going to be frightening, laborious, time consuming, and ego threatening. What you were most likely never told is that it can be emotionally troubling as well. This book will help to focus your concerns and serve as your escort and confidant. Get ready. In going through this process you'll learn a lot about what takes you up and down the emotional elevator of the career search. Stay with it. There will be times in your search when you will be confronting troublesome and discouraging information. The sections and exercises in this book are designed to keep you realistic, forward thinking, and in control.

2 | Eight Rules to Enhance Your Search

Maybe what we need is a brand-new set of rules.

—James Thurber

You're in for a Bumpy Ride

Simply put, change is bumpy. If you're like most of us, you don't want to remove yourself from situations that are predictable and comfortable. It seems easier to hold on to an unpleasant job than to take a chance on an unfamiliar one. People tend to vacation in the same spots, eat at the same restaurants, and maintain the same social relationships because unpredictability is stressful and makes life seem out of control.

However, if you're unwilling to change, you risk getting left behind in the career world. Vision, flexibility, and adaptability are necessities in today's job market. But why does there seem to be so much more willingness to make changes in job placement? The impending millennium has been witness to a "new careerism," a redefining of career and life plans. Young workers no longer pledge loyalty to their employers. Instead they use their companies as bases for skill building, with the goal of eventually parting ways. They crisscross the corporate terrain, migrating to new fields to acquire further skills that can be parlayed into stock options in another new and yet-to-be-public company. The career search is complicated by this conceptual transition.

There's even a shifting definition of "career." Passion for meaningful life work is being replaced in some sectors with a passion to make a financial killing early, and then move on to uncharted waters.

Ed had been a successful, popular college history professor and hoped his son would follow this path. He had been on the same campus for thirty-one years. However, Junior had other plans. He received his MBA and immediately joined the marketing department of a large soap manufacturer. He left after a year for an established food processor. With a well-honed set of marketing skills, he joined a soon-to-be-public Internet company. After eighteen months with the company, his stock was valued at more than his father's entire net worth. Ed reflected, "It's a whole new world. Junior made more in one year than I made in my lifetime."

You're a Survivor

Significantly, you've already gone through many life changes. You departed the hospital where you were born and went home. You left home one day to attend kindergarten or day care. You've graduated from one school to another and eventually moved into the work world. You've probably already had and lost a significant number of close relationships. You've survived! Congratulate yourself. Gather strength from your past. Build on your history. Realize that change is not an all-or-nothing, black-or-white experience. It's a process of self-discovery.

Many of you have made the transition from one job to another at least once. You've likely been promoted, and maybe even demoted. You may also have experienced a firing, corporate downsizing, reduction in force, cutback in production, or short-term furlough. Yes, you have shown you can change. You survived, but that doesn't prevent you from having sinking feelings of vulnerability. You wonder about the future, and you might even be terrified about what's next. Hang on. Let's begin by setting some basic parameters to keep your emotions in check.

Career Transition Rules

Here are eight rules that can help you weather your career search. They will more than just keep you afloat. They will propel you through the stormy seas of change and opportunity.

The eight rules are:

1. Accept the instability in the career world around you.

2. Use the people around you.

3. Use the resources around you.

4. Use your imagination.

5. Rethink your employment goals.

6. Don't panic.

7. Minimize stress.

8. Search only when you're ready.

Rule #1: Accept the Instability in the Career World Around You

By adopting this posture, you'll have realistic expectations. And you'll be prepared not only for this search, but the next one. You're going to do this again, guaranteed. Career paths can change dramatically, sometimes even overnight. Your company can merge or be sold, making it nonexistent the very next day. You'll find that you won't be able to fall back on past accomplishments.

After the merger of two firms, the new coupling will not do business like either of the old companies, no matter what you're told. When Nations Bank and the Bank of America (B of A) merged to form a "new" Bank of America in 1998, the old B of A chief was ousted within weeks. The top ten women executives at B of A either quit or were reassigned to lower-level positions. Twenty-three thousand jobs were lost. This new reality should be a warning to keep yourself alert and prepared at all times. By accepting rather than denying this reality, you remain in emotional control and prepared to act.

Jackson was the vice president of marketing for a small Midwestern automobile parts supplier. He was heavily recruited to be the vice president of sales and marketing for a large automobile power steering manufacturer. He accepted the job, sold his home, and moved his family to a new and larger metropolitan area. The very day he arrived on the job, his new boss, the executive vice president, told him there was both good news and bad. The good news was that the company had been sold and that the current employees would receive substantial benefits. That included Jackson because he was given a large stock option package as a part of his employment contract. The bad news was that the new company was not going to use any of the old manufacturer's sales and marketing people. That would duplicate staff work. Jackson was out of a job, the very day he started.

Jackson was very upset and sued the company for breach of contract. He settled out of court. While he had sufficient resources to live for the next six months, he had uprooted his family and now he was unemployed in a new geographical area.

To survive, Jackson began casting about for ways to create his own career stability. He joined a health club, repackaged his body, and entrusted himself to a job club. At the job club, he discovered how well his sales and marketing skills encouraged other unemployed workers. Club members encouraged him to consider a calling where he marketed people. Others concurred. Jackson began to appreciate the commonality between marketing products and marketing people. In a new city and in an unstable job environment, Jackson found focus and a new job goal. Soon after, he approached executive recruiting and outplacement consulting firms and did some informational interviewing. Then, after putting together a creative résumé, accomplishment portfolio, and marketing package, he networked and was hired by a major outplacement consultant. It took just over five months of searching. But Jackson had created a new job. He was more confident and passionate than ever.

Rule #2: Use the People around You

Job Clubs

Jackson joined a job club. If you want to participate in a group activity, consider doing the same. These organizations offer small groups where unemployed workers and career changers can tell their stories. It's a good place to vent your feelings, and you can get crucial, current information from other job seekers there. Meetings are regularly scheduled; members set goals, report accomplishments and frustrations, and receive suggestions and encouragement. At times, the club resembles group therapy and at other times, a twelve-step program. Joining a group can help remind you that you matter to others.

You can find job clubs at national organizations like Forty Plus and Experience Unlimited. Some local chambers of commerce sponsor them as job forums. Your state unemployment office can also refer you to one and may even offer one. Your local Private Industry Council may also be able to help.

There are other types of gatherings for unemployed workers. The business or classified section of your local newspaper often publicizes organizations that have support group meetings, talks, and open forums for job searchers. If you want to look at these from a national perspective, you can examine career events in the *National Business Employment Weekly*. Religious organizations, churches and synagogues, and the YMCA and YWCA also organize job clubs.

Whatever you choose, membership in a group can be a wonderful means of support to keep you upbeat and keep loneliness at bay.

Support Network

Jackson had recently moved and didn't have much of a support network. A support network is made up of people you know who can provide information and who can serve as sounding boards and cheerleaders. Members of your network encourage, listen, and offer ideas about your job search. They can help to keep you informed about emerging jobs and the "hidden job market," opportunities that exist that are never openly advertised.

Most people do not know how to use a network and refuse to acknowledge that they need one. But keep this in mind: Maintaining a support system is not a sign of weakness. It shows that you are connected. Joining with independent thinkers who will be honest with you and not just tell you what you hope to hear can expose you to possibilities that you never even considered. Some have even highlighted the idea of having your support network serve as a kind of board of directors to you. They can launch new ideas and innovative ways to approach your search.

To make your search as effective as possible, acknowledge your need for support and create a network of people who can listen, give you ideas, cheer you on, and suggest emerging opportunities. Remember, you don't have the time or the energy to canvass the changing work world by yourself.

Your network should primarily be made up of co-workers, mentors, helpful acquaintances, and at least one person who is Internet savvy.

Building your network is like building a positive multilevel marketing campaign. If you know ten people and they know ten people, then you're linked to 100 people. Your creation of a support team is quite simple but important. The team you build will be available for all kinds of consultation for years to come. So let's see who you can enlist.

Current and Former Co-workers

Current or former co-workers and workplace friends can share ideas with you. They have information about your company, field, and industry and can advise you on new trends you should explore. They serve as good listeners as you promote your fresh ideas and occasionally share your troubles. They can debunk industry rumors. And they can help appraise whether the organizations you are considering are a good fit.

Mentors

Choose a mentor from your profession. Everyone talks about mentoring, but many people are too embarrassed to pursue the fellowship of a special comrade. A mentor is a highly regarded member of your profession who knows you, believes in you, and takes an interest in your career development. Your mentor will keep you from feeling excluded. You can keep in regular contact by e-mail. There are listserv links to different ethnic groups that have on-line mentors across the country, so it is even possible to select mentors over the Internet and create a new and modern electronic family. Many of these mentors can help with the latest in corporate survival techniques. One of the greatest features of online mentors is that they are said to be available easily when you need them, even if they are halfway around the world.

Don't worry if your mentor disagrees with you sometimes. It's best to find one who challenges you to ascend to new performance levels. A mentor can give you straightforward professional advice to help you focus. Your mentor can be older or younger than you are, but should capture your respect.

Your mentor may also be someone you choose to place a broadcast letter for you. A broadcast letter is more than simply a letter of reference. It is a letter sent out to all of the people in your mentor's network who may be able to help your career search. The letter describes you and your unique qualifications. While a reference letter is a reaction to a prospective employer's request for information, the broadcast letter is conceptually more like an advertising or marketing tool. Because it is so personal and is sent to people who already know the author, it can be an exceptionally powerful tool to take advantage of during your search.

Even if you are without work at the moment, you too can serve as a mentor. There are literally hundreds of local people who could use your professional advice. You can mentor others through your professional organizations or through new listservs on the Internet. When you were little, you might have been told by your mother, "If you want to have a friend, be one." The same can be said for mentoring. If you want to learn this role, then try it on yourself.

Service Professionals

Enlarge and play hopscotch with your support network. People who provide you with personal services are an often unrecognized commodity. They may be able to give you new suggestions and assist you with gathering information. Your health care provider, accountant, hairstylist, receptionist, and letter carrier are people that you contact regularly, but you probably don't consider them to be in your support network. However, if they know you need help, they may provide you with something new.

To create a network of service providers, you need to remind yourself which service providers are actually in your life. To jar your memory, open the Yellow Pages to the alphabetical directory of categories and write down the names of people who come to mind when you read a particular listing like "accountant," "dentist," or "tree surgeon." You'll be surprised how effective this is.

To add to the list, go through your card file, the base of your contacts. Add others who are members of teams, clubs, or classes you attend. Some of the best network contacts may be people you have done favors for. Look through your date book or calendar to review your year and remind yourself about any of these people.

Internet-Savvy Support

If you aren't Internet-saavy, you should have at least one person in your network who is. This person can help you with new ways to use the Internet for career information. By last count, there were well over three hundred Web sites devoted to the career search. In addition, there are many popular media sites that you can segue or link into. If you don't know anyone who can help you use the Internet, extend your network to your local librarian. Your public library should have Internet access, and your librarian can assist you with learning to use it. Some adult education programs and community colleges will also help you to gain short-term Internet access.

Classmates

This difficult time can be an excellent chance to reconnect with people from the past who just might have an opportunity for you, in addition to being a part of your network. People that you knew from grade school can be as useful as your sorority friends from college. This part of networking can give you some refreshing links to your past. You might also want to contact old teachers, professors, or counselors. Many of you may have attended a college that can help you to access alumni in your area who may be an additional source of support. Some university alumni clubs have lists of graduates who are available and willing to do informational interviewing.

Friends

Your friends can be a useful source of support and are often more readily available than others on your list. Neighbors, people from social clubs and community organizations, and individuals that you have regular contact with—like friends from an aerobics class—are good places to start to add support.

Family

I put this one last for two reasons: it is obvious and it can be difficult. It may be hard to feel like the family failure right now. Still, family connections can be very helpful.

A Final Network Note

To sum up your network, try to focus on how it will connect you to the rest of the world, now and for the remainder of your working life. I used to teach undergraduate students how to network by showing them that they were only five phone calls away from anyone they wanted to meet. In the class, I had students draw names from a hat; they then had to use their personal networks to make a contact with the person whose name they had drawn. Afterwards they wrote up a short paper with a network diagram describing how they had arranged a meeting with the heretofore mysterious person from the hat. As proof of their contact, they had to obtain the person's signature.

Like those students, you can learn the process for connecting to people who can help you the rest of your life. Not only do you want to use your network to help you with the search, you want to use it to enable you to acquire problem-solving information over your life span. As you create your network, keep all of the names, addresses, and phone numbers available for ready reference in a Rolodex file. When you go to meetings, trade shows, conventions, or even when you get estimates for household repairs, get a business card and file it. Pick up cards at restaurants that you enjoy. You can never be certain when they will come in handy.

Career Coach

If job clubs are unappealing to you and you find, like Jackson, that you have a limited support network, consider meeting with a career coach. You might try this at least once during the search. It's somewhat different from visiting a career counselor, who can help you determine what line of work or education you ought to pursue. A career coach will help you with your search technique. You will receive assistance in packaging and marketing yourself, and you'll get evaluations of your interviewing style. After you've been placed, your coach can help you manage your career, job relationships, and communication skills. A coach may also be useful in helping to advance your career. The coach can streamline your skills and aid you in positioning yourself for your next career move.

Coaches have some degree of flexibility in the manner in which they consult with you. Of course most will meet with you in person, certainly at first. But thereafter, you might be able to stay in regular contact with your coach by telephone and e-mail. Coaches can help you to keep some degree of balance in your search, and they can help you to overcome personal barriers that you may have created for yourself.

Lists of coaches can be found in job clubs, the Yellow Pages, and at community college career centers. The Institute of Management Consultants can also provide you with information and referrals. You can also check out the International Coaching Federation's Web site (see Appendix).

For those of you who may be considering coaching as a field, especially the counselors, marketing experts, and consultants among you, you may be able to receive a free newsletter (see Appendix). Coaching may be just the right thing to add your current career or career portfolio.

Exercise 2-1   Using the People around You

In this exercise, you will begin the process of creating your network. This will ensure that you have support in your search, perhaps even more than you thought. In your journal, write in the names of individuals in each category who could serve in your network. Then rate them in the following manner. If they are good listeners, rate them with an *A*. If they are good encouragers, rate them with a *B*. If they are good sources of information, rate them with a *C*. Be sure to do the rating, which will save you time in the long run as you decide who can help you in different areas.

Name and rate the following:

- top ten relatives and friends in my network
- five professional coworkers
- mentor possibilities
- service providers and acquaintances
- Internet-savvy contact
- potential career coach
- local job club or job forum
- and job club meeting times.

Rule #3: Use the Resources around You

Continue learning by reading and experiencing new frontiers. Gather career information regularly and evaluate it. For example, try to read the career section of several Sunday papers, at least one local and one national. You can do some of this on the Internet at home or in your library. Examine copies of your local business newspapers for industry trends and new ideas. Study classified job listings for new ideas, career information, new job titles, and new words to use to describe yourself.

It can be an interesting adventure to make a weekly trip to a major newspaper stand. It's a good place to browse for ideas, because they'll have some of the best newspapers and trade magazines available for your search. You can discover publications that you probably haven't heard of before.

Research companies and search for new career information on the Internet. Don't stop this practice after you've landed a position. By the time you finish getting your new job, you may know as much about the career change process as a lot of professionals. Record it. Remember it. Continue it. You'll use the information again.

Don't Forget Continuing Education

Demonstrate to yourself and to others that old dogs *can* learn new tricks. Involve yourself in continuing or adult education, either for your current career or to prepare for the future. The new career countryside will demand new knowledge. You'll be expected to have the skills to sell your ideas, your company, and yourself. You'll need to understand new forms of information technology, and most companies will want you to understand spreadsheets and the bottom line.

Your community is undoubtedly full of adult education programs. Community colleges offer surprisingly cutting-edge courses. Another benefit is that by enrolling in any course at a community college, you're usually entitled to use the college's career services. You may be able to meet with a free or low cost career counselor or career coach.

Many colleges are creating satellite centers for new career developers like yourself. San Francisco State University started a downtown center a few years ago to house its fledging multimedia training programs and courses. This satellite program has turned into one of the most flourishing multimedia programs in the United States.

You can also take advantage of "distance learning," classes and programs that colleges, universities, vocational-technical centers, and graduate schools offer through the Internet. This wave of educational programs will bring learning directly into your home, and may even be the course of education in the new century. These classes can be taken at your own speed, on your own time, in your own home. They aren't expensive. A local librarian or college career center can give you information on accessing this material. You can check out one of these possibilities through the UCLA Extension (see Appendix). Keep in mind that virtual education will allow you to save on parking fees, commuting time, and day care, so it's a new way to receive some training upgrades for less time and money.

If you prefer to learn in a more hands-on manner, consider a volunteer position that will help to build some new skills while you get a pat on the back. Most communities have a volunteer bureau;

you can receive information about local opportunities from staff members. If there isn't anything to your liking currently available, create something on your own. Make a deal to work with a business for free for a while to learn a new skill, the same principle that an intern uses. It's also what a "walk on" athlete does in a college or professional sport. You'll have a chance to become a valuable player, an MVP type. Jackson learned that he had surefire motivational skills when he discovered them volunteering at his job club. He was able to take advantage of these and now they're a permanent part of his career development portfolio.

You can also try internships and apprenticeships to add new skills. Companies may have these programs already set up. Contact local trade unions, personnel departments at different companies, professional associations, and private foundations to secure information about paid and unpaid internships and traineeships.

Information and education are useful as regular career checkups, even when you have a job. Give your career the same attention and consistent care you give your body and your car. What you'll learn from this search will pay off today, but will also have a big payday later, when you make your next change.

It's useful to make a record of the resources around you. Sometimes these resources are so obvious or available that you never think of using them. For instance, did you ever really think that your local library might be a good place to work on your search?

Exercise 2-2   Listing the Resources around You

Take the time to identify the resources around you and make a list in your journal. If you don't come up with an answer immediately, try the library, a newsstand, a magazine shop, or the phone book to determine what is available to help you. This exercise will supplement the networking information that you have already gathered, but most importantly, it will begin to give you a sense of control over available information.

It's important to have at least one response for each of the resources:

- best local newspaper for me
- best national paper for me
- best local business newspaper for me
- best national business newspaper for me

- best professional trade papers for me
- adult education programs
- continuing education programs
- local community or junior college
- distance learning programs
- courses I might take
- volunteer agencies
- volunteer positions
- apprenticeships/internships

Rule #4: Use Your Imagination

Stay open to all change possibilities. Cabbage Patch Dolls didn't stay popular for very long. Neither will Furbies or Beanie Babies. Keep your new work and your job search interesting. If you focus your imagination, you can anticipate changes. Note how America's Yellow Pages have changed their logo. No longer will your fingers do the walking. Instead you're encouraged by the directory to "get an idea." It reflects the current workplace tempo of generating new and innovative ways of doing things.

Keep your facts straight, but think intuitively. Ask yourself, "How can I make the world as I want it to be?" Engage in divergent thinking, a thought process that allows you to come up with more than one answer to a problem. Jackson demonstrated that when you do make a change, it can be a radical switch in fields, but not necessarily one that demands learning entirely new tasks. He switched fields and industries but used old skills in a recycled fashion. When engaging in your search, consider new environments where your job skills can be used without much of a stretch.

Students often ask, "What's the difference between divergent thinking and convergent thinking?" An old Midwestern farmer's story illustrates the point. Suppose that three crows were sitting on the farmer's fence. The farmer got angry and shot one of them dead. How many are remaining? The linear, convergent thinker would say "two" because three minus one is just that. But the nonlinear, divergent thinker would say none, because the remaining birds would have flown away with the sound of the gunshot. Both are probably correct. Which answer would you have chosen?

Exercise 2-3   Assessing Your Divergent Thinking

You can test your capacity for divergent thinking with a simple little exercise. The results will show how much you need to practice to generate innovative approaches to your career.

Get a stopwatch and give yourself three minutes. Now, write down all of the possible uses you can think of for a brick. Be brazen. Really use your imagination.

How many uses did you come up with? Did you think of the different objects that you could build? Well, building is only one use. How about using the brick as a shape to make a block design? Did you use it as a measuring device? Could a brick be a potential weapon or an object used in a violent activity? Could it be an object of percussion? Did you know that the founding fathers used bricks to warm their beds?

Review your own list of uses. If you had more than ten different uses, your divergent thinking is probably in excellent shape. If you had fewer than five, you need to try to test your imagination more in your routine activities. Your support network can help you with this.

Generate new ideas using techniques other than just your recollection or intuitive processing. All the new resources you are in contact with will expose you to more input. Let best-sellers, magazines, and the Internet inspire you to become more imaginative. If you want to explore intriguing—and at times oddball—ways of looking at the world, read the local newspaper op-ed pieces or the letters to your local newspaper editor. These can be amusing and informative.

Exercise 2-4   Creative Job Development

Like Jackson, consider your assets like your skills, interests, personality characteristics, and values. What are some new and different types of jobs you could do with these assets and your education and experience? What new avenues could you pursue? Write down at least ten.

How did these answers compare to the careers that you thought you had within you?

Al was a psychologist, always seeking new possibilities. When he moved to another state, he wanted to explore different roles for himself. A spellbinding counselor, he wanted to conceive of doing something besides clinical work. He wrote down the following possibilities: clinician, professor, high school teacher, public speaker, hostage negotiator, disability rights specialist, corporate consultant, personnel officer, employee assistance specialist, health insurance case manager, corporate trainer, intern supervisor, hospital training director, focus group leader, psychological marketing consultant, radio talk show host, author, entrepreneur, futurist, ethicist, and critical incident stress debriefer.

Creatively thinking about your career possibilities can change your whole direction. Al related an interesting but painful story about not pushing one of his more creative entrepreneurial schemes. In college, he had roomed with George, who eventually became a psychology professor. In 1975, Al called his old friend to discuss a new career idea. He thought it would be fascinating to develop a firm that specialized in exploring social attitudes in different communities to help attorneys with jury selection. George had never heard of such an idea and, besides, he didn't want to invest in the start-up costs. The idea never materialized into a new endeavor for them.

When he noticed all of the consultants that were used during the O.J. Simpson trial, Al contacted his old roomie again to bemoan their missed opportunity. George was still a college professor. He admitted that not starting the firm was probably the most expensive decision he had ever made.

Contemplating the Future

So how can you be a bit more creative in imagining new possibilities? Contemplate the future, but do it with the imagination of a child. Children will invent solutions to almost any problem. They remain unblocked because they consider all possibilities. They don't stifle themselves with mental limits—and you shouldn't either.

Don't laugh at your own crazy ideas. Try to consider how you might feel toward a friend or your own child if either told you to stand out in the pouring rain, fly a kite with a metal key attached to a jar, and determine whether there was electricity in the lightning in the sky.

Exercise 2-5   Repackaging Yourself

Choose one of the positions that you listed in the last exercise and try to envision how you would package yourself. Prepare a résumé and cover letter that support the notion. What you learn from this exercise is that it does not take much physical effort to repackage yourself into a different role, but it does take mental effort and creativity. If this exercise was easy for you, then do another, with a different position. What you'll find is that by moving the text and key words of your résumé around, you can develop a good piece of advertising for yourself in a variety of positions.

Rule #5: Rethink Your Employment Goals

As you use your imagination, consider the portfolio career. The portfolio career is a composite career made up of more than one income stream. This can be developed in several ways. You can have a "day job" that accounts for the majority of your income, a "swing shift" or night job that supplements that, and a "job in creation" that is reflected in your educational courses or volunteer activities. Or you could have three part-time jobs that all provide similar income streams but demand different job skills.

Students have long had portfolio careers without calling them that. Lynn takes classes, waits tables, and works at a campus employment center. Joyce attends class, cares for a child, and works in a laboratory part-time. Unfortunately, for most people the portfolio career ends with graduation. Today's work world is ripe for reconsideration of this alternative.

There are compelling reasons to create a portfolio career. First, as the career world changes, companies recruit workers to join a clearly delineated project and work until it's completed. They are classified as "full-time temporary" workers. Organizations are pruning full-time positions as they move toward a "project economy." Second, the composite career provides you with some surefire risk protection. If you have several income streams, and one of them goes awry (through merger, acquisition, personal boredom, etc.), you still have two to protect you. Business consultants have known this for years and tend to diversify their work to keep up with market demand.

Third, the portfolio career lets you sell yourself and your talents directly. You can scout companies that may be interested in your skills on a part-time or project-driven basis. As you research companies that might interest you, you'll be able to refine and articulate the nature of what you have to offer. Engaging in this activity wastes no time, as you're learning about your own career portfolio as you begin to develop a portfolio career.

You can be your own company, and you can be on loan to other companies, even several at the same time. Categorize your information so you create or pinpoint a market niche. Divide your skills into subheadings so that you present yourself with some degree of diversification.

Janet was a trainer for a large health-care organization. She had been a schoolteacher for ten years but had become disenchanted with the pay scale. She was an avid runner who kept herself in good physical shape, and she had an interest in health care that motivated her to look for a job in the health insurance industry. She used her teaching background to promote herself and was able to secure the training job with an uncomplicated job search. While at the HMO, she trained staff and patients in smoking cessation, motivation, well baby care, asthma education, meditation, relaxation, and hypertension control. She was well received by all of her audiences.

The HMO went through a management change and the training program was seriously reduced. Janet was understandably devastated: she had created a series of classes she enjoyed teaching, she made more than twice her former teacher's salary, and she enjoyed health care education.

So Janet redefined her employment goal. She decided that she would start her own company and contract out her services. She wrote descriptions of her classes and collected performance evaluations and testimonials, then contacted a friend in marketing and advertising. With a little guidance, she put together a presentation book with examples of her training materials. She included areas where she had not actually taught. For example, she had served in a multiethnic, multicultural school district and had an interest in diversity training. So even though she hadn't actually taught that subject, she assembled a respectable course outline and included it.

Then Janet went off to sell her portfolio. Eight weeks later, she had companies interested in her training courses who were willing to pay her $1500 per day. She found that she could work fewer hours than she had at the HMO, earn more, and generate financial freedom. She wasn't doing anything substantially different from what she had done fifteen years earlier. But she *had* learned to repackage herself and sell the new products and services for a different price to a different consumer group.

She had created a portfolio career. She assessed the interests, skills, and experience that she had acquired, packaged them, and sold them to different companies, with the goal of securing several permanent part-time positions to use as a more secure financial base.

Portfolio careers are excellent, trendy, and can work in many fields, but are especially convenient for artists, writers, educators, and business consultants, to name a few. They are, of course, not for everyone. They demand confidence. Because focus is essential, they need to be a clear choice rather than a last resort. They require imagination, passion, and a futuristic orientation. You need to love to muse over and act on possibilities when you have a composite career. And you definitely need to enjoy marketing and selling yourself.

Exercise 2-6   Your Portfolio Career

This exercise will help you to determine whether a portfolio career is appropriate for you right now. Answer each of the questions below with either a yes or no response.

_____ I love thinking about the future.

_____ I enjoy selling myself.

_____ I can determine what kinds of businesses need me.

_____ I don't worry about the financial ups and downs of independent business.

_____ I make plans and set goals regularly.

_____ There are markets for my set of skills and experience.

_____ I know what makes me different from others.

_____ People like to include me.

_____ When I look at advertisements, I imagine who the ad is trying to reach.

_____ I have a vision for myself.

If you answered yes to at least eight of these statements, you should definitely consider the portfolio career. The career can involve similar tasks in different places—as is the case with Janet—or it can include different tasks with different organizations.

To begin to create a portfolio path, do the following:

1. Define what you want to do based upon your skills and experience.

2. Give your portfolio career a name.

3. Do research at a business library to help to determine its viability.

4. Do preliminary market research to determine whether there is an audience for your activities.

5. Describe how you will package yourself with a résumé, cover letters, broadcast letters, and a presentation booklet.

6. Gather support for your portfolio career by having it evaluated by a volunteer at a local SCORE (Service Corps of Retired Executives) office and by others in your network.

7. Have enough savings to last six months.

8. Create a business plan.

9. Market and sell yourself.

Starting a Business as Part of Your Portfolio

The current healthy economy in the U.S. is convincing more skilled job seekers than ever to start their own businesses. The media reports that about 10 percent of all executives who lose their jobs are considering portfolio careers or starting their own businesses. The American Counseling Association reports that new women-owned businesses are germinating at the rate of 1,400 per day. Available venture capital and strong consumer confidence are assisting many in making the decision to go out alone with a portfolio career or a new business idea.

Enrollment in entrepreneurial business school classes has increased steadily since the early 1990s. The Internet has made new dreams possible as the teens and twentysomethings of the millennium decide to take advantage of new technological changes. Job instability in traditional markets appears to have generated a whole new class of young tycoons. There is a new world of risks and excitement.

A good vault for information about potential venture capital money is the PricewaterhouseCoopers quarterly Money Tree Survey of 500 or so venture capital firms and the projects that they are currently investing in. You can reach out to them at www.pwcmoney-tree.com. At the time of this publication, the site was accessible at no cost and was loaded with fascinating data including industries, regions of the country, state of project development, and the nature of the financing. Another well-positioned resource is Venture Capital Resource Library, which includes not only a directory of resources but also provides different links to the home pages of venture capital firms (see Appendix). Another free site is the National Venture Capital (see Appendix). For those of you who prefer to look at money matters through established government resources like the Small Business Administration (SBA), you can get information about capital from their Web site (see Appendix).

While you will hear that it is difficult—close to impossible—to make a contact with venture capital firms, they are afraid of turning their heads away from a great idea, so it's worth a shot. If you can't get a foot in the door at these firms, contact a local university-based business school. Many of them have free forum nights several times a year where people with new ideas are given a short period of time to pitch their idea to faculty experts. Business professors often consult with Fortune 500 companies and should not be viewed as out-of-touch ivory tower types.

Keep in mind that the 1980s were the "me" generation. In the 1990s we met the generation Xers. As we move into the millennium, there is a growing trend toward independence, or what some are already calling the "I" generation. What you may find is that you want more and more independence, and starting your own business is a sure way to get that. Ernst and Young has already touted the idea that the millennium will see grand growth in entrepreneurships. For women seeking to start their own businesses along this avenue, there are new Web sites (see Appendix) that can help.

Regardless of your specific goals, the sites listed here can help you to spot new industry trends and position yourself for your future. Don't be embarrassed or ashamed to try to make a contact. Just be thorough in your research and marketing plans and be very, very concise. You can also consider using appropriate members of your network to help you promote an idea. If your network is insufficient, make a contact with the Service Corps of Retired Executives (SCORE), which is connected with your local Small Business Administration office. You can receive wonderful advice and encouragement from interested businesspeople who want to remain involved.

Rule #6: Don't Panic

Job searches are more threatening than you might have imagined. You probably expected that with all the right training, skills, and experience, everyone would want you. You read about the large salaries offered to others, so what about you? You may have lost your innocence when you realized that not everyone thought you were so special. Then, too, you may wonder about the choices that you have made. How many have asked themselves, "Gee, why didn't I take that job at Microsoft back in 1985?" Maybe you're in the group that asks, "Why didn't I buy Microsoft stock back in 1985?"

What is probably most personally threatening to you, however, is that the people who need to hire you are not necessarily very nice to you. You may think that you have a lot to offer, but time after time you are treated rudely by an executive recruiter. It's a real fall from grace. Recruiters don't return calls. They may not keep promises. If you're told a job offer will come in a week, you expect it. Well, it often doesn't come when you're told. Sometimes it's not out of malice, but because companies usually have many players who are involved in the hiring process. The hiring manager or the headhunter is only one person in the workplace menagerie.

It's also disheartening to find that the people who have the power to hire you have their own issues and problems. They may even feel threatened by you because they fear you want their job. They may take pleasure in humiliating you in a job interview or embarrassing you in a group interview. They may use the job interview to show off to a colleague. Be prepared for this, and don't allow anyone to bully you. See hostile interview experiences as your chance to use your own career search survival skills. As you notice more office dysfunction, remind yourself that it's an opportunity to learn street smarts. Instead of feeling humiliated or upset, learn to cultivate a new sense of humor about circumstances like these. The more you can laugh, the less threatening it will be.

Rule #7: Minimize Stress

Take a reading of your life stress. Change elicits stress. What you're doing isn't familiar and where you're going isn't known. So, instead of hanging on to imagined security, accept change as a natural thing. Begin to liberate yourself from your past and open yourself to the future. Create a rite of passage to make the career search easier and less stressful. A rite of passage could be as simple as taking time off to visit a new and unfamiliar place for a few days. It could also be an educational experience that you have always wanted to try. Some of my clients have created a passage rite by going through their closets and ridding themselves of clothes they didn't like. Others have created new wardrobes and hairstyles for themselves. These rites give you a more potent sense of yourself and your circumstances, as well as adding some feelings of being in control as you head through the transition.

Exercise 2-7
The Effect of Change on Your Life Stress

You can evaluate your stress level relative to your life changes with a simple instrument, the Social Readjustment Rating Scale (Holmes, and Rahe 1967). I've modernized the scale a bit. You'll find it's quite easy to use. Simply circle the score on the right if you've had experience with the life events listed.

		Value
1.	Death of a spouse or life partner	100
2.	Divorce	73
3.	Separation from spouse or partner	65
4.	Jail term	63
5.	Death of a close family member	63
6.	Personal injury or illness	53
7.	Marriage or life commitment	50
8.	Fired at work	47
9.	Marital or partner reconciliation	45
10.	Retirement	45
11.	Change in health of family member	44
12.	Pregnancy	40
13.	Sexual difficulties	39
14.	Gain of a new family member	39
15.	Business readjustment	39
16.	Change in financial state	38
17.	Death of a close friend	37
18.	Change to a different line of work	36
19.	Change in number of arguments with spouse or partner	35
20.	Mortgage over $100,000	31

21.	Foreclosure of mortgage or loan	30
22.	Change in responsibilities at work	29
23.	Child leaving home	29
24.	Trouble with in-laws	29
25.	Outstanding personal achievement	28
26.	Spouse or partner begins or stops work	26
27.	Begin or end school	26
28.	Change in living conditions	25
29.	Revision of personal habits	24
30.	Trouble with boss	23
31.	Change in work hours or conditions	20
32.	Change in residence	20
33.	Change in schools	20
34.	Change in recreation	19
35.	Change in church activities	19
36.	Change in social activities	18
37.	Mortgage or loan less than $100,000	17
38.	Change in sleeping habits	16
39.	Change in number of family get-togethers	15
40.	Vacation	13
41.	Christmas	12
42.	Minor violations of the law	11

After completing the inventory, add up the circled numbers. To interpret your score, refer to the table below.

Score	Interpretation	Susceptibility to illness
300+	Major life change	Major illness in a year
250-299	Serious life change	Lower resistance
200-249	Moderate life change	Depression
150-199	Mild life change	Colds, flus
0-149	Very little life change	No impact

How did this exercise feel to you? Did you discover that you were in fact going through a variety of changes? Isn't it interesting that even positive changes can also be viewed as stressful?

How accurate is the scale for you? Is your score higher than you anticipated? Do you feel as if you are undergoing more life change than others around you? What can you do to better manage the life changes? Are you afraid that the stress of the transition is going to make you sick?

There are several points to note about the scale. The first is the number of work-related questions. There are nine, suggesting that a substantial amount of life change is work related. The second point has to do with the connection between stress and illness. A person may be more prone to illness, depending upon the type and level of life changes. Look at your score, and compare yourself to the scale scores. Do you feel that you are in the midst of major or serious life change? Do you expect that this will influence your health? If you are at risk, what will you do about it? Techniques for taking care of yourself during the search will be covered in chapter 5.

Roxanne's situation illustrates how the stress of a career change can take a toll. Roxanne was in her third year of surgical residency when she began to have misgivings about her career direction. She was frightened of the changes taking place in medicine. Malpractice insurance rates seemed sky-high and her best friends from college were all feeling successful in their business careers. She had very little income and worked 75 hours a week. Several other medical residents mentioned to her that they too were considering leaving medicine. Not even thirty, they were burned out and carrying major debt from college and medical school. They couldn't see the light at the end of the financial tunnel and even worse, medicine just didn't seem fulfilling.

As Roxanne contemplated her future, she discovered that her live-in boyfriend, a successful bond trader, was having an affair. And when she called to tell her parents that she wanted to take a year away from medicine, her mother told her that her father had prostate cancer. Roxanne began to have chronic, although mild, symptoms of asthma.

Unfortunately, and with all kidding aside, the stress of change can make you sick. The mind can heavily influence your health. Hypertension, gastrointestinal ulcers, strokes, and heart attacks are all related to the stress and how well you respond to it.

Roxanne needed some quiet time. She needed to distance herself from her boyfriend. She needed a passage into a caretaking role with her father. Then, she needed to make time to explore her own career options. She asked her boyfriend to leave, at least temporarily, so they wouldn't be at each other's throats. With that handled, she spent a weekend visiting her parents. She discussed with them possible new roles that she could play in their lives. They wanted her to visit more and she agreed to greater contact. She then applied for a sabbatical from her residency. It was granted and she would begin her leave at the end of her residency term. She was then able to evaluate her career and different options.

Next, Roxanne fervently reached out to several friends from college and discussed with them the possibility of serving as a health-care consultant in their accounting firms. She also applied for a job as a part-time science journalist and television doctor for a hospital-based cable station. As she disconnected herself somewhat from her past and put a greater focus on her future, her asthma symptoms lessened. With time and proper diet and medication, her health came back under her control. After six months she was remarkably symptom free. Evaluating stress and choosing some life changes allowed her to begin to take care of herself and plan the rest of her life.

Emotional Sabbaticals

Give yourself an emotional sabbatical if you're feeling overwhelmed. In fact, it's a good time to evaluate your stress level and its relationship to your career search. Not only are you experiencing career change, you're undoubtedly experiencing other changes. When people tell you they have one problem, they usually have two.

If you've lost your job, one of the most difficult pieces of advice to accept is the advice to disconnect for a while to rid yourself of old patterns of behavior. Yet this may be the most productive thing you can do. It's not unlike a farmer letting a field lie fallow for a while, regardless of the lost income.

How can you start to disconnect from the past? First, try to get quiet with yourself. Roxanne did that when she asked her boyfriend to leave. Books on yoga and meditation can be useful here, as can quieting activities that you may never have tried before. (Some are covered in chapter 5.) Second, disconnect from old behavior patterns by trying new ones. Start a new activity. Since you're in a period of turmoil, try to engage in activities that redefine you. Attend a new group. Join a club for a sport like windsurfing, volleyball, tennis, or golf—anything that is different from what you usually do.

Finally, if you have children, become more involved in their school and after-school activities. Take pleasure in being able to drop them off in the morning or pick them up in the afternoon. You may never have this time again. It really does disconnect you from past work experience.

As you continue through the job change process, keep conscious of your mind, body, and spirit. You will want to care for all three and muster up support from all three. As you learn more about stress, relaxation, and healing, you will begin to have a far greater appreciation for utilizing all three of these personal dimensions of yourself.

Rule #8: Search Only When You're Ready

If you're currently unemployed, you're aware of so many activities that you miss, particularly if you've just been let go. Early morning breakfast meetings, late night projects with pizza, and "call out for sandwich dinners," off-site retreats, exotic travel, conventions, and corporate seminars are all activities that you miss. Maybe they seemed a pain when you participated, but now you remember them as a part of your work life. You may be quite surprised that you even miss your commute on public transportation. As difficult and as much of a hassle as it might have been, it still connected you to another group of people who were all in this together. More than one unemployed worker has missed the morning fellowship of the rush hour. They remember car poolers, toll takers, parking lot attendants, and the receptionist in the office building who greeted them each day.

Not having a clearly articulated schedule can create a feeling that's akin to withdrawal. Work can often be the very best game in town and without it, you aren't playing anymore. As you begin the career search, be sure that you have completed the withdrawal process. If you begin your search too soon, you will be substantially less effective.

Henri had a small, successful wine distributing business. He knew his wine products and winemakers. When a larger corporate distributor made him an excellent offer for his company, he sold his distributorship and was comfortable with the money he generated. But he soon became very depressed. Henri felt as if he had lost his life purpose. No one seemed interested in him anymore. His network of winemakers tolerated him for a while, but they really needed to attend to their own businesses. At meetings of the local wine merchants, he found that his opinions were not listened to like they had been in the past. He had plenty of money, but he had no game.

Having lost his identity, Henri thought it would be easy to get it back. He wanted to go back to work as an associate at another distributorship or at least act as a wine seller. He was quickly hired as a retailer by an upscale wine shop. It didn't work. The owners of the shop noticed that Henri was much more interested in discussing the wines with the customers than selling them. He had to be let go—a shocking experience for him. He hadn't realized that his withdrawal from the camaraderie of his business had left him lonely. By talking to customers, he began to solve his loneliness problem. He didn't need much income so his poor sales didn't bother him. He was insensitive to the needs of his employers because he was working out his own withdrawal issues. He had gone back to work too soon—before giving up his old identity. He was having a terrible struggle with his purpose in life.

One of his winemaking friends suggested that Henri go back to the basics of winemaking and sign on for something he had not tried before. He told him to learn how to grow grapes, to create a new coterie of colleagues and friends and with it a new identity. He could be a gardener and work in the fields. He had time and money and basic knowledge. It was recommended that he attend several wine gardening classes at the local community college. He needed to gradually reenter the work world. He did this and found that the new field kept him active and robust. He now had new information to share with growers and merchants. He had formed a new identity, tied to the old, but still new for him. And he had successfully gone through withdrawal.

Metamorphosis

The process of career transition is a metamorphosis. Regardless of who or what you call yourself, when you move from one career arena to another, one job to another, you will transform yourself. To help you transition, visualize the monarch butterfly. Every year in California, monarch butterflies from all over the country gather along the coast in Santa Cruz and Pacific Grove to spend the winter and breed in the spring. The monarch goes through four different life stages. It begins as an egg. Gradually it becomes a larva and looks like an ugly worm. Then it becomes a pupa or chrysalis, all wrapped up in itself. But when it emerges, it is a gloriously beautiful butterfly. In your transition, allow yourself to become the butterfly.

3 | Goal Setting

*It's the only dream you can
have—to come out number-one man.*

—Willy Loman in *Death of a
Salesman* by Arthur Miller

Getting Things Done

Everyone talks about setting goals, making lists, and getting things done. Unfortunately, not many people do it. The diet industry is a good example. Customers set weight-loss goals, hire personal trainers, and pop massive quantities of pills. All of this has questionable results, but people continue to spend billions in hopes of transforming their bodies.

What can you learn about goal setting with a passing glimpse at the nation's dieters? Weight loss and physique enhancing are clearly long-term projects, but many people have short-term expectations. The desired outcome is not going to occur overnight or even within a week or two, despite what the folks on Madison Avenue often imply.

The truth is that exercise and helpful eating have to become a part of your routine in order to be effective.

Similarly, career change takes time and good planning. The reinforcing, positive outcome of a long-term diet and exercise program is a reinforcing statement like, "Gee, I look and feel great." The reinforcing positive outcome of the career transition is something akin to, "I finally found a job that will give me purpose and passion and utilize all of my talents and interests." These are reinforcers at the end of the journey, but what is important is what reinforces you during the struggle itself.

Unfortunately, long-term reinforcers tend to be ineffective because they are not immediate enough. Behavioral science researchers have known for years that the sooner a particular reinforcer is presented after completion of a desired behavior, the stronger and more efficient is the change in the behavior. If your dog does a trick, you give the dog a treat immediately thereafter. The dog learns and maintains new behavior if the reinforcer is presented right after the desired response is observed. The longer you wait to reinforce the behavior, the longer it will take the dog to learn it—and the new behavior will not be as enduring as new behavior that is immediately reinforced. You don't train your dog very well by introducing a treat when the pooch is lying on a mat.

You're probably familiar with this concept in another context. If your goal is to train your puppy to stay off the furniture, you know that meeting that goal is going to take time and continuous, consistent reinforcement of appropriate behavior. You also know that you'll need to be consistent in removing the puppy from the furniture with some kind of verbal or paper rattling reprimand. Chances are good that you'll stay with this program. That's because you'll be immediately reinforced as well by having a limited amount of dog hair on the furniture. With consistent effort, your dog will end up staying on the pad on the floor, unless, of course, you discover you have lost a battle of will. If that's the case, then not only do you have a problem with goals, but also with your boundaries and willpower. (But that's another book.)

I have always found it interesting that although many of my clients had a very easy time with setting goals and limits while training their puppies, they seemed to have an extraordinarily difficult time doing the same kind of programming for themselves. Yet the behavioral principles are the same. With habit change, your willpower can change as well—that's why this is so important during your search. Remind yourself of the puppy experience. A puppy needs short-term behavioral goals with positive consequences and occasional reprimands in order to reach the final goal. So do you.

This is the behaviorists secret. You can help yourself to be more effective in weight-loss programming or in the career search by setting up or enumerating short-term subgoals, sometimes called immediate objectives. These subgoals can then be regularly and immediately reinforced positively.

This same principle can be used to keep workers productive. In some ways, project-driven work is most effective because the workers are reinforced shortly after a project is completed. In fact, if you think about this, worker raises might be more effective as reinforcers if they were given immediately upon completion of certain tasks rather than a month or two after a performance review.

There are many good reasons, practical and psychological, to highlight the goal-setting process during your job search. Becoming a goal-setting maven can help you in positioning yourself at different times during the search while also increasing your efficiency.

Setting Goals Is Practical

Managing Your Time

Let's look at some very practical reasons to set goals. First, goal setting gives you a way to account for and evaluate the use of your time. Regardless of what activities you're involved in, you're always aware of and motivated by your use of your time. You take special pleasure in saving some of it. For example, when you travel to a distant friend's house, you often describe the trip by your speed, sense of direction, and efficiency with words like, "We made good time." If you're caught in a terrible traffic jam, your focus is often on the "waste of time."

In our culture we value time with almost a religious fervor, perhaps because we know that our time on the planet is limited. As a career searcher you're especially aware of this sense of time as limited or running out. You can almost feel the clock ticking away as you experience increasing pressure to *do* something, to make something happen. If your monetary funds are limited, you may throw that into an equation with time: "If I don't get a job soon, I'll be broke, on the streets." If you have been in positions that you might describe as dead-end, you have even more personal coercion to get the job change right this time.

While you want to get it right this time, you're also aware that the search is filled with competing time-consuming activities. You may have to take time off from your current job to attend outside job fairs or meet for an informational or job interview. Given your limited time, which of these activities should you pursue? In fact, you can fill your spare time with obsessive questioning on what you should be doing. Should you be out networking? Or should you be updating your résumé? On top of that, you're often filled with anxiety because you don't have all the time in the world. The key is to use time appropriately and not obsess about it. Remember the acronym SAMS: Keep everything simple, achievable, measurable, specific.

Evaluating Your Choices

In addition to helping you understand your use of time, goal setting also allows you to intellectually process the different choices that you make during the search. Each of these choices has the potential for taking the search in a different direction, sometimes into uncharted waters. The good news is that appropriate goal setting can keep you focused and can also motivate you by giving you benchmarks of your progress during each part of your journey. This processing helps you to determine whether other variables are affecting the search. As already suggested in an earlier chapter, this type of monitoring demands that each day you do some minimum amount of work. That's been said a lot already. But even though it's clearly important, you still may find it difficult to do at least one activity per day.

Try to be aware of what seems so aversive to you during the search that you're unable to do anything. Do the tasks appear to be worthwhile? Are you concerned that you won't be able to complete the tasks? Are you fearful that they will not lead anywhere? Or does every activity seem to be subjected to unfair scrutiny, making all activity aversive?

If you're having trouble moving ahead, you may also be stuck in the murky quagmire of obsessive thinking. If that is where you are now, take a bit of a break from your obsessions and look ahead down the career path. Try to think of larger goals within the context of this search. Try a bit more fantasizing. The creation of a larger context may help to get you unstuck.

Bill was stuck. He had recently graduated from high school with a less than stellar track record. He planned to join the army and spend four years developing skills and determining where to take his career and life path. He wanted to work with people but the idea of a degree in psychology seemed unattainable at the moment. His army recruiter suggested that he imagine helping people right now. Bill knew a lot of drug and alcohol abusers in high school and mused that he thought he could really help them. The recruiter, on hearing this, suggested that perhaps Bill should consider a service organization like Americorps rather than the military.

The army seemed like a fallback position rather than one that would propel Bill along a more personally rewarding career path. Americorps would give him a chance to explore service roles immediately and help him to accrue experience that could later help him to decide on the "people professions."

As difficult as this is, goals and objectives serve as an inventory of what you have achieved during the job search process, and they can help you to organize your day and manage your time. Practically speaking, it's prudent for you to explore which of the different types of career search activities you seem to be willing to take on and see through to some completion. You also should think about whether or not your list of goals or activities continues to increase. If you keep adding more and more things to do without getting any closer to your goals, you risk frustrating yourself and eventually becoming a little depressed about your seeming lack of progress.

Looking to the Future

Goal setting should be moving you toward your ultimate goal of entering a particular field and finding a job that inspires some degree of passion and optimism. But monitoring your goals also lets you evaluate whether or not you actually achieve the "big bang." In the scheme of your life, getting a new job may be just a subgoal. The major life goal could have a different standard. Did you get the job you really wanted? Did you eventually contribute to the world what you wanted? Did you actually pen the great American novel as you had expected?

Goal setting will keep you oriented toward the future. As a career psychologist, I've always felt "future oriented" toward my clients even when they were oriented toward their own past history and sometimes even toward their unfortunate circumstances. I think they benefited most from my always having another new idea, one that came up on the spur of a moment during one of our sessions. Career counselors, coaches, and advisors are future oriented because they are goal oriented.

Psychological Reasons to Set Goals

Control Your Impulses

First, goal setting can keep you from being too impulsive during different parts of the search. That's not to say that you shouldn't move ahead quickly when there's a new opportunity. However, the new opportunities that come to you should be viewed in the context of what you're trying to accomplish. If you're looking for a position in Web page development and a terrific opportunity is presented to you to create marketing videos for a production company, you may want to see whether the creative aspects of this opportunity are consistent with where you want to be. The money may be good but the opportunity may not be related to your fundamental goal.

Jewel wanted to be a television and radio news writer. She had written a few short stories for children's magazines and had a friend who encouraged her to pursue writing for television. A small FM radio station not far from her home turned out to have a lower-level position as a sales and marketing trainee. She thought that she could get an inside track to news writing by working in the local station's sales and marketing department. She was offered a position there based upon her enthusiasm for the radio and television industry.

Jewel accepted the position in order to "get in from the cold" and make some money. But in only a few weeks she discovered that she hated sales, she wasn't doing any writing, and her department colleagues were aggressive in guarding their territories. As a potential support network, they weren't very helpful to her. She quit this job after only two months and has become disenchanted with the entire field of broadcasting.

Without thinking clearly about the skills you want to acquire, those you want to refine, and those you want to use, you may not be discriminating carefully enough. You also need to be careful in determining whether a terrific opportunity is available because the company or the industry is in trouble. Jewel found out that few advertisers wanted to be on her station. She also found out that the station had never been able to retain a sales trainee because the work was a "hard sell" and the sales manager wanted trainees to focus more on organizing the office rather than selling.

If your goals are well articulated, you won't get yourself into the bind of accepting positions that aren't suitable for you. All new opportunities should be evaluated with your current and life goals in mind. Be appreciative that a great job like one in horseshoe repair may be available, but it may not help you to become a horse trainer.

Say Good-bye to Frustration

Good goal setting will help you to determine which of your goals are going to be easy to reach and which may not be. The career search is not a one-size-fits-all process. Some activities will be much more arduous for you than they will be for another person, friend, co-worker, or family member. As you outline the activities involved in reaching your goals, make an assessment of their difficulty and allocate the appropriate amount of time and emotional energy to each task. By doing this, you'll manage your goal setting appropriately and position yourself admirably toward reaching the goals.

Not completing certain subgoals to your final goal will be very frustrating and stressful. A list of uncompleted tasks can leave you with the feeling that this job search is never going to end. It certainly won't feel like it will be successful. Goal setting will help you realize that you will have to make a substantial investment in the process. But you can be discriminating in the amount of effort that you are giving to the various goal-directed activities.

Plan More, Obsess Less

Goal setting will also keep you from agonizing and obsessing about what your next career search task is. If you have appropriate goals with realistic timelines, then you will have an array of focused, productive activities in front of you. You will be able to keep different subgoals and activities from competing with each other for your time. For example, you may want to make lots of personal contacts, but you still need to complete a résumé. You can't complete the résumé because you don't think you have the necessary experience to get the job you want. All of this creates conflict and stress, and it will also keep you from facing the job search as a whole that sometimes seems to be bigger than the sum of its parts. A job search that feels overwhelming can immobilize you.

Finally, goal setting will keep your search more fact oriented. With shorter-term goals, you'll weigh your accomplishments and then evaluate your search progress. You'll be focusing on reality rather than fantasy. You'll refrain from trying to read the minds or predict the behavior of people whom you're trying to meet.

Be alert to the fact that when people feel out of control, they have a tendency to interpret the behavior of others in psychological ways. You've probably said to yourself phrases like, "They probably will call next week" or "I had the feeling that they wanted me, but they don't want to call too soon and show that they're excited to have me." If you find yourself using phrases like these to feel in control or protect yourself from rejection, you're wasting your time. Learn to stay with the facts.

How Subgoals Relate to the Final Goal

Goals in combination with subgoals will help you create a winning plan, even when the subgoals seem unrelated to the final goal. Be aware that a winning plan might, on its face, appear to be a little odd and unfocused. When Bill Walsh was the coach of the San Francisco Forty-Niners, he reportedly always had specific subgoals for each game. While he wanted to win each game, he wanted to win it by meeting clearly defined subgoals. For example, one of his goals was to set the number of first downs he wanted to achieve by the end of the game. By striving to accumulate first downs, he knew that he could keep a strong, well-prepared opposing off the field. Thus, that particular goal was especially good against teams with a potent offense. He also scripted the first fifteen plays of each game. So, he put together a strategy and devised end goals that he wanted to meet. He broke his game plan up into subgoals and believed that if his subgoals were met, then he would achieve his final goal and emerge a winner.

This approach is certainly one way to set goals for yourself. You can create mental way stations and work toward achieving success in each of these stations. The end result will be achieving a job that you want in a life plan that you can script for yourself.

A Practical Approach

In many classic examples of goal setting, an outline is used to explain the process. It usually begins with understanding what the particular goal is. Meanwhile you can add the timeline for reaching the goal and list the information you need to complete it. Next you can look at particular options that may come into play, depending on how you work toward the goal. Then you go ahead and develop the activities and strategies that can meet the goal. You absolutely must have a well-articulated strategy in place for meeting the goal. Then you evaluate the strategy. If the particular strategy isn't getting you closer to your goal, then change it or drop it. Finally, you implement the strategies that are effectively related to the completion of the goal and evaluate the outcomes. In outline form it looks like this:

A. Define the goal or objective

   1. Create the timeline for completing the goal

B. Gather necessary information to help you reach the goal

C. Define the options to the goal that may take place, such as

   1. Different outcome

   2. Changes in the perception of the outcome

   3. Changes in the desirability of the outcome

D. Create a strategy to reach the outcome

E. Evaluate the strategy

F. Implement the strategy

G. Evaluate the outcome or the goal attainment

H. Change the strategy if the goals aren't met

I. Evaluate the new strategy

J. Implement the new strategy

K. Evaluate the outcome or the goal attainment using the new strategy

This method of goal setting and strategy planning acknowledges a couple of points. It's abundantly clear from the outline that goal setting is more than simply writing down a sentence about what you hope to accomplish in your search. Instead, goal-setting activities eventually give you a specific outline of what will need to be done strategically in order for you to meet your goal. Goal setting also implies evaluation. This can include an evaluation of the plan, specific strategies, or the degree to which certain goals and objectives were met.

From the outline, you can begin to set more specific timelines for the completion of certain activities. So you should have some idea of what you'll do today, this week, this fortnight, this month, the next six months, and the next year. You can even go further with your planning and decide where you hope to be in the next two years, three years, and so on and so forth.

Driving and Restraining Forces

In the middle of this you may again wonder why, with a strategy that appears to be so simple, it seems so difficult to meet the goals that you've set for yourself. The answer to that lies in part in what organizational psychologists have referred to as driving and restraining forces.

There are forces that you may not consider when you set goals that can nevertheless have a serious effect on the outcome of your work. Let's say that one of your goals for the day is to go to an informational interview at 10:30 A.M. You give yourself plenty of time to make your appointment. But then, when you go to start your car, the battery is dead because your teenage son left the lights on. So, you get the battery jumped and still think that you can make it to the appointment, when you realize that the gas tank is on empty. You need to fill up, but you have no available cash. You go to the ATM and a computer screen tells you that it's unavailable. It's on some sort of time-out. You sheepishly arrive at your appointment 45 minutes late and are told that you'll have to come back another time, because the person who was to see you has gone on to another meeting. Does this sound familiar? These are all examples of restraining forces, which keep you from meeting your goals or maximizing your effort to meet your goals.

Driving forces, on the other hand, are those forces that seem to speed you toward the attainment of the goal. You want to be not only aware of these but to actively look for them along the way because they serve as psychological propellers. In goal setting and strategy implementation, you want to maximize your driving forces while you minimize your restraining forces.

A driving force during the job search may be something as simple as the emergence of new opportunities in your field. For example, when your personal network begins to provide you the names of technical writers, that represents a driving force. Other driving forces could include: a favorable technical writing job market; a well-established, local professional association of technical writers; opportunities to teach technical writing at a local community college or trade or vocational school; or changing economic circumstances like a merger or acquisition that provides new opportunities.

Of course, restraining forces may be operating at the same time. One example of a restraining force in the technical writing job market might be that those personnel officers who hire technical writers want them all to have at least three years of experience, while you have only one year of professional experience. Another restraining force could be that local training programs are putting too many graduates into the labor pool, resulting in lower salaries and greater competition for positions.

The Internet could be seen as a driving force in your job search if you're in a field in which people are regularly recruited using this technology. There's also the added driving force that you can easily reach employers by circulating your résumé on the Internet.

But as is true in physics, for every action, there is an equal and opposite reaction. Posting your résumé on the Internet could be a restraining force. The restraining force might be that your current employer could discover your posting. If you're not particularly facile with a computer, time constraints could be another restraining force. There's more. Perhaps you don't know how to use the Internet, or at this moment you haven't put a résumé together. Those activities could take time away from personal networking or studying for an employment exam.

Exercise 3-1
Driving and Restraining Forces in Your Life

You can try this activity for a moment. In your journal, list five driving forces that help to propel you along the job search. These can be forces like encouragement from friends and mentors, excitement about putting new ideas to use, marketing a new educational degree, new opportunities you've heard about in your field, or simply the psychological lift you get when you think about entering a whole new work world.

After that, try to enumerate five restraining forces. These might include worry and anxiety that you won't get a job, the economics of your community or job world, poor job search skills, holes in your educational or work experience, poor technical skills, a badly designed résumé, or analysis paralysis. Now go ahead and make your list of restraining forces.

If you're like most of my clients, you had a much easier time drawing up your list of restraining forces. People in the job search often pay more attention to what they believe can and will go wrong, rather than considering what is going to go right. That's not to say that you shouldn't spend time understanding what may be an unanticipated problem, but you shouldn't let it inhibit you.

In setting your goals, it's important to recognize the power of driving and restraining forces. By recognizing the driving forces as well as the restraining ones, you can learn to retain a balance between them. If you have too many driving forces, it may be that you're deceiving yourself about the ease with which you're going to reach a particular goal. If you listed too many restraining forces, you'll find that you become more paralyzed in your attempts to meet your goal.

Goal setting can keep you from feeling victimized by the search. It's also geared to show you where you may need some outside assistance in reaching your goals. Probably the most psychologically beneficial part of staying focused on your goal is that it helps you feel in control of the planning, implementation, and evaluation process during your job search. It will keep you from feeling as if you're some kind of a puppet engaging in meaningless activity. In fact, it may feel like you're running a small company.

Behavioral "Shaping"

Another way of achieving your goals and objectives is to imagine what a final goal is going to be and then to create successive behavioral approximations to that final goal. With each new attempt at performing a particular behavior, you get better and better. In a way this is similar to what B. F. Skinner and other behaviorists used to call shaping. Goal setting in this fashion is actually putting a behavioral principle into everyday practice. Each of the behaviors is geared toward reaching some subgoal that is directly related to the final goal of creating a particular role in a particular career path that is appropriate for you.

The key to understanding shaping is to realize that you must break up the path to your final goal into a series of successive approximations or steps in order to reach the goal. It's similar to learning how to dance. Your dance will take its final form after a series of steps are slowly learned and then put together into a routine.

When you shape your dance, you need to look at a demonstration of the entire routine. Then you can break up the steps into manageable components and shape the appropriate behavior. To do this for a job search, you need begin with a clear, comprehensive outline of the job search.

A Brief Look at the Components of the Job Search

Before preceding much further with shaping and goal setting, let's look at the tasks that are a part of the search. There are entire books on the subject, but this list will give you a broad picture. It's divided into career search preparation and career search implementation. Regardless of how your search might vary from this, the model is probably a pretty good place to begin because it allows you to see the whole as well as the parts. What we'll do after scanning the whole model is show you how to take a few of the smaller components of the search and break them into subgoals.

Career Search Preparation

Self-assessment

    Health and physical characteristics

    Family history and parental and societal expectations

    Psychological characteristics

        Interests

        Needs

        Values

        Abilities, aptitudes, specific skills

        Transferable skills

        Beliefs

        Fears, worries

    Educational background

    Work and volunteer experience

    Economics

Occupational Assessment

    Nature of work tasks

    Ability requirements

    Need reinforcers, working conditions, location, climate, and compensation

    Outlook, advancement, opportunity

Sources of leads through networks, Internet, organizations, media

Environmental Support

Home and significant others

Institutions including community and religious organizations as well as service, political, and social clubs

Career Search Implementation

Networking

Informational interviewing

Marketing yourself with résumés, cover letters, portfolios

Interviewing, including speaking skills and listening skills

Negotiation for contract

Job placement

What you will notice from this list is that searching for a job is like painting a room. Painting is 80 percent preparation and 20 percent application. The career search is 80 percent preparation and 20 percent implementation. What you'll learn during the search will influence your decision making for the rest of your life, so a worthwhile endeavor at this time of the search is to set some life goals. You may be able to achieve some of these while you are actively involved in your current search. As mentioned in chapter 1, you will probably learn more about yourself and about the job search process than at any other time in your life. So let's begin by creating some life goals that will be useful regardless of where you end up.

Subgoals

Consider the types of charts that you might make for activities like becoming more Internet savvy, becoming a more sophisticated interviewee, or being a better listener.

You can develop your Internet-savvy personality by becoming more proficient with these steps:

- Learn the difference between the Internet and the World Wide Web.

- Learn to use an Internet browser like Netscape or Explorer, depending upon what is available.

- Sign up for an Internet service provider.

- Learn to use search engines like Yahoo and Career Mosaic.

- Sign up for an e-mail account.

- Enroll in a listserv, a type of mailing list that will get you some valuable career-related information.

- Employ a usenet if you want to have discussion online about career-related issues.

- Explore the myriad Internet career sites and Web pages.

- Make your own Web page to advertise or market yourself.

What you can see from this list of activities is that the idea of becoming Internet savvy can have a large number of components, all of which may be useful in your career transition or at other times in your life. You see how your work in the job search can have a positive impact throughout your life. Just remember that the key to effective goal setting is to break activities into smaller and smaller parts. You can even manage your time in this way. If you're stuck with what to do next, you can say to yourself, "In the next five minutes I'm going to _____ !"

Let's explore another goal.

Becoming a better interviewee can be broken down into the following subgoals:

- Collecting knowledge and information

Knowledge about your field

Knowledge about the company

Personal knowledge about yourself

- Preparing yourself for the interview, arriving early, noting the environment, attending to appearance

- Staying active during the interview

- Following up

- Handling tough questions about prior employment and compensation

- Doing a personal postinterview evaluation

A subgoal to your being a better interviewee is becoming a better listener. You could break this into smaller goals by trying the following:

Encourage your speaker with head nodding and occasional uh-huhs.

Appear interested by smiling at the speaker and maintaining eye contact.

Maintain short periods of silence after the speaker has completed a final thought.

Attend to your nonverbal cues.

Moderate your verbal speed and amplitude (loudness).

These three examples demonstrate how the goals of your search need to be researched and simplified. If your goals are too general, then each of the differential tasks of the search will appear to be too demanding.

Exercise 3-2   Life Goals

This exercise is a good way to set some goals for yourself that are related to your search and your own life plan. At this stage in the book, it's important to evaluate how the way you might try to reach these goals now is different from how you might have tried it before.

Goals as a part of prediction

Project yourself five years into the future. Where do you hope to be and what do you hope to be doing?

Goals as a part of disaster planning

You've just been terminated. What do you do now?

Goal setting is important and complex. It's much more than just making lists. As you expand your subgoals and objectives, you'll be able to create a map or chart for your job search.

Eight Basic Rules for Making and Meeting Your Goals

1. Keep a log of the goals and subgoals that you have created for yourself and monitor your progress toward reaching them. If you have children, you may already have done this to shape their behavior toward some goal. In your home office, create a wall chart with a large sheet of paper and illustrate your job search in a pictorial format. While there are computer programs that assist with this, there is nothing wrong with the simple butcher paper technique. Then, as

you complete subgoals in pursuit of a final goal, acknowledge your progress. Pushpins and stickers can be useful for
tracking your steps.

2. Tell people in your support group what your goals are and
report your progress to them. This technique is often used by
weight-loss groups and smoking cessation programs. The
pressure of performing in front of a group of interested spec-
tators will keep you honest.

3. When you meet each new subgoal, be sure to give yourself
some kind of positive reward or reinforcement. It might be
something as simple as an acknowledgment in a personal
diary, but it should be there. A more tangible reward might
be more powerful. When you reach well-defined subgoals,
give yourself a treat. The same techniques that work for an
animal trainer can work for you.

4. If you're not able to reach goals or subgoals, you are probably making the goals too large or you're not using appropriate reinforcement contingencies. Be sure that you break the
goals up into achievable subgoals—and give yourself enough
of an incentive to make this worthwhile. Demonstrate to
yourself that your work deserves the rewards that you have
chosen to give yourself. If you have trouble with this, maybe
you need to get a personal monitor or a mentor to help to
reinforce you. Select someone who you want to impress with
your search who can help you to put a value on your different activities.

5. Another reason you might have trouble meeting your goals
is that you've miscalculated how long a particular task is
going to take. Most of these goal-directed activities will take
longer than you expected. Career counseling clients regularly
ask me how long the job change process will take. You
should plan to spend about one month in the job search for
every ten thousand dollars that you hope to earn in salary.
So, if you plan to earn $50,000, then you should prepare your
search activities to last about five months.

6. The more extraneous tasks you can get rid of, the better off
you'll be. You don't always have to complete the little tasks.
Turn some of the smaller goals over to someone who can
assist you. For example, don't always wash the car on Satur-
day. Get someone else to do it for you, or tolerate a dirty car
for a while.

7. Use your goals to help generate alternatives. Don't think that just because you couldn't complete a goal that it was necessarily a failure. It might be the beginning of a whole new path. You're the author of this project, and you can let yourself be free to change the ending. One of the most beneficial outcomes of this search will be the creative alternatives that you have made for yourself.

8. Organize and reorganize your goals each day, and find a natural stopping point in your work. Haphazard quitting is time consuming because you'll be unclear as to where to begin when you start again.

PART
2 | Understanding Your
Career Identity and Beliefs

4 | Your Career Identity

*... but who am I ... Of this time, of that place, of some
parentage, what does it matter?*

—Lionel Trilling

Why Is Career Identity So Important?

Bill is a financially successful corporate attorney who has never been
happy at work. He dreams of being a high school history teacher and
basketball coach, but his law firm wants him to be the managing
partner. Until recently, he never consciously thought about his career
identity; he thought he was just depressed.

Gail has a degree in archeology but could never break into that
field. She took odd jobs as a food server, gardener, and child-care
worker but feels lost. She can't make her career identity a reality,
although she is clear about what she wants to do.

Jason wants to be an artist, but he home schooled himself as a
computer software developer to pay the bills. He now works fifty

hours a week as a software engineer. He rarely has time for his art and feels he is losing his artistic soul. Economic circumstances have kept Jason from making his career identity a reality.

Beth didn't know what to do when her company was sold. She had been an assistant to the sales manager for twenty-three years when she was abruptly told that her services were no longer needed. She instructed the company's outplacement consultant that she wanted to finally do something she loved, but she just didn't know what that was. She felt adrift because she didn't have a clear career identity. She was also angry, felt betrayed, and wanted to seek revenge by suing the company.

Your career identity is a psychological concept that seems simple on its face but is actually rather complex, because you may not discriminate between a job that you have, a career you're developing, and a vocational calling that embodies your spirit. Your job may be waiting on tables while your career development is as an opera star and your vocational calling is the creative and performing arts where you perform, compose, and direct. Even if you never earn an income in your vocational calling, you may always hold on to that as your career identity.

Bill, Gail, Jason, and Beth, like many people, are struggling with career identity. Your career identity consists of the various roles that you play in life, roles that can change radically from childhood to adulthood and from job to job. Sometimes life transitions make it tough for you to know who you are and where you fit in, especially when you change careers.

Why is career identity so important? It's the kernel of all that you hope to be or become, the nucleus of your workplace confidence. It represents the accrual and integration of your experience, skills, interests, values, and personality characteristics. It's an essential variable that aids in choosing a career path, getting a job, and sustaining authentic job satisfaction.

In this chapter, you'll learn about the importance of your career identity. You will learn where it comes from, how it changes, and how painful it is to have it threatened or to lose it. You'll also see how difficult it is to give up a career identity that you have been comfortable with.

Discovering Your Career Identity

Do you know your career identity? Try this. Imagine you're entering your local supermarket when a microphone and a video camera are shoved into your face and a reporter asks, "Who are you in the work world? You have thirty seconds to tell our audience."

What pops into your head? Can you even do this? Are you speechless? Most people haven't conceptualized their career identity. But being able to answer this question is necessary for eventual career satisfaction as well as a successful career transition. A strong, focused career identity can help you in the career search process. It can empower you. It can keep you from settling for work that doesn't represent you.

Your career search forces you to test new waters; experience alone can't guide you. It's easy to lose your passions and positive expectations, but a well-articulated career identity can help to preserve passion and direction in your search.

Most of the abundant career self-help literature tells you to focus on your skills, accomplishments, interests, values, and education. That's useful, but a focus on skills and aptitudes alone doesn't necessarily help you find a position that will be satisfying. Bill, the attorney, had all the right information about skills and aptitudes when he decided to become a lawyer. Nevertheless, he chose a career that didn't meet his needs.

When you engage in a job or career search, ask yourself, "Is this job or position really who I am? Will I fit in? Are the people who work here similar to me? Do they love it here? When someone asks me what I do for a living, will I be proud of my answer?"

Your career identity is an equation that helps you define yourself and gives focus to your work life. It consists of your personal, educational, and career goals; your achievements; and your affection for the work you do.

Now, how fluid was your answer to the reporter's inquiry? The question appeared to be straightforward, but the answer wasn't so easy. Your career identity is like that. But you can learn to create a smooth answer to a career identity question. Afterwards you will feel more self-reliant in marking your career path.

Exercise 4-1   Creating a Sound Bite

Let's create a thirty-second sound bite describing who you are in the world of work. The sound bite is the first step in defining your career identity and can be used to describe yourself to people in your network and to prospective employers. Rewrite the paragraph below in your journal, replacing the words in parentheses with your answers.

> **For the past** (years, months), **I have worked as a** (job title) **for** (your place of employment). **In that time I have been able to** (describe accomplishments). **I am best known for** (personal worker characteristic). **My proudest moments in the** (place of employment) **have been when** (list what you want to be remembered for) **which shows that I** (describe your impact). **In the near future I plan to** (describe your plans). **It's my expectation that in the next five years I will** (predict the future).

This brief sound bite exercise can have a powerful impact. Jason refined and refocused his career identity, which helped him solve his own career issue. Here's what he wrote:

> **For the past** six years, **I have worked** as a software developer for a large electronic game producer located in California. **In that time I have been able to** produce some of the most creative electronic game software in the field. **I am best known for my** imagination. **My proudest moments in the** company **have been** when two of my games sold over 300,000 copies, **which shows that I** have good engineering skills, creative skills, artistry, and the capacity to work with a team of software developers. **In the near future** I plan to bring my artwork into computer graphics. **It's my expectation that in the next five years I will** seek to add my artistic skills to some of the computer graphics that we are working on.

By using this exercise, Jason began to appreciate that he has used his artistic bent in his present job. His artistic soul could surface in work environments that were not strictly artistic. Gail created the following:

> **For the past** year, **I have worked as a** gardener, waitress, and child-care aide **for** a variety of part-time companies, including Manpower, Inc. **In that time I have been able to** refine my archeological skills by taking classes at the local university and volunteering to assist my instructors in examining material from their digs, while applying for research opportunities in all parts of the world. **I am best known for** my perseverance and stick-to-itiveness. **My proudest**

moments in the different jobs that I have had **have been** developing a closely knit group of friends and supporters **which shows that I** am an excellent team member. **In the near future, I plan** to continue to take classes and increase my archeological network and apply for positions in research at the local museum. **It's my expectation that in the next five years I will** be on an archeological dig in the Middle East working as a research assistant and cook.

By using this convenient device, Gail realized that her team member skills created opportunities. She was able to add this skill to her refocused identity. Her sound bite inflated her optimism.

Jason and Gail both have a focus, plan, accomplishments, and a combination of activities that reflect their different interests and experience. A career identity sound bite captures who you are, what you can do, and what you hope to be. It takes you from confusion to clarity, without being heavy-handed. It adds new twists to the way you view yourself.

Practice your own thirty-second sound bite aloud to yourself. Voice it to a mentor or friend for further tailoring. Afterwards, evaluate it. Does it tell you who you are in a clear and concise way? Does it feel like you? If it does, then you're on your way to establishing your career identity. If it doesn't, you may be blocked. The following career identity exercises are essential for you.

Exercise 4-2   Naming Your Position

Have any friends asked you what kind of a position you are looking for? People who want to help you will ultimately ask this. Your response will help to apply your career identity to a specific job. In your journal, rewrite the paragraph below, filling in your answers.

> **I'm looking for a position as a** (job title or description). **That gives me an opportunity to use my skills to** (describe what you want to do). **I prefer a** (small, medium, large size) **company in a** (small, medium, large) (metropolitan, urban, rural) **area.**

When Jason was first asked what kind of position he was looking for, he said, "I'm looking for a small start-up company that will give me good stock options that I can exercise when the company goes public." This answer was offensive to people who were hiring him and was of no guidance to the networkers who could help him. This was quite different from his eventual response, which was:

> **I'm looking for a position as** a graphic designer **that gives me an opportunity to use my skills to** create interactive art work on CD-ROM disks. **I prefer a** medium-**size company in a** large metropolitan **area.**

This answer gave people enough information to consider their own network and who they might know in companies that are attractive to Jason. With a little effort, Jason had a description of himself and the environment he wants to work in.

The Family Approach: The Career Genogram

Where do you think your career identity comes from? How have your family roots colored your career path? How much are the jobs you want to do and the environments you want to do them in affected by your family?

For many years, family therapists have used a type of family tree that allows for the exploration of family dynamics. This tree is called a family genogram and is a part of standard practice in helping individuals, couples, and families understand their family dynamics.

More recently the genogram entered the domain of career counselors, helping individuals understand the origin of their clients' career choices. It's engrossing to examine your career choice as it fits into the fabric of your family. The career genogram is a marvelous tool to put you in touch with the career attitudes that are rooted in your family. It can help you decide whether your career identity, or lack of one, is represented in your family of origin.

The career genogram doesn't merely give you understanding. Instead, it "untraps" you. It helps get you out of a family attitude rut of expectations and judgments.

Let's focus on your genogram, or family tree. By the end of this process of exploration, you should have access to information about the following:

- Origins of career expectations in your family

- Family judgments about career choices

- Your family's definitions of success

- Congruence between your expectations and those of your family

- Patterns of career choice in your family

- Ideas about possible passions to explore

Why is this information so essential to you? It's because you'll be able to separate your choices and your life path from those of your family. With this information you'll be able to create a career path that's appropriate for you.

Exercise 4-3   Creating the Career Genogram

In order to create the genogram, you first need to gather some family historical information. Create a simple chart in your journal like the one below. Ask relatives or family friends to help you fill in pieces of information. Begin by listing the work of your four grandparents. Then add their children. That includes your mother, father, aunts, and uncles. Then add yourself as well as your siblings and your cousins.

Mother's side	Grandparents	Father's side

Aunts and Uncles

Cousins

Parents and/or stepparents

Brothers and sisters

From this information you can construct a genogram that looks like the one that is included here. There is a key in the genogram that shows you how to handle different genders, deceased members, stepparents, those who are married or living together, and those who are divorced or separated. There should be five lines in the genogram: your grandparents, aunts/uncles, cousins, parents, and brothers and sisters.

The process of creating your own genogram can be very useful; it can also be fun. Try to use oversized sheets of paper when you create the genogram. Use different colored crayons and pencils to add information. You can use regular pens and pencils to make comments about different relatives as you go along.

You might find it revealing to do your genogram with a sibling or another family member, like a cousin or an aunt. Those who can talk about the family from a somewhat different history, birth order, or environment can speak to issues about their career development that were influenced by the family. You may find that your interpretation of family career history and life roles is quite different from that of a close family member.

When you finish your genogram, answer the following:

- What family patterns do you notice?

- Which family members had a clearly formed work identity?

- Whom do you most admire? Whom do you most identify with?

- Whose career aspirations were most consistent with their achievements?

- Who was most influential in the creation of your own career identity?

- What pressures do you feel when analyzing the genogram?

Take a look at Beth's genogram. Compare your feelings about your genogram to Beth's. Beth was an assistant to the sales manager for twenty-three years. Her family appears to have incredible staying power regardless of the work tasks. Her maternal grandfather was ill and never held a permanent job, which seems to have set a tone of fear and persistence for the family. Career identity was not considered to be as important as job stability. Her maternal grandmother worked as a seamstress to make ends meet. Her paternal grandfather was a store owner and combined hard work with personal contact. Beth's mother was a homemaker and her father was a factory foreman. He had worked in the factory since his high school graduation

Beth's Genogram

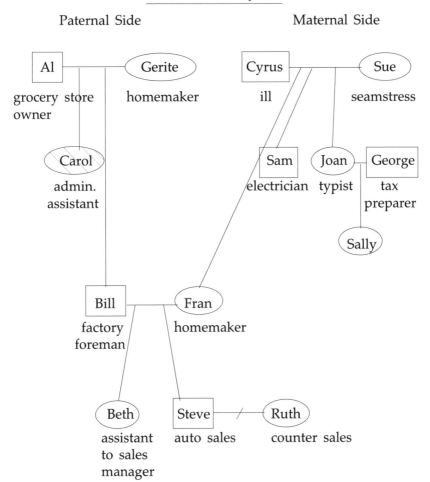

Paternal Side

Maternal Side

Al — grocery store owner

Gerite — homemaker

Cyrus — ill

Sue — seamstress

Carol — admin. assistant

Sam — electrician

Joan — typist

George — tax preparer

Sally

Bill — factory foreman

Fran — homemaker

Beth — assistant to sales manager

Steve — auto sales

Ruth — counter sales

Key

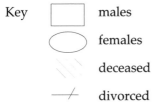

males

females

deceased

divorced

and evolved into his management position gradually. Like the others, he believed in stability and hard work. Jobwise, Beth never thought that her parents were very happy. Like them, Beth had job stability but wasn't very happy with what she did. Only after constructing the genogram during outplacement counseling did Beth begin to give herself permission to pursue something that she loved. Later you'll see how the genogram in combination with another exercise freed her from her family expectations.

Other Uses of the Genogram

If there's tension between you and your partner or spouse that you believe is due to your career identity, suggest they do a genogram. This may help to elucidate the source of their career expectations for you and lifestyle expectations for themselves. Career expectations that another person has for you may not coincide with what you have in mind for yourself.

People often forge a career identity that is based upon a new partner's career needs rather than upon their own. This path is a recipe for disaster. Although it may lead to painful discussions, an exploration of career demands on the front end of a relationship will, in the end, be far less difficult than a separation or breakup in the future.

Many of the conflicts that come up in intimate relationships have to do with career choice. In fact, some family therapists find that career issues are a more common cause of separation and divorce than infidelity. Exploring the career aspirations that a partner has for you is most enlightening.

The genogram can also be used to pinpoint times in your life when family members gave you information about their career aspirations for you. Statements like "Someday that little girl will go on to run the family dry-cleaning business" or gestures like placing a violin in the arms of a toddler can exemplify the types of family pressures that affect a person's career journey. Look at your genogram again, particularly with your parents in mind, and recall what they had hoped for you.

Mark is a successful political science professor with a Ph.D. in Government. His parents had hoped he would be a pediatrician. He feels accomplished except when he visits home. His mother still refers to him as "the son who is not the real doctor." The overwhelming number of physicians in the family genogram still haunts his mother, and she does not stifle her disappointment in Mark. The genogram helped Mark understand where his mother was coming from. He can now joke about a situation that was once painful and embarrassing.

If you're currently changing jobs, search for examples in your family genogram of people who went through career changes. Frequently, job changers believe that most family members didn't have the same kinds of traumatic career struggles that they themselves experience. They don't feel entitled to much family support. On the contrary, exploring the genogram might help identify family members who could be a source of support. It's quite useful to survey the critical incidents that led to these family members losing their jobs and finding new ones. It's comforting to know that within the family, you aren't alone.

Although the family contributed to your career identity, it's still uniquely your own, because it evolved from the landscape of your personal development. It's beneficial to take a look at how it all happened.

The Developmental Approach: Critical Life Events

Remember when you fantasized about the rest of your life, particularly your working life? Which of your characteristics made you feel special? In understanding your career identity, it's possible to take a life-stage, developmental approach.

Approaching your career identity from a developmental perspective takes into account your family experience but adds the influences of peers, educational programs, the media, and social and economic status. Dividing your life into increments or stages exposes critical incidents and points that influenced the career path you took. It allows you to focus on the barriers that emerged during each period. Like roadblocks, they forced you to switch from one direction to another. A developmental perspective helps you to understand how, when, and why you chose your career path.

Bill, the unhappy barrister, investigated his career path developmentally. He found that throughout his first twenty years, his parents just wanted him to be "happy." He loved to learn and was a three-letter athlete in both high school and college. He had lots of friends and was seen as a social, popular guy. In his last year of college, during the height of the Vietnam War, he was advised by his college counselor to attend graduate school to avoid the draft. He considered a physical education master's degree but opted instead to go to law school. After all, he'd protested against the war and wanted to be able to defend those who chose to defy their draft boards. "I want to defend the little guy," he argued. He excelled in law school and afterwards received attractive offers from large, prestigious firms. Encouraged by his family, he accepted one of the offers. He joined a business law firm as a junior associate and moved up. His clients were all corporate, and he had no time to defend the disenfranchised clients as he had originally envisioned. Each developmental stage was filled with great success, but Bill was unhappy.

By examining his career developmentally, Bill realized that his own success was his worst enemy. He unconsciously narrowed his own choices and created a career path and identity that was inconsistent with his earlier dreams. After reviewing his history, he decided not to become the managing partner of his firm. Instead he became the head of the firm's pro bono (or volunteer) unit. He also volunteered to assist the basketball coach at his local junior high school. The developmental exploration showed him alternatives he needed to take to keep his career path consistent with his career identity as an athlete, community servant, and lawyer.

Exercise 4-4   Recording Critical Incidents

Now, explore your career identity developmentally. Draw a vertical timeline representing your life from birth until the present time. Break up the timeline into five-year intervals. In each five-year interval, write down five specific critical events or personal experiences that took place. These can include obviously traumatic events like the death of a loved one, the breakup of a relationship, losing a job, failing a class, or moving from home. They can also be happy events like a new relationship, the birth of a child, or success in school. Bear in mind that you are creating this list of events to help you better understand your career identity.

Now that you've listed your important life events, evaluate their emotional impact, with a simple scale, ranging from one point for an event with slight emotional significance to five points for a life-changing, emotional event. These ratings will help you to become aware of incidents that affected you in the past and may push your emotional buttons now.

Keep in mind that some events may not look important to others, but are especially significant to you. For example, if you did poorly in your first algebra or geometry course, it might have convinced you that you could not compete academically. On this basis you could have given up some career goals prematurely. A new relationship may have been significant only to you, but it may have made you feel adored and loved in a way that you hadn't experienced before. A class that you were able to get into in college may have dictated a particular awareness of new interests. Not being able to enroll in a class that you wanted may have forced you out of a college major or a program that you'd hoped to join.

After you've completed the timeline, with the appropriate emotional response evaluation, determine how these events affect you now as you look for a new job or assess your own career circumstances. Finally, determine how these events add to or detract from your career identity.

When Jason recorded his incidents, he remembered the struggles he had in elementary school. He never felt he fit in. He wasn't athletic and preferred solitary activity. He spent hours by himself painting and drawing. At school, kids called him Jumping Jack Jason and made him high-jump over different yardsticks, beating him up if he failed. The experience scarred Jason, and even in his adulthood, he still felt he had to keep on jumping corporate hoops just to survive. He recalled the delight he felt with the song "Jumpin' Jack Flash." It didn't heal anything, but he felt a lot better when the name was associated with a popular singing group.

If you have difficulty remembering particular events or activities, you can research historical information from local newspapers. Use the Internet to research papers, if you like. Historical research might serve to prick your memory about events that were significant to you in the past. You can trigger memory by recalling friends, colleagues, teachers, and bosses from years ago. Reviewing old report cards and resumes and collections of artifacts can also help. Using the relaxation exercises in Chapter 5 can also help you to visualize earlier circumstances.

Identity, Fantasy, and Expectations

Besides the critical life events, it's important to also review your fantasies as you moved through life. Issues of self-perception and self-worth are reflected in how well your particular career identity matches your career expectations. Psychoanalysts refer to this process as matching your real self with your idealized self.

The closer your idealized self and your real self are to each other, the greater is your chance of experiencing career and personal satisfaction. People who don't experience this feel like they never measure up. They feel they have failed in some way even though society might view them as personally, vocationally, and financially successful.

Albert Einstein was one of the greatest astrophysicists of his generation. On the basis of his brilliance and certainly in no small measure on the basis of his fame, he was asked to become the first president of the new state of Israel. He turned the opportunity down. With all the notoriety, he felt it detracted from who he was. It was inconsistent with his career identity and career expectations. His expectation was to be the best and most productive astrophysicist he could be; it was not to become the head of the government of Israel. Einstein achieved congruence between his career identity and his career expectations. Had he taken the political position and not done well, he would probably feel that he failed both himself and Israel.

Exercise 4-5   Making a Fantasy Chart

Let's explore the consistency between you career expectations or fantasies and your career identity. Make an educational time line by writing down what you hoped to be at the following ages or educational periods:

- Five years old or your first days of kindergarten

- Twelve years old or the sixth grade

- Fifteen years old or ninth and tenth grades

- Eighteen years old or graduation from high school

- Twenty years old and second year of post–high school education or work

- Graduation from college or first promotion

How do these different career expectations and fantasies contribute to your career identity ? Were there times when you had no idea who you were or what you wanted to do? If you were unclear about your expectations, was it because you couldn't make decisions, had no appropriate information, received no guidance, or had no mentoring? Any of these issues can make it more difficult for you to embody imagination and expectations. How consistent is your current life path with your earlier fantasies? Remember that it is possible to make your next move more consistent with your fantasies.

As you go through this exercise, you might find that you compare yourself to your siblings, friends, and peers. This comparison can elicit vivid emotional reactions. You may resent others who seem to have their predetermined career paths. You may believe that others, for whatever reason, received more support than you did in your career planning. Your family may have said to you that they wanted you to "just be happy." But perhaps they gave you no guidance or direction that benefitted you.

You might also find that some of the circumstances, decisions, and choices you thought were irreversible may in fact not be. Some of your choices may have necessitated a compromise. Maybe you were unwilling to compromise earlier but are more willing to now. For instance, some students aspire to be physicians without ever considering the vast number of other positions available in the health field. But if those individuals can't get into medical school, they rarely consider other health-related jobs like nurse practitioner, medical technician, clinical health specialist, psychologist, researcher, emergency medical technician, or hospital administrator. These are a just a few of the potential positions in the health field. Unfortunately, the pain of rejection from medical school often results in an applicant's refusal to consider other health-related fields.

Developmental Barriers

As a final piece of the process of exploring your career identity developmentally, list the most significant barriers to your achieving a fulfilling career identity. Barriers can be exemplified by a lack of funds, poor early education, prior arrest record or early military conscription. It's important to recognize these now because they're often the excuses you use to prevent you from taking the risks that make significant life changes. Hold on to the list. How to eliminate these barriers will be addressed in chapter 6.

The Narrative Approach: Writing Your Story

A third way to explore your career identity is through narrative work, which involves focusing upon the development of your career identity as a story (Jepson 1993).

Career counselors have known for years that the career search unfolds like a yarn. Since storytelling isn't a terribly difficult task, and most of us grew up having other people tell us stories, you might find that with a little structural assistance, you could write or tape record your career development as an interesting story. You can tell your whole career story or you can attend to a specific event or recollection.

Exercise 4-6   Career Drama

What elements go into a good yarn? The conventional wisdom says there should be a scene, action, some purpose or goal, and at least one character. The story doesn't need to be long. Career drama can keep it interesting.

Write your story for yourself, a mentor or a mythical counselor. Try this simple structure that narrative therapists use. Just write your initial story in four short sentences, beginning the sentences as follows:

It all began, so we are told, when . . .

And then . . .

So . . .

And finally . . .

The story as a writing exercise can force you to think about not only yourself but other influential characters who you want to put into the story. You can describe the characters, protagonists, and antagonists in whatever fashion you want.

Your career story can help you to define some of your aspirations and interests. You can expand it and change it as your perceptions evolve with your exploration. In addition, you can edit it and reinterpret it to fit in with outcomes that are consistent with who you are or want to be. Beth wrote the following story:

> **It all began, so we are told, when** mother said that I wouldn't amount to anything. She worried that I wouldn't be able to support myself. **And then,** after I cried, I decided that I would go get a permanent job that no one could take away from me. **So,** I joined a local company and stayed there twenty-three years as an assistant to a sales manager who treated me terribly. **And finally,** the company was sold and I had nowhere to go so I decided then and there to prove that mother was wrong even though she'd been dead for five years.

Beth was able to express a great deal about her career identity with her story. She showed how emotionally tarnished and frightened she was. She also demonstrated how, even with her planning, things don't turn out the way that you expect. She ends on an optimistic note and lets us all know that her new career identity has yet to be established. The story has sadness, perseverance, and hope.

If, like Beth, your story doesn't end with the career identity or outcome that you want, add fictional content. Establish yourself as the main character and eventually the hero, if you choose. Envision your career identity as evolving, flexible, and subject to change and renewal. Storytelling can instill new hope as you resurrect your career identity.

The story of your career allows you to see how much control you had—and still have—over the formation of your career identity. It also allows you to explore your own intentions and foibles, where you had power and where you did not, and to visualize how you might have done things differently. It acknowledges the nature of the choices you have and how you can maneuver yourself to take advantage of these choices.

Exercise 4-7   Winning the Lottery

What would you do if you won the lottery and were now and forever financially independent? List ten activities that answer this question. After you make the list, ask yourself what has prevented you from doing these things already.

This exercise is extremely valuable because it dwells only upon the moment and who you want to be. If you answer the lottery question by indicating that you would probably keep your current job, then you've undoubtedly achieved a strong career identity. Your expectations and career identity are consistent with each other. Who you are is who you want to be.

There are some common answers to this question; perhaps you share some. Many say they want to travel for a few months. Others want to spend time in volunteer work. If you share these kinds of answers, try to take the activity deeper. If you want to travel, determine where you want to go and why you want to go there. Also ask what you would do when you got there. If you want to engage in a volunteer activity, figure out what the activity would be and where you would like to do it.

What If I Can't Describe My Identity?

For many of you, this chapter has given you insights regarding the origin of your identity. But the exercises herein are not necessarily going to solve everyone's problems regarding who they are or ought to be. Many people do not know who they are and have no idea what they want to do. Their career path is somewhat akin to driving nails into a hundred-foot board; there is no structure. Like Jason, they've gotten jobs to survive. But the jobs bear no relationship to their understanding of who they are. Others have developed career paths simply by falling into something. They did not do any serious looking, searching, applying. Jobs appeared through friends and with luck.

When people without a clear sense of their own identity and purpose compete in the job search process, they regularly encounter the feeling that they do not know who they really are. Why does this happen?

Indecisiveness

Some people do not have a clear concept of their own identity because they are and have always been indecisive. The indecisive person often has a whole complex of associated issues that have made it impossible to develop a career identity. This state is called role confusion. A lack of clear identity can stem from a life of ineffectual involvement in a variety of activities, a feeling of incompetency and/or poor decision-making skills. The inability to settle on an occupational identity is terribly disturbing.

Beth was highly anxious in the work world and came from a history of fear about career instability. Her lack of personal security and ego strength caused her to stay put on her job. Anxiety, undoubtedly from her family history, kept her from moving. So when she had to find new work, she couldn't make a decision. She wanted something she loved, but when she tried to make a choice, her indecisiveness set in. She gave herself permission to search for what she loved. But she had trouble identifying it because of her indecision. Beth's indecision and identity issues stared at her with an unrelenting persistence. Her self-confidence wilted at a time when she needed it the most.

There are many explanations for indecision. The most plausible is that indecisive people were not given much support for their childhood decisions. They were unattended to, criticized, negated, or abused emotionally. Decision making became filled with high anxiety. Criticism made it impossible for them to get a clear understanding of their own interests, values, and goals. The options they generated for themselves were disparaged, so they stopped creating options and took what was given to them. This dysfunctional history results in an indecisive person, who lacks in self-esteem and clarity.

Other indecisive people feel that they can never emulate their parents, so they give up trying. Camille's mother had won numerous awards for journalism. Camille felt that no matter what she did, she would never be as good as her mother. She couldn't decide on any career because she felt she could not begin to accomplish what her mother had. Too paralyzed to pursue activities she might love, she gave up.

Indecisive people are different from undecided people. Undecided people simply lack information about their characteristics or the job market. They haven't been cut off from their identity by parental or supervisory criticism.

There is, of course, hope for the indecisive. If you're indecisive, you need to begin to reexplore your childhood in a supportive atmosphere and work through the stages that have been described earlier in this chapter. Go back to the developmental stage chart and recreate an early fantasy life. Experience the reopening of your curiosity and imagination to new possibilities. Reading vocational biographies that are available in most career libraries will be useful. Creating a story can help. Talking to others who have rehabilitated their indecisiveness generates support. These techniques may take some time, but the payoff in the formulation of a clear career identity will be priceless.

Multiple Talents

Another group of people do not have a clear sense of their identity, not because they come from difficult family circumstances, but because they do everything well. They are people with multiple talents. Each of the talents is strong and equally potent, a state called multipotential-equipotentiality.

These are the Thomas Jefferson types. Once President Kennedy addressed a White House dinner of American scientists and began the evening by exclaiming that on this occasion there was more talent in the White House dining room than on any night except those when Thomas Jefferson dined there alone.

People with multipotential-equipotentiality, like the indecisive, also suffer. They feel successful, brilliant, and competent. But they may lack a clear career identity. Most importantly, they often refuse to relinquish any of their potential career talents.

Vinny majored in art in college and then considered art graduate school along with medical school and business school. When he received his graduate degree in art, he regretted he had not chosen medical school. So, he applied to medical school, got in, and then wrestled with whether to go. He wanted to complete medical school but also wanted business knowledge to facilitate running a practice. But then, if he completed a business degree, he wondered, was legal education far behind?

In brief, these are people who have stellar education and educational potential but have an extremely difficult time launching a career because they are unable to choose between different aptitudes and abilities in order to keep focused. For example, they don't relinquish musical talent in favor of mathematical skills. They continue to add on to their potential career choices without career discrimination.

If you fit this type, you need to find some way of integrating your education into a new identity, or you need to pursue some activities and education vocationally while you pursue others as recreational or leisure activities. If this is not possible, then you need to consider splitting your work identity into parts and creating a job network that is more part-time, portfolio, or project-driven. For example, you could be a fill-in physician on the weekends for a large HMO, while you spend three days a week engaging in tax and investment advice for health professionals. You could be a firefighter with a one-day-on and two-day-off schedule and practice dentistry as a fill-in dentist. You could be a roofer and a substitute teacher.

Identity Loss

Unemployment

Job loss creates identity loss. It also creates a new identity as "unemployed." For an unemployed worker, the job search has the added dimension of incorporating an identity (unemployed) that is disparaged by society. Unemployed job seekers may feel they are losers or have-nots. Time has passed them by. They may have made poor career or institutional choices.

So what do you do about an identity if you're unemployed? If you are looking for work, develop a transitional identity. Call yourself a "job changer" or an "explorer." After all, you're attempting to reinvent yourself. Some job changers refer to themselves as consultants, entrepreneurs, private investors, project workers, or temporary employees.

Even though you're unemployed, try to use a positive label to identify yourself. Be a "worker in transition." Speak to others about that. Find those similarly situated to support you. Find self-help groups of other transitioning workers with whom you can share a common bond that leads to the affirmation of an identity different from the one you left. Make the job search process a distinguished interlude. Share with others the experiences you have as you continue through the transition. Take note of those who created new paths because they were without a job.

Should you be able to create an identity that gives greater comfort during the career search process, it is important not to hang on to the "unemployed" identity for too long. Some unemployed people who attend self-help career groups like Forty Plus begin to enjoy the identity they have in the group. While this can be affirming, it can also hinder the job search. Organizations like this can be so supportive and may offer members such a safe identity that they do not want to leave and reenter the job market. It's curious how much we need an identity and sense of belonging, even when both may be detrimental to our success and to moving on.

Promotions

While it may be obvious that job loss is painful, it may not be so obvious that a promotion can also be painful. In fact, both experiences involve loss and, as such, demand a readjustment period. When searching for a new position after a termination, you're forced to engage in a job search when you are not emotionally available to yourself. You are in shock, depressed, and disoriented. Promotion can bring a similar sense of loss and disorientation.

After a promotion, you may be surprised to find how difficult the adjustment is, especially if you're joining a new organization. You have lost an identity and series of labels that you were familiar with. Studies of depression show that rapid increases and decreases in wealth and prestige result in similar rates of depression. If you were recently promoted, give yourself adjustment time. Join a cohort group in a local management association. By all means stay in contact with the person who held the position before you.

The Dream versus Practicality

There are those who strive to achieve a certain goal but never reach it. Aspiring actors may never get the opportunity to act in the roles they want or the venues they aspire to play. Most talented, well-trained painters never sell a completed work. Few classically trained musicians ever play in a professional, large city orchestra. These types have a most difficult dilemma. If they leave the world of the artist in order to take a job with security, they generally experience a loss of identity as they give up their artistic pursuits. They also have the problem of never knowing whether or not, with a little bit of luck, they could have achieved career success.

Fear of Failure or Success

There are some who have difficulty establishing a career identity because of fears. These feelings can be reduced to two types—the fear of success and the fear of failure.

Fear of success disrupts your career identity development because you utilize avoidance behaviors to keep from achieving lofty goals. The fear may be related to undercommitment, but it's usually due to having to compete in an unfriendly environment. Success puts you on unfamiliar terrain.

If fear of success is your backdrop, you refrain from putting your talents and abilities out where others will scrutinize them. You curtail your talents and are careful to bring little notice to yourself. You stifle your potential identity development and instead function in a work life that is free of some of the pressures that a promotion entails. If you continue in this pattern, you'll never realize your potential.

The majority of people who experience the fear of success are new to success in the institutional setting. They may be first-timers: first in their family to receive a college degree or first to get a management position in a factory. The best way to address this fear is to meet with others who also may be in the first generation of highly successful people in their families. Civic organizations and service clubs are good beginning professional associations to cultivate.

Similarly, fear of failure leads you to avoid the behavior that could result in success. If you fear failure, you would rather be seen as capable of ascending to new heights than to be told that you don't have the right stuff to be successful. To maintain this illusion, you avoid difficult tasks, and your progress stagnates. To break this pattern, choose a mentor at work who can be watchful, helpful, and encouraging. You need to be told regularly that you will be okay.

When people suffer from fear of success or fear of failure, they'll never experience their best work efforts. They won't be able to add higher-order accomplishments to their identity. They'll wonder throughout their life about what might have been.

The Identity Paradox

In school, as you progressed, you eventually looked forward to graduation. It may have been junior high school, high school, an apprenticeship, a vocational training program, college, or graduate or professional school. Upon commencement, you were supposed to move on. But two adjustments occurred. First, you *lost* something that was comfortable and familiar, the identification with the school or program. Second, you *kept* part of the old label that identified you with this experience. This is the paradox of your shifting identity.

Different illustrations suggest the complexity of developing an identity and transitioning away from it. For example, soldiers become vets, always entitled to veteran's benefits. But the soldier identity is lost. Vets generally don't fly F-18s, lead a corps of cadets, or have the satisfaction of defending the country. But vets keep their soldier part. Whether carpenters or lawyers, vets are likely to be holding on to soldier memories. They will feel comfortable with other vets who share similar military experiences and attitudes.

Likewise, when you graduate from college, your identity as a student should graduate with you. But at social gatherings, professionals ask each other, "Where did you go to school?" Most significantly, your alma mater wants to reinforce your old identity; it will always claim you, most notably around fund-raising time. Even though you lost student status, you kept your identity as a "Tiger," "Badger," "Trojan," or "Gator." You may never hear your high school nicknames again, except at a class reunion, but it reinforces that old identity. You had it. You transitioned from it. But it's easy to get back into it, with the right environment and circle of people who share a common experience.

When you move from one realm to another, you make choices, and with each of these choices you give up your old identity. By doing this, you lose the identity that you have developed for yourself. This loss can be painful and disorienting. It is one of the uncomfortable aspects of transitioning.

The paradox of the career identity adds to the emotional baggage of the career search. With a precipitous career transition such as a layoff, reduction in force, or firing, the loss process is disconcertingly painful. To prevent feelings of loss, you try to hold on and not move forward. Trying on a new work identity is demanding. It's not like changing your daily clothing. It's more like changing a wardrobe: you throw out a lot but you keep a few outfits that you like best and believe will last a while longer.

Some people are perpetual students. They want to stay in school as long as possible, maintaining that identity. Some college professors joke that they never wanted to go to work for a living—they wanted to stay in school forever. Some soldiers never dare leave the service. If they do, they may find that they spend their social times at clubs around their former military bases. Others maintain their military identity and stay connected with their base by remaining in the reserves.

John Glenn exemplifies some of the confusing aspects of establishing an identity that stays with you long after you take on a new identity. Glenn was an astronaut who was the first to circle the earth, an American hero and legend. He later became a United States senator. But he'll always be a hero and recognized for his work in the NASA program. Recently John Glenn returned to space as an astronaut. So how would you define his worker identity?

Unlike some astronauts, Glenn was able to make a transition to a new career and appropriately embody some of the characteristics of the old career. Several astronauts have not been as successful in moving on to new careers, and have been chronicled as very depressed.

Jane Fonda is a prominent individual who has gone through several identity transitions. She may seem like an enigma to you. Would you characterize her as an activist, an actress, a workout video producer, a mother, or a traditional wife married to a wealthy business tycoon? She moved from one identity to the next with what appears to be relative ease. That's not to say that she did it without struggle. But each time she dared to leave a career identity behind her, she took on another different and challenging one. She could discard much of the old identity without needing to hang on.

The above examples are all about successes. But what about people who fail in work or school or the transition process? People who flunk out of school or are terminated from their work positions experience a loss of identity and probably do not feel comfortable with holding on to the previous identity. A dishonorably discharged soldier presumably maintains little military identity. A high school dropout rarely returns for reunions. College dropout Bill Gates probably did not suffer the loss of the college student identity. Of course, his alma mater welcomed his financial contributions even though he did not graduate.

So you can see that creating, losing, and hanging on to an identity is complex and multifaceted. It is not a simple linear process, but a paradox full of both loss and hope.

Career Identity and Self-Worth

How important is your career identity to your self-worth? Do you describe yourself by your worker characteristics or job skills or instead by your individual interests, values, and physical and personal characteristics? When your friends describe you, what characteristics do they focus on? How do your neighbors or co-workers view you? Do they reflect upon your personal or your workplace characteristics?

Generally we make judgments about the careers of other people without knowing much about them. Perhaps you've traveled and been seated next to someone on a plane or train or bus. If you begin to have a conversation with the person next to you, invariably your work status is brought up as a common denominator of understanding. You're engaged in measuring and comparing yourselves to each other.

Your assessment of another person's career path is a projection of your concepts of success and failure. But rarely do you know what that person actually does. A person sitting next to you sharing a transportation experience may say that she is a psychologist. Light bulbs go off. But what do you think that means? That's partly based on your personal experience with a psychologist, or a psychology professor at school, or a talk show psychologist, or television characters like Bob Newhart or Frasier. So your labeling of that person is based upon your own experience as well as your preconceived idea of what goes into that person's career. Unless you ask, you have no idea what this person's career is really like. But this doesn't stop you from thinking you know. Sitting next to a psychologist is intriguing for many, threatening for a few, and boring for others.

Compare the experience above with how you feel when someone tells you she's a teacher. What are the different perceptions you have of the two different roles? Now, it's quite conceivable that the same person is both a psychologist and a teacher or professor. Still, what does the word "teacher" bring up for you? All of us share the common experience of being with a teacher. That makes the evaluative process likely to be more tangible and experiential with the teacher as compared to the psychologist.

Exercise 4-8   Judging Career Identities

Try this last activity, which you can do any time you're out of the house. Explore your judgments to a variety of occupations. As you ride the bus or walk along the street, talk to others and ask what they do. Make note of the kinds of judgments you make about career choices. What you're doing is exploring how you evaluate, label, sort people into different categories. Now, notice what you do when someone says they're recently unemployed, or that they've been looking for work for several months, or that they're a student who's just starting to plan a career in a particular field. What judgments do you make?

The manner in which you judge the career choices and aspirations of others is often a good predictor of how you'll judge yourself. All of this informs career identity. If you're a job seeker, you may judge yourself as inadequate because you don't currently have a position. On the other hand, you may reward yourself because you're trying to make a change that's better for you and the people around you.

A pervasive difficulty with career identity is that your worth in contemporary society is based upon the prestige of your work. You may buy into this. If you do, your career may be inconsistent with what you love to do. A provocative column in *Newsweek* was titled "What's your real job?" One sentence illustrated the theme: "I'm an actress with a Harvard degree and my family worries I'm wasting my education." There was a conflict in the family over the worth of the author's career identity. The Harvard grad actress pressed a lot of readers' buttons.

The next week, *Newsweek* published several letters responding to this one-page article. One letter was from an unsuccessful medical school applicant. He said, "I firmly believe that I cannot be happy doing anything else." Another said, "I completely agree with following your heart." In contrast, another was from a mother and father who had a child who was a theater director. They said, "It never occurred to us to question her choice of a career."

Like the Harvard grad actress, there are many examples of people who took winding paths to be happy with their work. Your happiness and satisfaction come when your work identity meshes with your work. A final success story supports the point. Michael Crichton has a medical school degree. He chose to become an author, not a doctor, and is currently both a writer and movie director. He followed his heart, and people now view him as successful. How would you view him had he not been financially successful but continued to write? What judgments would you have made about him?

5 | Your Career and Personal Beliefs

I want to be a lady in a flower shop stead of sellin'
at the corner of Tottenham Court Road. But they
won't take me unless I can talk more genteel.

—Eliza Doolittle in *Pygmalion*
by G. B. Shaw

Tuning In to Your Career Beliefs

Eliza Doolittle has a well-scripted career belief. It's likely that you have more than a few of your own. Most career beliefs have something to do with how you think people will respond to your credentials. Now, Eliza has clearly convinced herself that she can't attain her job of choice without some major reconfiguring of her transferable skills. Further, she believes with some confidence that if she were to make the requisite changes in the way she spoke, she would secure the position she desires. Both of the beliefs may be true, or one or both may be false. Regardless, her beliefs frame and guide her career decisions.

Eliza hesitates to apply for work in the flower shop because she's obsessed with the belief that she won't be accepted. She probably has visions of people scorning her or mocking the way she speaks. Unfortunately, her belief will limit her view of her options, and she'll never arrange for other types of work in the flower business that don't require articulate language skills. Eliza is blocked by her unyielding belief, convinced that she can't have what she wants. How familiar is this pattern to you? How many times have you been unwilling to risk rejection because you believed that you weren't qualified?

Notice how Eliza is also setting herself up, so to speak. She believes that with improvement in her linguistic skills through continuing education, she'll succeed in working in a flower stand. There may be none other than anecdotal evidence to suggest that this is true. Other skills are surely required. Clerking in a flower stand, like working in other small businesses, demands more than simply improved articulation skills. But her belief drives her to focus on a goal that will be time consuming and, were it not for Henry Higgins, expensive. She risks the possibility of being sorely disappointed.

Your Beliefs Can Change Your Life

Career beliefs are powerful determinants in career decision making. They reflect what you accept and reject about your prospects for work. They help to motivate you forward or push you backwards, stifling your search. They can encourage or depress your efforts.

Beliefs can be global or specific. You use them to explain the particulars of your life circumstances. For example, if you perform poorly on employee or scholastic aptitude tests, you can explain this with the belief that you're not very smart or that you just don't do very well on tests like these. That's an internalized belief about your innate test-taking ability. But you can also have certain beliefs about external events and how they affect you. Maybe you think you did poorly on a test because you were tired, distracted, or just not able to relate to the questions. These beliefs about your performance relate to circumstances that might not be so internal to you.

Preparatory programs and review courses for different professional board examinations brazenly exploit the often pessimistic career beliefs, both internal and external, of high achievers. They seem to threaten you with failure or embarrassment. As a state psychology oral examination commissioner, I am shocked by promotional literature claiming that you can't possibly pass your "boards" without review courses, regardless of your personal preparation, education, or plain old exam "smarts."

Your beliefs can be long-term dispositions. They can be rational or irrational. They can promote or deny you. Beliefs that are illogical, irrational, or just plain wrong can seriously affect you career search—and they need to be confronted. How many times in your career have you made the "right" decision only to find out later that your decision was based upon inaccurate data? How many seemingly stable companies did you consider joining only to find out afterwards that they were in some financial distress? Sometimes we disregard the very best objective information available to us because we hold very strong beliefs about a person, company, or personal characteristic.

By the way, there are many infamous business blunders based upon erroneous beliefs and inaccurate data. A case in point: In the early days of computing, IBM believed that a little upstart company named Microsoft could never really have much impact on a company with a history like IBM's. Well, if wise old IBM had not permitted Bill Gates and Microsoft to keep the original licensing rights for the early PC internal operating software, a sprouting Microsoft would probably never have been able to swell and capitalize as it has. And Bill Gates would probably not be a household name. Some call this IBM's greatest misstep, based on an erroneous belief about itself.

Three Common but Erroneous Beliefs

Here's a list of three of the most common generic career beliefs that I have heard coming from the minds and lips of career searchers. You've probably heard them yourself. Maybe they reflect your own beliefs. Regardless, they're worth pondering as you explore how particular thoughts about yourself and your career beliefs can discourage you from moving forward in your search. Look at the belief and then pay attention to how the belief can be confronted.

"It's too late for me to start over again."

The youthfulness of the high-tech future probably has taken its toll on you. The fact of the matter is that it's never too late to jump-start your career. Your career path can have a lot of leeway, more than you've imagined, and the seemingly unstable, futuristic workplace is ready for new ideas and innovation. It's also ripe for new directions that are based upon wisdom and proven skills. Your years of experience can be put to use in the generation of new approaches to doing things.

Let's remind ourselves of a few newsworthy examples. You may not agree with or appreciate eighty-year-old *60 Minutes* curmudgeon Andy Rooney. But this sagacious reporter still comments on life and work in America every week, infuriating some, amusing others. Senator John Glenn went into space again at seventy-seven, to the chagrin of his family. Coco Chanel was seventy-one when she introduced the woman's suit that eventually captured the interests of the fashion design world and made her famous. Venerable Harland Sanders, the all too familiar Colonel, pulled together his Kentucky Fried Chicken (KFC) enterprise when he was sixty-one. Gordon Liddy left prison to become a successful talk show host, the same line of work that former California Attorney General Dan Lungren connected to when he lost his bid for the governor's mansion.

Jerry Brown was the governor of California for eight years. He was an unsuccessful presidential candidate and, like the two aforementioned politicians, became a talk show host. At age sixty, he decided to make another campaign run, this time to be mayor of Oakland, California. He embodies the spirit of taking new risks and staying in touch with new opportunities. He takes care of himself, lives simply, and puts his energy into creating opportunities that are important to him. His political drives resurfaced after his stint as a media host. He never adopted the belief that he couldn't win another election. And he ran in a multiethnic city that had not had a Caucasian mayor since the mid 1970s. He demonstrates that it's never too late to create. Now that he is mayor, he has turned over his management staff to begin afresh, with a whole new team.

There is some evidence that unemployed executives are taking potential new opportunities more to heart. They're using their wisdom and experience to launch new ideas. A recent study by the Chicago outplacement consulting firm Challenger, Grey & Christmas noted that in the last quarter of 1998, 11 percent of the executives and managers who had lost their jobs were making the decision to create entrepreneurial endeavors for themselves. In part, this is due to the current availability of venture capital. It may also be due to the economic stability some people are enjoying; the stock market has done well recently and many households have two incomes. A side benefit is that people who keep active and take on new adventures stay healthier and live longer.

Well-known urban universities are in the process of creating graduate programs for people who want to expand their career land-scapes or retool their skills. Many have "executive" MBA programs. Others, like the University of Phoenix, promote degree programs nationwide to assist career changers in reinventing themselves through education. These are frequently geared to older workers. They are popular enough for other, more traditional universities to copycat their course offerings.

After he had retired from his work as a history professor, Leonard began to take courses in poetry writing at a local community college. At the age of seventy-two, he still felt he had strong internal productivity. He has just signed a contract to publish his first compilation of poems inspired by his experience of the aging and retirement process. He has also signed on to develop travel suggestions for retired educators, on a new Internet site.

In light of what's been documented so far, it may come as no surprise to you that the fastest growing group of new computer purchasers and users are fifty-five- to seventy-four-year-olds. San Francisco is home to a large organization called Senior Net (see Appendix) whose mission is to teach computer skills to seniors. At this writing, there are 150 learning centers in thirty-five states. An astonishing 70 percent of computer owners over age fifty-five have access to the Internet, a number that will only increase. (Contrast this with a comparatively meager 17 percent in 1995.) SeniorNet offers book clubs and bulletin board discussion groups on current events. It's clear that seniors wish to continue to learn, and they don't appear to be computer phobic. E-mail seems to be the primary reason, however, that seniors purchase and use a computer. Seniors can also access for-profit sites like Third Age Media (see Appendix) to explore romance, relationships, monetary issues, and travel. Health and caregiving information are also on the site. The American Association of Retired Persons (AARP) has a Web site (see Appendix) and there is another popular site for people over fifty called SeniorCom (see Appendix).

Finally, it has become abundantly clear that older workers are needed now more than ever before. There are documented shortages of experienced workers in many different occupations, and these can easily be filled by people with not only experience, but also strong, transferable skills. Nationally certified career consultant Norm Meshriy tells these older workers to "wear their experience with pride." He believes that when modern elder-friendly workplace techniques and information availability combine with a youthful and energetic presence, the world is their oyster.

"Midlife is a time of career and identity crisis."

You've heard of the midlife crisis. Maybe you've had one, or thought you did. Despite this stereotype, people between forty and sixty years of age appear to be quite a happy bunch. In fact, the baby boomers appear to be happier than ever. Sure, maybe it is all in the current economics. But people in midlife today have a greater sense of their own physical, mental, and emotional well-being, according to Orville Brim, project director of a ten-year, $9.5 million MacArthur Foundation research project.

What are the ingredients for this bliss? Evidence suggests that a good relationship with a life mate, satisfaction with one's children, and security at work all play a part. By the way, some of this change in the attitudes of the boomers and the elderly may be related to recent, popular, pharmaceutical developments like Viagra, melatonin, hormone replacement tablets, and minoxidil. There's also a growing interest in over-the-counter mood enhancers like Saint-John's-wort.

What you may be more aware of at midlife is not so much a crisis, but rather that your approach to life is different. This new attitude makes midlife an attractive time to engineer some type of career change or development. You may have a better idea of what fulfills you, and because you may also have fewer responsibilities, you can pursue exciting challenges. What you will almost certainly find as you search for a richer experience or environment is that people around you may feel threatened, which can keep them from being supportive of your attempts at fashioning a new career and life plan.

You should try to develop a support group of people who are making changes similar to yours. Some can be found on the Web sites listed above; others might be at your local chamber of commerce or unemployment office; and still others may be affiliated with religious or civic organizations. You need support in these times, and if those around you cannot provide it, then you need to create supportive associations elsewhere.

"It's natural for people to get sadder as they age."

Another belief that you can confront is that people become sadder as they get older. Years ago this had a fancy name—involutional melancholia. New research suggests the opposite is true, according to

Mroczek and Kolarz (1998). Aging certainly is full of life changes, as our physical problems increase and we lose intimate relationships and significant others. But this study suggests that older individuals seem to be able to regulate their emotions more readily than people who are much younger. They have a better handle on their boundaries, exert more control, stay away from a frenetic life pace, and, as a result, seem to be happier, not sadder. The study goes on to say that older men, if they are married, appear to be the happiest group of all.

The Power of Beliefs

Sometimes beliefs are derived from data, however scant, while at other times superstitions and spiritual beliefs are their foundation. They can and often do develop without much scientific evidence. Theologians have explored the power of beliefs for centuries, as well they should have. Religious and spiritual beliefs have influenced the way people make decisions about their lives despite the arguments against the existence of God or a supreme being.

Like religious beliefs, career beliefs can influence your path in life. In the eighteenth century, career and religious beliefs merged, for work was viewed by theologians as a means by which God could be served. A Protestant work ethic emerged from this belief; the harder you worked the more God was served. During the gold rush, belief in striking it rich provoked massive career migrations to California and Alaska. Wall Street's love affair with any stocks that end with ".com" created an early belief that Internet stocks would only go up.

With a little reflection, you can bring beliefs into the context of your career. John Krumboltz (1991) defined career beliefs in the manual to *The Career Beliefs Inventory*. He suggested that career beliefs are reflective of our past experiences and that they help us to form a consistent and cohesive reference frame, which assists us in figuring out ourselves and our world. The exercises in this chapter will help you to understand and clarify your beliefs.

Beliefs about Ourselves

There are essentially three kinds of beliefs: those about ourselves, those about our environment, and those about our interactions with our environment.

First of all, there are our firmly held beliefs about our individual selves. We make self-observations all the time in the form of personal appraisals. "I'm not very quick; I'm not very smart; I'm a multitasker;

I'm a lucky person"; all exemplify the type of appraisals that you've made about yourself at one time or another. Interests, skills, values, personal characteristics are all assessed by you regularly throughout your life. As the examples above show, they can be self-promoting or self-defeating. But they aid us in appropriately positioning ourselves for the career risks that we hope to take. Our beliefs can also be the instigators for us to consider professional therapeutic interventions, as reflected by, "I need help. I can't do this alone."

Beliefs about Our Environment

Second, there is the belief or appraisal that we make about the environment. We can say, for example, that particular environments are more intellectually difficult than others. Other environments are more physically dangerous and still others are more fiercely competitive. We can gather data to determine whether a particular environment is hostile toward us or not. For example, you've probably heard companies referred to as friendly toward women, or having a policy that truly supports a multiethnic, multicultural, or diversified workforce.

Our beliefs about the work environment affect our decision to apply or not, to join or not, to stay or not. We use our beliefs to predict whether it's safe to venture into a particular territory. We decide whether or not to apply for a position because we think we may or may not be considered. Beliefs like Eliza's, "They'll never consider me," are uttered with regularity.

To be sure, acceptance into certain institutions is fueled by applicants having cleared specific hurdles. Some professional organizations, such as exclusive law firms, are characterized by certain pedigrees. They only take people from the top ten law schools. Other companies are known to save a few seats for the graduates of the president's alma mater. Both public and private universities cater to historical legacies and admit people who may not be as competitive or qualified as others they admit.

We also gather beliefs about industries that are booming and those that are fading away. Any dunderhead knows that hot new jobs are in technology. But what beliefs do you have about work environments that may be in trouble? I suppose that you can figure out by yourself that if the Internet is taking over the way we buy and sell, retailing as we know it may be on the way out. ATMs seem to be taking over most bank teller positions, and companies with heavy assets in tobacco are probably not burning up with new jobs. But what you need is evidence to validate or confront these beliefs.

Beliefs about Our Interactions with the Environment

Third, there is a type of belief that is related to how we interact with the environment. In this case, our belief is based on a judgment of how a particular interaction between ourselves and the environment is going to turn out. So, if you experience yourself as a poor speaker, your expectation about public speaking in the work environment suggests a belief that it's not going to turn out very well. You either avoid jobs that demand this skill or you pursue some continuing education to gain skills and position yourself better.

Krumboltz called these "task-approach skills," although they really are beliefs that you have about how well your skills will relate to particular job. They include beliefs about yourself and beliefs about the work environment. Examples include a person saying that since she can't interview people very well, she probably can't be a good psychologist. Or, since she can't add or subtract, she probably can't work in the financial world. Dyslexics don't often apply for copyediting jobs.

Eliza Doolittle may have had the following type of general self-observation: "My language skills are poor." She may have had the following belief about her chosen work environment: "The most successful flower shop owners seem to have excellent language skills." She may have had the following type of belief about her task-approach skills: "Since my linguistic skills are so poor, I will never be able to own a flower shop and sell flowers." All of these beliefs may be in error or may be true. But rarely do people check out whether their beliefs are true. They accept them as fact and then, sometimes foolishly, make their decisions.

Determining Your Career Beliefs

Now that you understand the power and the development of career beliefs, it's most important to understand what yours are and where they came from. What are your career beliefs? Hopefully, you've been able to establish or put into words your career identity, based on your work in chapter 4. If so, then you can begin to put some fantasy beliefs into what that identity will mean as you continue in your search. Your identity and your beliefs about yourself can assist you with your own self-appraisal. You can use your career identity and your beliefs to give you a benchmark for reliably understanding your skills, interests, personality characteristics, and the like.

You also need to get some knowledge of the work environment that corresponds to your identity and beliefs. You can gather information about work environments through resources like the *Dictionary of Occupational Titles*, *The Complete Guide for Occupational Exploration*, and the *Occupational Outlook Handbook*. You can find these references in any career library in your community and especially those on the campuses of a local community college. You can also access this information from an unemployment office and on the Internet through the Web site of the United States Department of Labor.

If these resources don't help you, then you can gather more tangible facts from informational interviewing with those who are in your field of interest. You can also attend meetings of professional associations. And if you enjoy reading about workers in different occupations, inquire at your local career library about the resource titled "Vocational Biographies." This series of thirty-five books contains 875 true-life career success stories. Remember as well that you can learn a lot about companies and their work environments by exploring what they offer on their own corporate Web sites. While these will clearly show bias favoring the company, they are still important, free resources to consider.

Exercise 5-1
Establishing Your Career Beliefs—Self-Appraisal

In your journal, write down the career beliefs that are reflective of your self-appraisal. These can be beliefs about your characteristics. You might say, "I'm a high achiever. I'm more creative than most. I'm happiest when I'm working outdoors."

After you have completed the self-appraisal, indicate your personal beliefs by answering yes or no to the following.

_____ I believe that I need a feeling of accomplishment in my work.

_____ I believe in my abilities and ideas and want to use them.

_____ I believe that I need to be active and busy.

_____ Variety at work will help my productivity.

_____ Steady employment and security are necessary for me.

_____ Fair compensation is very important to me.

_____ I believe in taking initiative and I don't want to be told what to do.

_____ I want a voice in determining who I will work with.

_____ I believe that the best workers seek out up-to-date and appropriate training.

_____ I just can't do the same task all of the time.

_____ I believe in being able to move up the career ladder.

_____ I work best by myself.

_____ I want my employer to be honest with me and others.

_____ I believe in setting my own work pace.

_____ I want flexible work time.

_____ I believe that I am qualified to supervise others.

_____ I want to assist others on the job.

_____ Working conditions are important to me.

_____ I want to know how I will be evaluated.

_____ I don't follow my career path in a specific sequence.

_____ I need to have clear goals.

Exercise 5-2 Establishing Your Career Beliefs—Environment Appraisal

In your journal, write down the career beliefs that you have about your potential work environment. These might be similar to the following: "I need an open-door policy with my boss in order to be productive. I need deadlines and pressure in order to be most effective."

After you have completed this, respond to the following with a yes or a no.

_____ I believe a comfortable work environment is conducive to my creativity.

_____ I believe that people need to be able to work together.

_____ I believe in a work environment where independence is encouraged.

_____ I want my company to invest in workers, not environmental trappings.

_____ I want a company that is in the area where I live.

_____ I want a work environment where there are many employees.

_____ I want a work environment where everyone has at least a college degree.

_____ I want a work environment where everyone has postgraduate degrees.

_____ I want the company environment to be a social one.

_____ I want the company to promote free continuing education and training.

_____ I want the company to promote diversity and an aging workforce.

_____ I want regularly scheduled brainstorming activities.

_____ I want management to act in a timely way on innovations and suggestions.

_____ I want to be taken seriously.

_____ I want to feel like an individual who has links to others in my field of work.

_____ I don't want the company to influence my career path.

_____ I don't want to relocate.

_____ I don't want a company where there are obstacles blocking my future.

_____ I want the environment to be pleasant.

Exercise 5-3   Establishing Your Career Beliefs—Task-Approach Skills

Your task-approach skills will depend upon your knowledge of the career world and how closely your self-appraisal aligns with the skills that you think you need in order to be successful. Here you will have to spend a bit of time exploring the closeness of fit between you and the work environment. But with factual information, you'll be able to have a more accurate appraisal of your current circumstances while confronting inaccurate career beliefs.

By examining your responses to the statements above, you should be able to determine how your self-appraisal interfaces with your work environment. Based on what you've learned, write down the career beliefs that you have about your task-approach skills. For example: "I get my best ideas from others but I need to be alone to finish my creative projects. So part of the time I need to be around people and part of the time I need to be alone."

As you complete this exercise, try to recall the basis of your career beliefs. How do you know whether or not your appraisal is an accurate one? For each of the beliefs that you have in each of these sections, write down the evidence that you have that these are true. Support your evidence with examples or literature.

Career beliefs are guidelines. But they also give you confidence that you'll be able to adjust to the future. Your career beliefs will help you to forge new relationships and to make decisions in highly intuitive and complex ways.

Steve Case is the current chief executive officer of America Online. This Internet guru is immensely successful because of his career beliefs and, in particular, his task-approach skills. He had an idea, a marketing plan, and, most importantly, a belief that his ideas for hooking up people to the Internet would create an entirely new marketplace, a new way of advertising and selling products. He took a lot of heat for his vision. But his own self-appraisal allowed him to withstand the critical attacks. His predictions about the future and his belief that he could develop a whole new world of communicating allowed him to stick to his beliefs and his long-term plan. He was able to keep his critics at bay, proving many of them wrong. Today AOL has surpassed everyone's expectations, as it purportedly competes for market share against the three original television networks.

Career beliefs are mind-sets that we use to organize our career world. They're usually developed over the long term and may not always be in our immediate consciousness. But they help us to find a position for ourselves. They give us faith, hope, trust, and some confidence regarding how we will function in the future. Our beliefs allow us to look at alternatives as plausible rather than impossible. They're formed from a constantly morphing cognitive process that allows us to create conceptual conclusions about how we can fit in to our career world.

Career beliefs can lead to productive or counterproductive thoughts. Contrast the two different sets of thoughts that can arise from your career beliefs.

Beliefs

Counterproductive	Productive
Emotional Blocks	Creativity
Stress	Innovation
Low Creativity	Risk Taking
Poor Performance	Strong Performance

Clearly, you need to get around counterproductive thoughts while energizing yourself with productive ones. Beliefs can have a great deal of power over your thinking and your planning.

How Productive Beliefs Can Transform a Career

Careers are always changing—even those that seemed in the past to have some stability. Johnson was a certified public accountant. An ordinary guy, he had done well as an undergraduate business major, graduated, and decided to start his own business. He chose accounting because of his belief in its long-term stability. He passed all of the licensing exams and for twenty years kept up with the major tax law changes. He never believed his career was threatened by Internal Revenue Service changes. In fact, he felt that in some fashion he had a relationship, however peculiar, with the IRS.

Then the computer age hit. New tax programs were inexpensive and readily available. His clients could buy Turbo Tax for a tenth of the price of his fee. And after a few whistleblowers helped to make the IRS more client friendly, clients would go directly to them rather than call him and pay his fee. Soon he noticed his accounting colleagues began to leave the profession and reroute themselves into financial management, financial operations, and accounting for different corporations. A number contracted with Accountemps, the temporary placement agency.

Johnson didn't follow any of these paths. Instead he became more curious about the changes in the field. Johnson's expectation in the tax accounting environment was that there would be less tax work. He had always wanted to assist with financial advising and tax planning, so he also appraised his accounting skills and financial planning skills and gave himself strong marks. He knew that the environment was changing, so he changed with it.

When he sent out his yearly engagement letter in 1997, he added some tax tips. He then prepared a quarterly tax letter that he sent to clients about tax law changes and continued tax planning.

With the strong economy, Johnson had a lot of clients with tax and investment concerns who wanted to use him for hourly fees. What he discovered was that his clients relished having the personal contact with him. He was now able to set up new investment strategies, help people plan for retirement, and do more professional advising. He had examined his skills, his expectations, and the interaction between his skills and the marketplace to create something new for himself. His career beliefs not only didn't stop him, they propelled him into more satisfying work. Now with many of his clients experiencing mutual fund mania, he has the chance to do sophisticated tax planning and retirement strategizing. He enjoys helping people to make the transition from work to retirement or another job.

Let's explore how Johnson confronted his career beliefs. The first thing that he did was to gather some information about himself and his career world. He had a pretty accurate self-appraisal. He liked people, had a pretty loyal client base, and liked to work with numbers and the computer. He was fascinated with the economy and the stock market. And he relished the thought of saving people money, especially earnings from the stock market.

Even though his colleagues were leaving the accounting field, evidence both about himself and the accounting world kept Johnson going. He didn't form sweeping generalities; instead he tried to be specific. He wanted to know which of his specific skills could be put to use in a manner that would continue to be satisfying and to generate income. There is a lesson here: Don't let your generalized career beliefs dictate the particular position for you. The belief is a generalization, and there is always an exception to the generalization.

The second thing that Johnson did was to prevent any blocking of his career path. He decided to use the changing work world to his advantage and to strike while the iron was hot. He made a worthy assessment of his current and potential work environment. The lesson here is to create opportunity by making a change in your career world. There is always something exceptional that can be created in a changing world.

The third thing that Johnson did was to take some action to integrate his skill set with the environment. He spent little or no time obsessing about his career belief but instead moved into a problem solving mode. He did an appraisal of himself. He looked at his environment and at the interaction between himself and his environment in the form of task-approach skills. The end result: He was able to reinvent himself because he did not fall victim to the beliefs that others had about accounting.

Using Beliefs to Improve the Interview Process

Let's look at another example about career beliefs that comes from the arena of the job interview. All of you will be interviewing for new work, and you'll all refine these skills with friends and intimates or with career coaches. What beliefs do you have about yourself and your capacity to interview well? Have you thought about how your beliefs will affect this process?

You may have a particular belief about the tried-and-true, face-to-face job interview. Today, however, you may first go through a prescreening interview on your computer, with your responses sent electronically to the company. More and more corporations and institutions are utilizing these methods because they appear to be efficient and to save money and time. You will be called in for an interview only if you have been allowed though the prescreening process. When you reach a face-to-face interview, the people who make contact with you will know a great deal about you because they will have your responses from the computer interview. They'll know all kinds of things about you: your interests, your capability of working alone or on a team, and aspects of your personality.

Incidentally, some companies are now conducting their initial interviews through video conferencing. You may end up interviewing in front of a video screen with no chance to see the reactions of others in the room. You'll have some added pressure to learn how to "perform" in front of a camera. And, in some cases you may have to agree to let the tape be played to others in the company you're interested in joining.

Regardless of the interview format, imagine for a moment how you'll respond to the questions that are asked of you. Most interviewees have the belief that they can give the company what it wants from its employees. But here your career beliefs may be wrong. You may be generalizing from your own experience, and that may not be what the company's looking for. You think you know what everyone wants—and that's based upon your projection about the work world or the particular company. But what the company may be pursuing is simply a good fit. They may even be looking for something that is unique or odd among the applicants. You think that they're trying to see if your head is screwed on correctly, but they may be looking for a lot of lopsided people to make a well-rounded work force.

Think of tough questions that you have been asked in the past. For example, if you're asked about your weaknesses, standard texts tell you to not expose any. But the company may want to know about your level of self-awareness—including your weaknesses. To say you don't have any will probably kill your chances. You may be asked what you would do if you couldn't solve a problem. Would you ask for help from your boss? Many people are taught to avoid asking for help because it shows intellectual weakness. However, the company that is interviewing you may want someone who is unafraid to ask for assistance and honest about their capacity to do this.

So what is the solution? Simply be honest about who you are. Be aware of your own self-appraisal; know your career identity. Be clear and sincere about what you hope to be able to accomplish in a new organization. Don't generalize. It can keep you from being specific and focused.

You may have legitimate concerns about hostile interviewers. it's natural for people to get nervous when they interview. You may believe that the fear and the anxiety adversely affect your performance during the interview process. Most of you believe that you would perform better in front of a supportive audience that wants you to do well. Well, new research suggests that people may be better performers when they're in front of their harshest critics (Butler and Baumeister 1998). Empirical data indicate that people who face a hostile or critical audience may try to develop new strategies for completing the task effectively. They feel that they may have less to lose, since they already appear to have strikes against them. They're already disliked, so why not use the opportunity to be a little more creative?

Interestingly, there may be an increasing tendency for you to slip up or "choke" in front of a more supportive audience because the audience has certain expectations that you're trying to meet or exceed. To be sure, "Mighty Casey" struck out in front of the home-town fans.

Watch Out for Counterproductive Beliefs

There are a number of personal career beliefs that are definitely counterproductive. These can be beliefs about yourself, the job market, or the job search itself. While these are not as specific as the ones that have been explored so far, they allow for an examination of attitudes that are not simply erroneous, but also stifling, depressing, and unmotivating. Here are a list of those beliefs and what you can do to confront them.

"My career search is a hopeless, oppressive endeavor."

This is the most common complaint that people seem to make about their search. Usually it's held by people who are paralyzed and unable to engage in meaningful job search activities. If you're feeling hopeless, you've created a generalized belief about your search and you've let this belief take over your emotional well-being. So what are the activities that you need to engage in to give yourself a sense of hope and eliminate feelings of oppression?

To confront this counterproductive and bullheaded mind-set, you might go back and try to figure out how you learned it. There is much speculation that a hopeless career belief—or any hopeless belief for that matter—is a learned one. So, who was your tutor in helping to create this belief? Who plucked your optimism and injected you with pessimism? What is the evidence that your circumstances are hopeless? Can you document the facts that have led you to believe that there is no longer any hope?

So let's say that you can't find any good reason for feeling hopeless about the search. You just are. Then you have to use another strategy. Begin to document everything that you've learned about yourself by going through this search process. This can help to put a little hope into your soul and give your search a new meaning.

Exercise 5-4   What Have You Learned?

In this exercise, check off the statements that apply to you. At the end of the exercise, in your journal write down the specific new information that you learned about yourself.

_____ I have learned how to take risks.

_____ I have developed new interpersonal skills.

_____ I have developed new job-search skills, including interviewing and problem solving.

_____ I have new insight into myself and my strengths and weaknesses.

_____ I am aware of the effects of negative thinking.

_____ I am becoming realistic about the work world.

_____ I have learned persistence in my search.

_____ I am able to put my job-search difficulties in proportion.

_____ My job search has enabled me to think in a futuristic way.

_____ Being in the search has allowed me to learn my life purpose.

_____ I am able to present myself more easily than in the past.

_____ I have new transferable skills from my search.

_____ I feel that I have a life and pleasure away from work.

_____ I have a new appreciation for job searchers.

_____ I have learned to be honest with others in telling them about myself.

Now expand on any information here that acknowledges how you've expanded and grown and does not make your search feel helpless. To finish, just for documentation, write about the people who foolishly made you feel that your search was hopeless.

What you learn from this is that you can confront feelings of hopelessness rather than letting them swamp you. You can take the positive search experiences and use them to add meaning to your identity. The search will introduce you to new people and new environments, and it will expose you to the work world the way it currently is. You'll have new business terms to share and your knowledge of the work world will keep you more creative in your new endeavor.

You can also confront those negative people and update them. Lots of well-intentioned people have erroneous information. Don't accept everything that you hear, especially things you hear about yourself or your career world. It just may not be as accurate as the assessments that you have made on your own.

"I'm helpless. Who would hire me?"

Like the hopeless belief, this too is an overgeneralized self-assessment that is linked to depression. You can't change the particular situation that you're in. Sure, a difficult search experience is a tough hand to draw, but you have to play the cards you're dealt. So what can you do to remind yourself that you're not helpless?

The most important point to remember during the search is to engage in at least one productive activity each day. Make each day of the search matter. It's ludicrously simple—but it can keep you from being blocked.

Recently, novelist Elmore Leonard was touring the country to promote his latest project. At one of his readings a listener asked how he continued to be so prolific. His response was telling. He explained that he wrote at least six pages every day and that he kept his notepad with him. He wrote in longhand so that he was not computer dependent and could jot down ideas as they came to him. He appeared to love his life as a writer and had almost a droll sense of humor about it.

Maintaining a record of your activity is one way to confront the belief that you're helpless. A second way to feel less helpless and more empowered is to take on activities where you can actually change something. When you're out of work, the habits that you have cultivated over time seem to disappear. You get lazy, in part because you're a little depressed and you're out of your routine. You become much more dependent upon your own capacity for motivation, and if that is missing, you're in real trouble. An old athletes' adage says that motivation gets you started while habit keeps you going.

Sometimes new activities that are unrelated to your search will keep you from feeling helpless. You can try to improve your eating habits or start exercising. If you lose some weight or sculpt your body, you are doing something that is new and potentially helpful. You can also try to add to your community by volunteering at a service club, hospital, library, or school. This activity will help to cultivate your network.

The recent past president of the American Psychological Association, Martin Seligman, has written widely in this area. He suggests that you try to confront hopeless thoughts by disputing them. He thinks that there's a tendency for people to create explanations for the tough things that happen to them. In a lecture at the APA convention in 1998, he outlined steps to confronting your own internal dialogue. Most important was to stay specific to the circumstance. Get the facts and don't fabricate. Rather than blame others for your predicament, empower yourself by accepting responsibility for the things that are your fault. Also, don't let one event ruin your whole life. For example, just because the job search is difficult doesn't necessarily mean that you can't have a good relationship with a life partner.

There's also evidence that you can change your motivation by opening up the sources of your psychic energy. Your motivation is internal, and to release it you need to create new rituals that will help you focus and motivate yourself. Tai chi classes in the morning are one way of doing this. Learning how to rise and stretch yourself is another. As you arise for another day, stretch to the sky with your arms extended and give yourself an affirmation. "Every day I get a little closer," might be a good beginning. Simple words like "soar," "rise above," and "seek" can help to change your attitude and assist with motivation. Some people have also found that yoga with stretches, and vigorous activities such as kickboxing, can increase motivation while shaping your body. In any event, these activities simply take planning and organization. If you're able to partake of them, they will provide tension relief while eliminating your feelings of helplessness.

Evelyn found that her job search was particularly discouraging. She was trying to find a position in benefits consulting but since she did not have an MBA, the more prestigious firms were not interested in what she had to offer. She tried to keep her sights high but rejection was taking its toll. She noticed one day how her golden retriever got up and stretched each morning and always seemed to be in a good mood. He romped down the stairs on the way to his morning walk. She tried to imitate the dog's behavior. To her surprise, she felt more positive. She tried the simple dog stretch three times a day and each time seemed to perk up. This inspired her to enroll in a stretching class at a local YWCA. She found that she felt better, was more focused and productive, and she able to use the class to help with her networking. Interestingly, she was taught a yoga stretch that was strikingly similar to the stretch of her golden.

"I can't start at the bottom again."

For whatever reason, when people begin a job, they feel that at some level they're starting at the bottom. Even the company president or CEO feels this way; they are both at the bottom with respect to their knowledge of the feelings of the board of directors. Like a new CEO or company president, you need to keep focused upon what you are going to contribute, not where you are going to start. Over the course of our lives, we have learned to start at the bottom. This is the time to take advantage of that training. Sure you're going to be new, but right from the beginning of the interview process you can frame yourself as a person with innovative ideas. Remind yourself that you have the experience to bring in a host of new ideas and methods. Make sure to keep your creative linkages going.

H. B. Gelatt (1989) believes that everything in the work world is connected in some way. By starting at the bottom again, you might realize a new connectedness. Your goal might be to see how different components of a new organization are linked. Your attitude toward your world right now could be one of observation and tying together. How can certain products be used in new ways? How can a work force be better utilized? You want to be able to see new possibilities and to communicate these possibilities. Each interview should be a new challenge, a time to launch into your creative ways of handling problems. Your belief system defines you as a person with new solutions to old problems.

With this type of attitude, you won't be thinking about beginning again, you'll be focusing on how you can help solve problems. There always will be a new problem at work, and creative thinkers will be handsomely rewarded for developing new solutions. Use your experience and know-how to help companies see things differently. You rose before, you'll rise again.

"But I can't keep up."

One thing you are learning about the career world is that change is rampant. How do you feel about your ability to keep up with change? It's everywhere, so the trumpet blares, and everyone seems stressed out by it. A positive way to look at it is that because of a rapidly changing world, all of us are equal in that we must all adapt to new tools and career landscapes.

For example, let's explore the kinds of things that you buy. You probably own a bunch of gadgets, but do you know how to program and use all of their features? If you're like most people, you probably don't use all of the features on any of the gadgets you own. You most likely learned the bare minimum except with those items that were of most interest to you. This is true in the work world as well. People are hard pressed to keep up, so they learn just enough to get by. You'll find that you won't need much of the new technology, so you don't need to stress out about it.

Richard Bolles, the minister, columnist, trainer, and popular author of *What Color Is Your Parachute?*, has a clever retort to people who question their skills. He says that all of us are born "gifted." We're all endowed with skills that will allow us to keep up. He then recommends that career changers explore three kinds of skills: their skills as verbs, their skills as nouns, and their skills as adjectives. Their skills as verbs he calls transferable skills. Skills as nouns are subject or knowledge skills, while skills as adjectives are personal trait skills that can be used in your daily career search management and promotion (Bolles 1999). This simple, uncomplicated idea allows you to envision your uniqueness. Having trust and confidence in your uniqueness can be a key part of your belief system.

"I'll never get work."

Chances are that you think the career search process is like a game—you either win or you don't. It's generally evaluated with an all-or-nothing outcome. You either get the work that you want or you don't. There's no balance sheet. Career counselors often fall victim to this belief because their clients want the counseling work done quickly and then to get a satisfying job. Rehabilitation counselors fall victim also. Their goal is to vocationally rehabilitate disabled clients. But the forces that finance the work, including the state, the insurance carrier, and the private rehabilitation company itself, expect that the rehab will be done efficiently and with a positive outcome.

Think then of how this contrasts to the belief imbedded in the practice of mental health professionals working outside the career arena. Those counselors can work for years on issues of growth, relationships, self-esteem, and whatever else is a part of the current psychotherapy world. They're often given an unlimited amount of time, and are not held accountable for an outcome evaluation. (How, for example, do you determine whether or not your self-esteem is in place?) Therapists receive a lot of latitude in the assessment of their effectiveness.

So how can you shift away from a belief that immediate and satisfying results are the norm? Rather than evaluating your job search with respect to the outcomes involved, reevaluate the job search with a different or more unique standard. Be a tad more like a therapist than a career or rehabilitation counselor.

For example, you might evaluate your search relative to the effort that you are putting out. Instead of feeling each day like you have failed because it is another day without work, evaluate the day at its end by the time and the effort that you have put forth. Think of this period of time as a chance to develop a whole new expertise. Focusing on the process will keep you from feeling like you have failed because you've not yet attained a job. Allow your search to be an affirmation of your strengths and your weaknesses, the beginning of your understanding of your own "emotional intelligence," to use Daniel Goleman's term (1995). Try to discover how your assets and foibles are going to work in a complementary way with another group of people or an entire organization. Use this experience to develop more empathy for yourself and to listen to and acknowledge others.

In our society we're taught to value the accomplishment, not the education. In the search, you'll become more mindful. You can focus on your learning process and your capacity to relate to others and hear criticism. You'll hone and refine your relationship skills and learn how exposure and experience can help you grow. These are lifelong skills that you can put to good use.

This brings to mind the work of athletes. We know of the enduring successes of athletes, but rarely do we think of their failures. When we remember "Joltin' Joe" DiMaggio, we think about his triumphs on the field, not his difficult marriages. Rickey Henderson has the record for most stolen bases, but he also has the record for being caught the most while trying to steal a base.

There are some academic researchers who seem to receive the greatest number of important research grants. When you talk to the successful ones, they say their success is mostly based on trying harder than others. They submit more proposals, and they too are rejected a lot. If you only submit one proposal and are turned down, then you may never submit another, and you are left with the perception that grants are almost impossible to get. But if you submit ten proposals and one is funded, then you have the belief that maybe one in ten of your ideas will receive the professional and financial recognition that you want it to. But you must learn to accept the rejection with some resilience. Furthermore, you can at least weigh the pleasure of learning something new, even if it did not materialize into something with a more tangible reward.

What's the bottom-line measure? Which belief system do we hang as our banner? Should you focus upon the effort or nurture desirable outcomes? We don't acknowledge Henderson's failures with even a passing glance. We focus on his unmistakable success. But maybe the focus should be on something else, like his training. Perhaps we would give him even more respect if we understood how he learned to do his job so well. Maybe we should acknowledge the risks that he took. In the world of rewards, successes, and outcome evaluation, shift your focus to the important material, the enduring lessons.

"I need to be certain about my search techniques."

Give up the belief that you'll experience certainty. In 1989, H. B. Gelatt wrote a marvelous paper. It launched a whole new decision-making strategy that challenged the notions of certainty that people in the job-search process seemed to need. He called this strategy positive uncertainty and emphasized that this new concept would drive career searchers to "accept uncertainty and inconsistency, and utilize the nonrational and intuitive side of thinking and choosing." He added that decision making is a process of arranging and rearranging facts and information that can easily become obsolete. Ironically, more information and more choices increase your uncertainty. So to be truly mindful and present in your search, remember that the more you do to help yourself, the more you are going to increase your own uncertainty. Gelatt's recommendation is to give up rationality and look for greater possibilities.

Redefine Success

In a fashion similar to some of the material already covered, Gelatt emphasizes the redefining of success, embracing change, and forging new partnerships. Interconnectedness and change become the new beliefs.

In order to redefine success, you must understand interconnectedness. Careers are no longer like a ladder or a linear progression but are instead more like a matrix. That abstract concept suggests that what may emerge as your strongest asset is your capacity to change and to be more fluid and less rigid, more creative and less pragmatic.

Embrace Change

Second, it's important to truly embrace change. Einstein once said that imagination was much more powerful and important than information. Imagination is the force that utilizes information. In one year there is more information made available than was available for the entire lifetime of your grandparents. You can give yourself some leeway in your quest to absorb new concepts and knowledge. While you may be tempted to take in a larger spectrum of data, your real learning will take place when you learn to embrace change, have a new vision, and not accept things the way they are.

Find New Partnerships

Armed with this new belief, it's essential to forge new business relationships. Think about this: What are the attributes that you have now that can be put to use in new creative environments? According to Gelatt, you can't always change your skills, but you can change the attitude that you have about your skills. Brand-new fields evolve, with skills used in one field being applied to another. Look at the common household gadgets that were developed as a part of the space program. The Internet didn't develop in a vacuum; it was developed to help scientists stay in touch with each other. The

Internet seems to exemplify the four paradoxical principles of positive uncertainty. You need to be focused but also flexible, aware but also wary, objective and optimistic, and practical yet magical.

There is an emerging field called competitive intelligence. Many factors contributed to creating this field. Innovative companies try to keep track of their competitors, and in a similar vein, venture capitalists want information on the hottest new companies. Thus, innovative marketing executives and consultants, investors, and information technologists have all interlocked their experience to create this new, emerging growth field. All around you, other types of new relationships are emerging as well.

There are groups of Internet trollers who bottom-fish the Internet to get added muck on competitive companies. They are a bit like the old clipping services, but they troll for rumors as much as competitive data. Even these new companies compete with each other. Electronic service monitoring firms like Cybercheck, Cyveillance, and Ewatch all compete for market share as they sign up new and well-established companies.

Wellstone was a football coach who became a motivational speaker after his college coaching was over. He had a delightful career, but in retirement he wanted to give his best information to another group—young entrepreneurs who needed some guidance about how to motivate themselves and others. He enjoyed the work, but found that it was more emotionally draining than he had suspected. If he worked one-on-one or in a small group, he accomplished a lot and was paid accordingly. But he mused about having a much larger impact, working with more people, and making a far greater income in his coaching retirement than he had ever imagined.

Wellstone knew a bit about computers and the Internet and was curious as to whether he could create a motivational coaching practice that was entirely virtual. In order to formulate this idea, he had to gather some new information, but he already had most of what he needed. He knew that he wanted to have a lot of bang for the buck. He wanted to use information he had but distribute it for a fee to a much larger market. He wanted to be geographically free to do the coaching anywhere so that he and his wife could do it from their vacation spots. And he wanted to be appreciated for his resourcefulness.

He did some research on other job arenas that have emerged with virtual coaching. He determined that he could put together a business based on low-cost audio teleconferencing. With a very small investment, he could create a virtual audience. He used his personal name recognition (Wellstone is hard to forget) to create a Web page where he advertised and sold his coaching package. Since hundreds of people could sign up for this, he could charge individuals a reasonable fee and still make $20,000 per month for four hours of coaching. He found that he had more fun, more influence, and substantially higher income by using this coaching framework rather than one where he had to give workshops and consult in person with other coaches and teams.

What is interesting about this case is that there is nothing "proper" about the way that Wellstone put together a new opportunity. He got his program going by being creative and intuitive and not by following any particular rules of order. He had done what Gelatt suggested: redefined success, embraced change, and forged new partnerships.

Gelatt also reminds us about zeteophobia, a profound fear of seeking out that which is new or different. If you have trouble with change, you may not just be rigid—you may have a bona fide fear of it. Chapter 7 can help you with some of the issues that you may have about change.

"I feel as if I've failed."

Failure is almost always a part of the career search. If you're looking for a job because you just lost the one that you had, you have lots of company. If you're looking for your first real job and you're just starting out, you're likely to find that your idealized expectations are not going to be acknowledged. You may not get the position, salary, office location, or geographical location that you had expected. If you're new on the market or if you've been searching for a while, the same is likely to be true. So the all-encompassing fear of being a failure may be setting in. Unlike that which was discussed in the last chapter, the fear of being a failure is a global feeling that is paralyzing. What if you gave it your best shot and you failed? This is scary stuff. You've always been told that if you try hard, you'll succeed. But now, what if you take this advice and you don't succeed? Then, lo and behold, you are shown as the failure that you have feared to be.

If you feel that you have failed in some way, it's likely that you've kept this quiet. People rarely talk about feelings of failure, except to their counselors or coaches—people who are paid to listen. If you're typical, you also feel that you're the only one who has gone through this kind of experience.

Something happens when you have an atmosphere of failure around you. All of those characteristics that you like about yourself now seem to annoy people. If you're perceived as loquacious, suddenly you're seen as talking too much. If you're hardworking, now there are those who characterize you as workaholic. If you have been touted as creative, now you feel like you're a maverick. So this upbeat, positive, energized soul is now an annoying, abrasive newt.

So how can you confront this belief other than by saying that it just isn't true? The fear of being a failure is a global generalization that is really meaningless. What do you mean that you have failed? The job search is simply taking longer than you had expected, and that is probably all you need to say to yourself. But there is a richer, more creative plan you can use to address failure. Try this: Pick a task that is going to be difficult to do but one that may also be fun. Let's say that you pick a new sport like golf or another activity like portrait painting. Both of these activities would be useful ways to dispose of excess energy in the search. But let's say that you use these for no other reason than to work very hard at them and still fail.

Try golf. Buy or borrow some clubs. Take some lessons. Go to the driving range for exercise several times a week and then in three months, try to break par on three of nine holes or on six of eighteen holes. It's almost certain that you won't be able to do this. You'll have a goal and you will work and try very hard, but you're still going to fail. That is real, bona fide failure.

Or try painting. Enroll in some classes. Take oils, watercolor, charcoal, or pastels. Create three portraits in three months and then try to sell them for $250 each at a local garage sale. Unless you are truly unusual, you won't be able to. Again, you've tried very hard, you've put in the time, and you've failed.

Now compare these feelings of failure to the ones that you had during the job search. On the job search the feelings, whether global or specific, were paralyzing, eliciting a mild state of catatonia. But here the feelings seemed to be unrelated to the effort. You knew you would fail, but that didn't stop you. You forged ahead for several reasons. Your ego wasn't tied into these other activities. Your lifestyle and income weren't either. In addition, you knew all along that you were learning something and you were getting more skilled. You could allow yourself time—something that doesn't happen during the search.

Still, there are lessons to be learned here. You need to feel more in control, so you should break up your search into controllable activities, much like you do when learning a new recreational activity.

There is another thought that can be useful to consider when you're in failure mode, which is that most successes have come about only after significant failures. Edison had well over two hundred failures before he was able to come up with the incandescent light bulb. Failing is simply a part of the process of moving toward your goal. The issue you struggle with is the degree to which your feeling of failure overpowers you and creates a paralysis. If you can see failure as moving you ahead rather than stopping you, then you will be able to keep moving forward in your quest.

"I feel worthless. So how can I decide what salary I deserve?"

During the job search there is a continuing tendency for you to believe you're worthless, because you tend to equate your self-worth with other kinds of worth. Doing this can be confusing and will distract from your search efforts.

How do you put value on yourself? Do you think of your self-appraisal and determine your worth through your interests, skills, personality, and so forth? Or do you determine your worth by the contributions that you have made to your friends and the community where you live? How much impact have you had in changing the thinking of others? The film It's a Wonderful Life explored how a person who felt worthless was given the opportunity to see how he had impacted the lives and well-being of so many others. Your value as a human being must be kept separate from your worth as an employee or your net worth as a money manager or investor. If you don't do this, you're likely to experience panic and a sense of worthlessness.

If you need to inventory your characteristics as a part of your self-appraisal, then do it. Consider your appearance, the way you relate to others, the contributions that you make to your friends and community, the relationships that you have with your immediate and extended family members, and the unusual, idiosyncratic interests that you have that belong to you and nobody else.

After this, if you feel the need, calculate your net worth. Add up your savings and checking accounts, investment portfolio, and real estate. If it is worth a lot, what have you done toward putting a will together? If you have a solid net worth and you have no will, then maybe your net worth isn't as important to you as you think it is. Consider what you need to do to understand what your net worth means to you.

As an employee, what do you think you're worth? If you're demoralized by the job search, you might equate all of the worths together and come up with very little. But let's try to be a little more scientific and put some energy into an analysis of your employment worth. In the process, you might even find that this "research" opens up new job search avenues.

Try the following activities to determine what kind of salary you could command. Look over your résumé and be sure you have a strong sense of your accomplishments and the amount of time that you have logged in each of your positions. Then, with this in hand, get information about your potential salary from one or more of the following:

- Executive recruiters or headhunters

- Associates in professional organizations you belong to

- Advertisements in local and national trade papers and newspapers (paying particular attention to the fit between your résumé and the key words in the classifieds)

- New emerging growth industries and smaller companies that offer stock and options rather than high salaries

- An assessment of how much you can generate by having two or three part-time positions rather than one full time position (the portfolio career)

This roundup of your worth will give you some empirical data on your value in the workplace. A concrete figure can replace the belief that you're worthless and give you the knowledge you need to become a better negotiator for yourself.

PART
3

Handling Your
Emotions during Your
Career Search

6 | The Perils of Self-Doubt

... too many of the wrong things happen somewhere.

—Margaret Mead

Are You a Doubter?

In my work, I've spent more time than I like to think of with clients who are willing to apply for anything and submit their credentials to anyone, even when they weren't close to being qualified. And I've counseled others, immensely talented and creative people, who were convinced that they would never be considered for a particular position, so they just wouldn't apply for it. For example, I've had occasion to work with a brilliant, prolific songwriting client who chose to stay in his family's leisure consulting business rather than risk finding out how the market would evaluate him. I've seen lawyers who fashioned themselves to be warriors in court but who broke down in tears over the mere thought of losing.

There are some people who have a glaring absence of self-doubt. I've watched consultants who seemed to have résumés based on quicksand become wildly successful in their businesses. Why do some people seem to be so crippled by self-doubt while others are uncontaminated by it? What differentiates people with confidence in their career path from those who lack it? Consider the following examples.

A Tale of Two Careers

Willard had just completed his business plan for a new marketing company he was forming and was understandably delighted. He enthusiastically punched in the phone number of the venture capital firm he hoped would fund his project. Then it hit. Like a hailstorm from nowhere, the self-doubt pummeled him. His usually well-lubricated motor mouth dried up, and his hands shook a little. He placed the receiver back into the phone cradle. He let out a sigh and then reluctantly but probably foolishly decided to wait another day. Although he was quite conscious he was procrastinating, he decided that the finishing touches of his plan could be inserted tomorrow. His efforts suddenly felt at once both brazen and incomplete. The meticulous snippets of inspired detail he had incorporated into the plan suggested a winning formula. But tonight he waffled like he had so many times before. The pattern of self-doubt was relentless and all too familiar.

Willard had all the right credentials. He also took ownership of a strong career belief that he could be successful on his own. He was well known and respected in his field and had for some time resented the fact that his higher-ups seemed to make quite a margin of profit from his hard work. He had decided that now was the time to break out on his own, but he had doubts that made him seem almost catatonic, unable to take a risk or move ahead.

Meanwhile, Pietro had an eighth-grade education but an epicurean's love of good food. He started working in his father's Brooklyn delicatessen when he was fourteen. By the time he was eighteen, he was a food purchaser and personnel specialist. His charismatic way with people made him popular throughout the neighborhood. When his father retired from the deli business, Pietro stayed on as the new owner and proprietor. He loved the work and his customers.

Pietro took his first major risk when he decided to expand the business. He found a few backers, had his lawyer draw up a contract, and let the business grow. He never had a doubt as he branched out into new areas. He even started a mail-order confectionery business on the side.

As he looked to new horizons, he lost touch with his old contacts in the neighborhood. He began to consider running another business, in part to prove to himself that he could diversify his businesses. He also wanted to create something by himself without the assistance of his father.

The opportunity arose when one of Pietro's deli investors approached him. The investor had good money-managing skills, but when it came to people skills, he was characterized as a good bean counter. He needed someone like Pietro. He invited Pietro to invest in and join his fledging retail appliance company, specializing in high-end kitchenware for the boutique restaurant business. Without much hesitation, Pietro sold his delis for a handsome profit and moved on. He is now the manager and 20 percent partner in the restaurant supply business, and is developing a new plan to purchase a wholesale restaurant furniture business. Pietro has no business plan, no contracts, and, significantly, no doubts about whether or not he will be successful. He said that even if any of his businesses fail, he will be able to develop another without much fearful, obsessive rumination.

With little formal education and professional training, Pietro appears to lack self-doubt; he isn't consumed with a sense of doom or rejection. Yet when people are asked about the risks of starting their own business, almost half of those surveyed say that the risk of failure keeps them from going ahead. So what makes this new process so much easier for Pietro than for Willard? Why does one have self-doubt while the other does not? Why does one foresee failure while the other does not?

Various human qualities and self-understanding are involved, but unfortunately, we don't pay enough attention to these basic human considerations in the career search. Instead, we remain fixated on only the job market, our personal characteristics, our appraisal of our skills. What needs to follow after the establishment of your career identity and an understanding of your career beliefs is a method of keeping self-doubt at bay. Not allowing self-doubt to intrude will be crucial in the process of actualizing yourself and meeting your career goals, especially if these involve some sort of large ego risk or financial risk.

Watch and Learn

The newly elected governor of Minnesota, Jesse "The Body" Ventura, is certainly a person with little apparent self-doubt. Jesse was a wrestler. His chances for pinning down an election were not taken very seriously by the pundits of the upper Midwest. But he threw off no less a hero than the offspring of former presidential candidate, vice president, senator, and "favorite son," Hubert Humphrey. After being elected, Jesse has stayed visible and has been unafraid to speak his mind. In fact, he has gotten himself into some difficulty with comments about "drunken Irishmen" and street design made on the David Letterman show. But notwithstanding that, when a recent scandal broke out involving Clem Haskins, University of Minnesota basketball coach, the governor flexed his political muscle and brazenly expressed himself. He proposed that perhaps student athletes shouldn't be students at all and that the public should not expect them to attend or do well in academic programs.

Whether you agree with the governor or not, he certainly exemplifies someone who has charisma, chutzpah, and little, if any, self-doubt. He says he believes he could be president if he wanted it. He has excellent communication skills, visibility, a willingness to work with handlers, and the ability to use his experience with media exposure to launch his positions. What keeps him from self-doubt?

Trust in Your Success

The above examples illustrate a concept called career self-efficacy (Betz 1992), which is an application of Stanford psychology professor Al Bandura's (Bandura 1977) theory to the career search behavior of individuals. You can use this theoretical framework to understand your self-doubt and then confront it, thereby keeping self-doubt from infiltrating your thinking during your search.

Your self-efficacy expectations refer to the attitude that you hold regarding your capacity to successfully perform particular or demanding behaviors. Governor Ventura really believed that his past wrestling ring experience, media exposure, and local elected office politics qualified him to be governor.

Your expectation of the probability of your success determines whether or not you will even begin the endeavor. This expectation also influences how much effort you will expend attempting to be successful. Further, the expectations help to determine how long a particular behavior will be sustained when there are demanding career hurdles to jump. Your efficacy expectation can influence your career choice, as well as your success in staying with the search and reaching your goals. Efficacy expectations are also apparent in the performance of your duties in your new job, and they impact the job tenure that you might accrue.

Bandura's theory lists four sources of potential efficacy expectations:

1. Performance accomplishments

2. Vicarious learning or modeling

3. Verbal persuasion and encouragement from significant others

4. High level of arousal or anxiety. As your anxiety level increases, your self-efficacy decreases

Gender plays a role as well. It's been known for years that women tended to stay away from work roles that were held up as traditionally male because they had the expectation that they could never succeed in such a career. The socialization patterns of young men and women are markedly different and as such, the efficacy information available to men yields a substantially larger array of career choices than that available for women. While this is certainly changing, a brief look at the *Dictionary of Occupational Titles* gives information suggesting that the vast majority of the jobs still appear to have stereotypically "male" qualities attached to them.

Count Your Accomplishments

So how can you begin to increase your career self-efficacy expectations and eliminate (or at least reduce) the intrusions of self-doubt?

It often helps to enumerate your performance accomplishments, so let's begin there. By exploring your personal accomplishments, you'll get raw, vivid exposure to your basic skills and talents. This is evidence that you can use over and over again to help keep the self-doubt demons away. Your accomplishments represent any activities that you have done especially well and that you are proud of. They should also be activities that you enjoy or that inspire you. If there was nothing but drudgery involved in the accomplishment, it is probably not something that you wish to repeat. In today's work world, people seem, more than ever, to be looking for an enriching experience and not the highest possible salary for an unfulfilling job.

Exercise 6-1   Significant Accomplishments

As you did in chapter 3, take a stroll through your past and recall at least five significant accomplishments for each decade of your life. You may want to have close friends or family members help you with this, as they can often recall events that you might have forgotten about. Even an examination of old photo albums, home movies, or videos can help. Be sure to keep an open mind. Your accomplishments might be in areas that are not always obvious, like community or neighborhood service or involvement in school activities.

After you have listed your accomplishments, try to analyze them by exploring the type of transferable skills that are highlighted by these accomplishments. If you find that you are having difficulty with this exercise, you might consider having someone else write a letter to you about your accomplishments. Jill was having some trouble with this exercise, so she asked her father to write to her about her accomplishments over the years. To her surprise, she received a lovely five-page letter filled with remembrances of event that she had completely forgotten. She later called to talk to him about the letter, and he spent two more hours on the phone describing her special chatacteristics.

Transferable Skills

_____ Creative skills

_____ Physical or athletic skills

_____ Verbal, persuasive, or argumentative skills

_____ Social and friendship skills

_____ Culinary skills

_____ Intuitive skills

_____ Decision-making skills

_____ Leadership skills

_____ Teaching skills

_____ Numerical, mathematical, engineering, analytical, or computing skills

_____ Observational skills

_____ Calming, meditative, or spiritual skills

An analysis of your skills can enhance your expectations for yourself. In career counseling and during a career search, so many clients feel that they have failed and should just quit. They feel that with all of their effort, they have not amounted to much of anything. As they reflect upon this, they also say words like, "Now, I don't actually think I'm suicidal ... but ..." Even the utterance of that phrase points to what sorry shape they're in. It's like nothing they have accomplished has meant very much. That's why it's so important to list your skills. It allows you to begin to think constructively about the next position you pursue and how it is going to be more fulfilling. Maybe in reality, you want to walk away from the current career that you hold or held and pursue something that is totally different. The skills analysis is a good way to start taking stock of yourself.

Exercise 6-2   New Skill Development

In addition to enumerating your old but familiar talents, try to add some of the accomplishments that you accrued through your current job search activities. Add these to your skill bank account. These shouldn't be particular goal attainments like sending out a certain number of résumés, but rather should refer to skill accomplishments that have come about because of the search. Have you made friends or picked up new social skills or writing skills? Have you developed skills through a new hobby? What about skills developed while volunteering or interning? Write down the skills, and then determine what transferable areas these new skills fall into.

Consider how you might use these new attributes in your search.

The Value of Vicarious Learning

When you read or hear about somebody opening a new store, like Pietro, you probably wonder how they had the internal fortitude to do it. Or maybe you ask why they can do something you can't. Part of what makes them different is that many of them learned a trade, not in the classroom, but on the job. They experienced workplace immersion from an early time in their lives. With this immersion, they also had a chance to model someone else. That's one reason successful businesses can be passed along in a family—because so many of the family members have worked in the business and learned new models of operations. Pietro was someone who learned his business vicariously. He was also given a great deal of encouragement to keep a family business going.

But what about you? If you don't come from a family of entrepreneurs, how does vicarious learning take place? The answer is that unless it is a part of your history, you need to plan for it just like you plan your educational program.

The story of a young entrepreneur who was starting an allergy products store called Gazoontite is an intriguing case in point (Sinton 1999). Noting that the $6 billion nasal allergy business was "nothing to sneeze at," Sinton described what it took to form the new business in terms of vicarious learning. The business owner, 33-year-old Soon-Chart Yu, had developed an interesting set of credentials. Born in Taiwan, he emigrated to Davis, California at age three, and eventually received a degree in electrical engineering from the Davis campus of the University of California.

Yu started his business career by working at Advanced Micro Devices. But since he was thirsty to work with clients rather than computers, he joined Bain & Co. and did a two-year stint at management consulting in San Francisco. While there, he decided that he wanted to work for himself—he just needed to find a business that interested him. He wisely noted that he needed more experience and an education with a different focus. So he obtained a blue-chip MBA at the Stanford Business School and then worked for the Clorox Company as a brand manager. This work and the company's competitive spirit helped to develop his interest in air quality. Since he came from a family genetically endowed with allergy problems, he thought he could combine his personal and business interests into a venture that capitalized on both. He could tap early experiences with allergies as instances of modeling allergy treatment.

Now for the vicarious learning. In 1997, Yu left his position with Clorox and worked as a sales associate at Crate and Barrel, taking an 85 percent salary cut. That was a daring move. However, he found that while he was daunted by the emotional and physical demands of the sales work, he learned how to "be with" customers and to treat all of them with courtesy and attention, whether they were his very first or last customers of the day.

It was the vicarious learning that added to his résumé and confidence. He observed other workers throughout the day and modeled the sales force. He learned the subtleties and nuances of the work by standing beside and observing others with substantial experience. He saw what it was like to have to be "nice" to everyone all day long. Then he added to the vicarious learning with his own experience. He learned about the exhaustion salespeople feel after a day on the floor. You can't teach exhaustion. You can only experience what it is like to have to be nice all day.

Yu didn't just start his business out of nowhere. He had pulled together vicarious learning opportunities, including family home remedies. All of the learning gave him the expectation that he could create this innovative new business. He called his new company

Gazoontite, because he thought that most Americans could spell and pronounce it phonetically rather than using the German word *Gesundheit*, which means health but which he wisely doubted could be spelled correctly by most. They might not be able to find him in the phone book. (Besides the phone book, you can find him on the Internet.)

So where are the examples of vicarious learning in your history? You probably have more vicarious learning experiences and modeling than you're aware of.

Exercise 6-3
Vicarious Learning and Modeling

In your journal, enumerate the modeling or vicarious learning that you have experienced in your life. It could be volunteer work, internships, or traineeships, or even work for pay that tells you something about yourself that's related to the building of your self confidence and the elimination of your self-doubt.

As you look at the information that you've just generated, does it affect your confidence level? Do you feel that you have a better handle on understanding how you can put your experiential learning to use? You will see that not only do you have skills that you hadn't thought about before, but in doing this exercise you have learned how to learn from experience—an essential skill.

But this is not all you need. Maybe you got all of your skills and experience from volunteer work and you don't think that the real work world is going to take you seriously. Even though most professionals have to do some kind of interning, job searchers often forget this and think that unless they have real world experience and the right education, they can't begin to have the expectation that they will succeed. Some additional ingredients are required to break through this mind-set.

Encouragement Is Key

Who do you remember ever encouraging you in your endeavors? Most people recall that their parents had some impact on their feelings about themselves, but they don't necessarily remember it being in the form of encouragement. Many remember it being in the form of expectations of the impossible. Others remember it being filled

with dampening judgments; still others don't recall any encouragement at all. Chris still recalls being dropped off at college with these
parting words: "We expect Phi Beta Kappa at graduation. Anything
less and you shouldn't expect us to attend." Rob recalls being called
"dog breath" by his father and he still, after thirty-two years, has to
work at not covering his mouth during a job interview.

Most of the career counseling candidates I've worked with have
trouble with risk taking because they don't feel that they were
encouraged to be themselves and to follow their particular paths.
They are saddened that they chose to follow a plan that was set out
for them by someone else. Others find that they resent the pressure
that they felt growing up. Still others feel that their parents let them
do whatever they wanted because they really didn't care about them.

Everybody wants positive feedback. Behaviorists have said for
years that appropriate behavior is shaped by positive reinforcement.
A lot of people don't easily recall positive reinforcement from the
family. However, they can easily recall the expectations.

At times, it may be easier to recall positive feedback from the
workplace. Many people have received good feedback in the form of
performance evaluations at work. And still more recall awards given
for academic, scientific, or athletic accomplishments. Some others
recall praise and applause for creative performances in theater or
music.

If you're in the midst of a job search and the last evaluation you
had caused you to lose your job, then you're probably not feeling terribly encouraged by those around you. All of you in this predicament
need some extra form of encouragement. In this exercise, it's important to think about the group of people who gave you important and
positive feedback about yourself.

Exercise 6-4
Remembering Encouraging Messages

Think about your past and enumerate the people in your life in the
last ten years who have been encouraging to you. This should go
beyond just reporting positive feedback on a project well done.
Instead, it should focus upon those who have been real cheerleaders,
people who believed that you were special in a particular way and
that some of your ideas, even if they were of the oddball variety,
should be considered. It is especially important if it was something
that you were going to do on your own with little or no help or guidance. Try to recall three of these experiences. Write the name of the

encourager, the message of encouragement, and your approximate age at the time.

How does this recollection affect your perception of yourself? Do you feel that the recollection of encouragement helps you to feel more confident?

Exercise 6-5   Fantasy Support

Pick out five fantasy figures you would like to put into a small room with you to give you encouragement. You should be able to imagine them doing this, even if you have never met the people. For example, if you're in the creative or performing arts, where you had few if any people encourage you, whose encouragement would you most appreciate? Who would you want to positively critique your work? Would you like to hear their stories, tales of well-known creative people who were not very well known until later in their life or even after their death? List five people who you would like to have as your encouragers and how you think they would encourage you to give your very best performance.

What have you learned about the kind of people that you want to support you? If these people are not currently in your life, can you find similar people in your environment who can become a part of your life? This fantasy exploration tells you about some instances where you are missing out on potential support that could be helpful. Now your career search work involves locating the appropriate support.

Keep in mind that there are support groups everywhere. You can find them through local business and professional associations, businesswomen's associations, chambers of commerce, and civic groups like Rotary and Kiwanis. You can search the Internet for chat rooms. The Small Business Administration can offer some guidance. It is all a matter of seeking out your encouragers. Even people in your network, friends, neighbors, professors, teachers, classmates, can assist.

Of course, there are still a lot of people who refrain from actually applying for positions that others suggest could really make them happy and keep them satisfied. Some of this is due to anxiety, the last variable in career self-efficacy theory.

All Riled Up

Arousal and anxiety are not good partners for you in your career search. Throughout your search, you want to be in the position of keeping your anxiety and arousal at a level that is optimal for you.

Does seeking something that is new seem to automatically create a state of heightened anxiety? It may be related to zeteophobia, mentioned in chapter 3, the fear of seeking out change or the fear of change itself. But it also may be related to a fear that you're fraudulently pursuing a position that you don't feel entitled to. You fear you'll be found out as an impostor. Even high achievers feel this way. But why?

In some cases, people become anxious about their career change because they haven't been entirely honest about themselves. They are so anxious about meeting the requirements of someone else or positioning themselves competitively that they tell either half a story or a story and a half. They don't give an honest representation of the facts. This can backfire and end up causing more than just a simple problem. How do you think you represent yourself? Do you feel you are giving an honest portrayal of who are? Or do you subscribe to the thesis that you should fake it until you make it.?

On the other hand, there are many examples of people who feel like they are impostors who are on the verge of being found out. When you accomplished something that really was quite impressive, did you have the feeling that it really wasn't so great and that soon people would find out that it didn't amount to much? When you talk to people who have gotten into some of the name-brand colleges and professional schools, many of them fear that they will be found out to be unqualified. They are the institution's major mistake. This type of self-doubting anxiety is daunting and long-lasting—and yet it's also a fabrication.

Career self-efficacy theory demonstrates the different ways that people can form a backbone of self-control. Self-efficacy overrides self-doubt, especially when you have no control over the reactions that others will have about you or your accomplishments. For instance, you can't be sure what will happen to you when you apply to a very competitive college. You apply because you're encouraged, you're smart, and you have specific talents. That's self-efficacy at work. So even though there's been a selection process where you have been positioned as one of the many educational elite, you can't be entirely certain why you were or were not chosen. The same is true in the job search.

Controlling Anxiety Reduces Self-Doubt

There is a movement among some behavioral science researchers to question the value of self-esteem, especially in controlling
behaviors like aggressiveness and violence. What *has* come from the
research seems to be even more pertinent regarding the job search:
The heightened state of anxiety and arousal that can allow for the
intrusion of self-doubt may be related most closely to feeling out of
control, not to self-esteem. The idea that the future of your working
life is in the hands of someone else probably makes you feel out of
control. This may help explain why individuals with high self-esteem
are often quite anxious during the job search.

So, learning new ways of feeling in control, disciplining, or
regulating yourself can be a way to begin keeping self-doubt out of
your job search. Your sense of being in control can begin with good,
honest knowledge of what you offer. You should be able to back up
your offerings with data that suggest that you know what you're
doing. Nationally certified career consultant Sheila Weisblatt has
referred to this as career search clarity. We'll tune back to this issue
later in the chapter.

Vicarious learning is useful in reducing anxiety because you
walk away from an encounter with the notion that you really have
learned something through experience and modeling. You also walk
away with some sense of understanding about the work world and
the structure of different organizations.

All right then, let's say that you don't embellish the truth about
yourself, you have clarity, and you feel in control of your emotions.
What can you do about feelings of self-doubt? Probably the most
important thing to figure out is the reason for it. If you've received
good encouragement, know yourself, your identity, and your accomplishments, aren't a terribly anxious person, and have experienced
vicarious learning, what is the problem? This takes some digging.

The following sections can help you uncover the nature of your
self-doubt. They come from the different clinical issues that my own
clients have brought to me over the years.

Commitment Counts

You've probably encountered this one in another context. Think
about all the times you have heard a man or a woman say about the
opposite gender, "They just can't make a commitment." You've
probably seen people get into inappropriate relationships for the sole

purpose of avoiding any commitment. Roberta did that for years to ensure that she could maintain her independence and pursue different professional opportunities that afforded travel to far-off lands. Why do you think that people get so apprehensive on their wedding days even after all of the planning? It's the commitment.

Getting a new job is making a commitment to more than just one person. You're committing to yourself, your employer, a new profession, professional organizations, and all the people who have helped you along the way. Of course you want it to work.

So it could very well be that the self-doubt you experience may not be self-doubt at all—it just feels like it. But it's really an avoidance behavior that keeps you from a commitment. As discussed earlier, people in volunteer services like Forty Plus often have a difficult time leaving for a real, paid position. That's because there is no commitment in the volunteer business. You can easily leave whenever you want. That's not the case with a real job. The real job is a part of a permanent life record. The real job has components of evaluation. And should you fail in the real job, you have this feeling like you're failing in the game of life.

Commitment anxiety shows up when you're asking yourself such tough questions as, "Do I really know what I want to do?", "Is this job really the right one for me?", and "Will I ever be happy on my job?" These are all questions that don't really have simple, immediate answers. To that extent they're probably a waste of your time. If you've done your search with appropriate goals in front of you and you are clear about what you're doing, then you have to just let the chips fall where they may.

But why then do you continue to ask questions like these? Frankly, it makes you feel like you have some kind of control. You may not want any direct answers. Instead, you only want to ask the questions. The questions, too, for the most part are not easy to answer and probably add to your feelings of self-doubt. Looking at your commitment issues may be a much more useful exploration.

More than one first-time job seeker has said that the anxiety they felt was not really about whether they would get a job. They were fearful that after getting their first job, they would not be able to feel like a child anymore. One nineteen-year-old boy admitted that he was a Peter Pan type, choosing to not grow up.

Relinquishing the Dream

Making the final decision to accept a job also takes away your dreams. Sure, you're back in the workforce, but perhaps what you wanted was something a little better than what you got. The loss of this dream is a difficult one. You undoubtedly have lots of dreams for yourself in this search. Now, you're faced with an unfortunate truism of the search: "What you're going to be, you are." You've found that the process of letting go of the dream is painful. To avoid some of this pain, you may keep yourself in a constant state of doubt about your decision making. If you refrain from committing, you've kept your options open. It's at this juncture that you need some outside help with a reality check. Maybe you hold on to the dream, but the dream is inappropriate for you. It's like holding out for that perfect prom date only to find out that the person was never interested in you in the first place. Dreams are important in relationships and in the job search, but you don't want your dream to become your nightmare. You don't want your dream to stifle your possibilities.

Commitment can also be problematic and anxiety producing if you are the multipotential-equipotential type that was described in chapter 4. Having a series of strong skills and interests does force you to make a decision. And give up a possible occupation. The same person can be an investment counselor who wants to pursue an advanced business degree as well as a secretly internalized jazz musician who wants to pursue an advanced musical degree.

Gary was a student who loved the field of counseling—group counseling in particular. But Gary was also a very creative filmmaker. He had excellent skills in both arenas and had a terrible struggle trying to choose one passion over the other. He eventually chose to receive advanced training in counseling, but the passion for filmmaking never ended. He later began to produce videos about the group counseling process, and he eventually created more of a portfolio career. He indicated that this process allowed him to reach out toward two occupations that didn't have stable or even comfortable salaries. By later combining the two, he has been able to develop a fine career.

Avoiding Failure

If you have just lost a job, especially one that you were fond of, be aware of the natural human tendency to avoid repeating unpleasant experiences. Reentering the workforce after an unfortunate termination is a clumsy experience. So what can you tell yourself to reduce your search anxiety? First of all, remember that you can leave a job if things are not working out. Try to make an employment contract with yourself. Give yourself a year to determine whether you want to stay in a particular job or industry. After that, focus upon the skills that you are accumulating and consider whether the job will provide important new experiences. Then, make more of a commitment to the learning process than to the position or the company.

Also, consider the expectations that you have for the new job. Your new work isn't going to necessarily solve your old workplace issues, just like a new relationship doesn't solve those old relationship issues. Look to the nature of the work tasks and what they're going to do for you. A realistic appraisal should give you some indication that you can do the work in a way that is satisfactory to the employer.

Examine the rewards of the job. If the position is not going to offer the rewards that you need to fulfill your specific needs, then, no matter what, you're just not going to be satisfied with the work. You could be working with a great, supportive staff, but if you have a need for the company to give you strong supervision or new skill development and you don't get it, you aren't going to stay very long.

You also engage in failure avoidance when you neglect your search. This is a far too common litany among job searchers: "If you don't apply, then no one can reject you." "If you don't take the civil service exam you can't flunk." This is not just a fear of failure, but an avoidance of anything that could possibly lead to failure.

What does this dilemma stem from? It can be related to a childhood without much encouragement to succeed, but with a lot of punishment for failure. This can lead you to avoid any experience where there is going to be a judgment made about you and what it is that you have to offer. More than simply a fear of failing, you just don't want the experience of feeling unwanted.

Are You an Explorer?

Your relationship with your parents and the degree of attachment that you have to them plays a significant role in your willingness to engage in creative career and environmental exploration. Think of what Joseph and Mary might have said to their son. "You have a wonderful career as a carpenter laid out right in front of you and you're going to do what?!"

If you feel secure in your relationship to your parents, you're more likely to take on somewhat riskier career exploration. What this suggests is that if you did not have strong bonding experiences with your parents, you may have a tendency to settle for what's put in front of you rather than creating something new and different for yourself.

Attachment theory (Bowlby 1980) adds something else to the mix. It suggests that even if you did not have positive bonding and support from others, you may be able to create it for yourself. Mentoring, career coaching, and counseling can be useful pursuits for those who did not have strong and supportive parental relationships.

Break It Down

For many of you, the entire search process is, in a word, overwhelming. When you have to approach an overwhelming experience, you can't seem to break it down into smaller pieces. How many times have you said to yourself that you just didn't know where to begin? And what did you do? You did nothing, because you just didn't know where to begin. There are lots of other career books that can help you with the step-by-step process. If your anxiety is related to this feeling that the career search is just too big, then your work is to break it up into very small steps. You can even write out the steps and make a flow chart of your activity. But you need to know where to begin. The chapter on goal setting can help you to keep the search from being so overwhelming.

Learn by Reading

For many, vicarious learning about careers can take place by reading how other people established themselves. Often what you find is that there were a few critical incidents or serendipitous meetings of people that led to individuals establishing their careers. As mentioned, the series of Vocational Biographies can be useful in gathering information about how people found their careers.

Take Advantage of Serendipity

If you are one of those people who can't make any order out of this and you don't want to follow any guidelines, then you are going to have to take a more serendipitous approach to the search. There are several points to remember in this. The first is that new opportunities will come to you, but you may not notice these as good opportunities. The second is that you need to keep a diary of your day and potential new opportunities. You need to record all of the different activities you do, the people you meet, and the ideas you have for what you want to create. And finally, you need to be able to meet regularly with a person you respect so you can run these ideas by them. With these three steps you can find that you're a part of the job search without following strict guidelines. You are gathering information, networking, and evaluating possibilities. You're just not doing it in a way that appears to be linear. You are also much more dependent on networking.

Perhaps the hardest part of serendipitous experiences is knowing whether there is a viable opportunity available. In Detroit, my great-great-grandfather owned a large carriage company, the E. Chope Carriage Company. The company was a successful enterprise. One day Grandpa Ed was approached by an entrepreneur named Henry Ford. Mr. Ford had an idea, a career belief really, that he thought Ed would like to be a part of. He thought that putting a fossil fuel-powered engine into an E. Chope carriage was a remarkable opportunity for Ed to enter the incipient automobile industry. My less-than-futuristic relative turned him down. He thought that the idea of carriages with engines just wouldn't sell. And it would certainly scare the horses. E. Chope was out of business in five years. The serendipitous opportunity was presented to Grandpa Ed, but he did not take advantage of it.

So opportunities abound in the career world. But like my grandfather, you need help to decide what is valuable to pursue and what is not.

It's Not Whether You Win or Lose

As has been mentioned before there seems to be an all-or-nothing quality to the career search. Face it—you either get a job or you don't. The job you get is either satisfactory or it isn't. But what is also true about the search is that you are creating a new knowledge base about the work world that will be a unique personal asset. It has often been said of people who are receiving their advanced degrees (like an M.D., Ph.D., or J.D.) that at the time of their boards, final orals, or bar exams, they probably know more about their field than they will at any other time in their life. Sure, they will specialize and develop a new expertise. But at those moments just before the qualifying exams, they have a vast array of knowledge.

This is also true for you in the work world. As a part of your search, new job ideas, business opportunities, and ways of acquiring information should be coming to you. If you frame your search as a process of building a new base of knowledge as well as getting a new position, then each day of the experience will be filled with new ideas about career opportunities and new ways of fitting in. Your self-doubt is coming from your all-or-nothing feeling. You have convinced yourself that there is only success or failure, rather than focusing on acquiring a new array of possibilities.

In a way, we are surrounded by all-or-nothing life events. Think about final sporting events like the NCAA College Basketball tournament. Do you remember the Final Four for the men and women? Usually you remember the winners but rarely the losers. You don't recall that sixty-four teams enter these contests, all with successful seasons. Can you name any of the losers? (Can you name the winners?)

What you learn from this is twofold. First of all, winning or losing is transient. Others will not remember much about your failures. Nor will they remember much about your success. You will remember them more than others. Second, what gets ingrained is that winners get it all and no one remembers a loser, except fans of the Chicago Cubs and Boston Red Sox. Who remembers the loser of the World Series, the Stanley Cup, or the Super Bowl, even though they were the second-best team? While it is true that the loser gets little recognition, those who were on those second-place teams know that they had a great season.

What this comes down to is finding some sort of balance between winning and losing. This balance can come in the form of evaluating your job-search process. Keep your focus on your learning, your optimism, your capacity to handle adversity, your new skills, and the new people that are a part of the processs.

Don't Learn to Be Helpless

Some of the characteristics of intrusive self-doubt stem from feelings of helplessness that you feel when you have lost control. Learned helplessness is not like any other feeling of helplessness. It was discovered by watching how animals became unusually passive and unable to act appropriately when they were punished with uncontrollable shocks (Miller and Seligman 1976). If animals are positively reinforced when they engage in a simple act like pressing a bar or jumping a hurdle, their behavior is shaped and over time they learn a new behavior. But if an animal is punished by an aversive stimulus like an electric shock, especially a powerful shock, the animal begins to reduce its active behavior and to then actually stop responding. In a sense it appears that the animal is shell-shocked. Punishment is going to be inflicted and there is nothing the animal can do. So it does nothing. Experiments in psychology over the years have drawn attention to this loss of capacity to respond. Interestingly, even when the animal is given an opportunity to escape the presentation of an aversive stimulus after being regularly and unavoidably presented with the stimulus, the animal does not respond. We are able to create a nonresponsive animal that appears to be helpless and depressed. This is called learned helplessness because the animal has learned that behavior will not influence the presentation of the aversive stimulus.

There are two components in learned helplessness. The first component is the destruction of the motivation to respond. If you are going to get a shock anyway, why would you respond. It is just going to be futile. There is a second and more upsetting component as well, which is that when there is the chance to escape the aversive stimulus, the animal just sits. Learning takes place during uncontrollable events. The animal learns that responding will not help. The animal learns to be unmotivated and the animal takes on a passive role even when there is an opportunity to escape.

The key issue here is that people also can develop the belief that no matter what they do, they will be ineffective. Remember, this takes place when there is a feeling that things are out of control. It is understandable during the job search, when so much of what is going on around you seems to be out of your control. That is why it is so important to keep working, to keep on responding even though there may be a tendency or predilection to do little or nothing.

Some people who are punished or who have a history of abuse (also the very old, the very young, the disabled, and the incarcerated) feel that there is little they can do to help themselves. So they stop responding. They may feel that they are just too stupid to solve the problem, or they may feel that whatever the problem is, it is not one that can be solved. What, for example, is your reaction to the lack of a callback or to a rejection of your credentials? What keeps you from persisting? If you can come up with reasons for why you were rejected, then you have some degree of empowerment in your responses. But if you just never ever know or can never figure out what went wrong, then you begin to take on the attribute of helplessness.

You can also decide whether your situation is one that is stable or unstable. For example, if you are rejected because you lack a particular experience, then you can see that you exert control over the outcome and go get experience. But if you see no way to ever be competitive in a career that you want to pursue and are continually rejected from even entry-level positions, your tendency is to become helpless and depressed. These are places where volunteering may come in handy to give you the feeling that you are able to develop new skills and get some control over making yourself more competitive.

Negative Thoughts and Self-Talk

Any number of situations may have elicited the thought patterns that led to your self-doubt. Certainly some of these ideas come from the first teachers you had—your parents. The degree to which your ideas were supported and reinforced had some impact on the thought patterns that you created for yourself. But simply signifying that supportive or unsupportive parents helped to shape your thoughts is not enough. The size of the family you were reared in can impact your thinking. If you had to share time with others in a large family, maybe you didn't let your needs be known. If an older sibling put you down a lot, maybe you learned not to express yourself and suffer the consequences. Whatever the case, it is usually reflected in your self-talk. Pay attention to the messages you hear and then try to validate them with facts. For example, if in the background you hear a voice that charges you to get married because you'll never be able to hold a job, look with pride at the jobs you have held. If you did get married, appreciate the many reasons why you chose to marry rather than letting unconscious thoughts take over. You can look at some of the phrases below and consider adapting them when you have intrusions of self-doubt.

Negative Thought	Appropriate Response
What a disaster!	This is a situation that needs attention.
How could you have done this?	Let me go through my thoughts step-by-step.
This can't work out.	Perhaps there is no good solution.
The search is a failure.	At which activities have I failed?
You're out of money, fool.	Who can help with this problem?
It's not going well, idiot.	I've got great ideas and coping skills.

Confronting self-doubt in this way can keep you feeling positive about the search as you force yourself to gather more evidence that certain things are not going the way that you had hoped.

Taking Care of Your Needs

We all have needs, but some people confuse needs with wants. While your wants are those goods and services that would be nice or desirable to have, your needs are conditions that are related to your survival. Abraham Maslow (1954) formulated a hierarchy of needs almost fifty years ago. They began with physical needs like oxygen, food, and water and moved up five levels to self-actualization and cognitive understanding. In the middle of the hierarchy there were safety needs, the need for a sense of belonging, and the need to experience some sort of self-esteem.

In the career search as well as throughout life, self-doubt emerges when you feel that your needs aren't going to be met. This can occur at all stages of the search, and it seems to occur in all parts of the need hierarchy.

Physical Needs

If you have just been given notice that your work is to be terminated, you probably have an uncomfortable reaction that is first related to your survival or physical needs. Your reaction may also be related to your capacity to provide for others. Your response is basic, and you probably feel that if you don't get a job in a hurry, then you are going to be on the street. You experience doubt. But what is really happening is that you're afraid that your physical needs are not going to be met. If you are at this level of worry, then you need to develop a way to ensure over a period of time that your needs and the needs of the family will be met.

So, what do you do? Obviously, you need to make a budget for the search and determine how long you can hold out. Include savings, possible loans, equity lines, second mortgages, and borrowing from friends. None of this will be comfortable, but it does need to be done. If you can understand that the initial self-doubt is related to your needs, you will be able to address the needs rather than obsessing on the self-doubt.

If you're like most people, you tend to throw money at your problems. But when you're out of work, you have the time to deal with the problems yourself, and it's not going to cost you anything. Take advantage of the situation. This is a good time to deal with your personal problems and issues.

To empower yourself a bit here, think about what it cost you to work. List the expenses that were directly related to work. Did you make a daily stop for breakfast and coffee? What were your commuting and clothing costs? What supplies did you get for work that weren't reimbursed? Did you buy flowers for your office? What about lunch? And of course there is child care or pet care, transportation and parking expenses. You'll be surprised at how quickly it adds up, and the figure may reduce your sense of panic.

Safety Needs

If you're in a job search, your need for safety is not being satisfied. If you've been pushed out of an organization for whatever reason, you certainly don't feel safe. And in the job search, the territory is uncharted, which doesn't feel safe either. Sure, maybe you were a telephone pole climber, day trader, or parking control officer and that didn't feel safe either. But the activities of the search are different because of the control issues. It is more like climbing the pole when the weather is inclement or the ground is unsteady.

Much of your personal work in your search is to find different emotional safety nets. You need to have the feeling throughout the search that you can be safe. Safety is created when you can make things familiar to yourself. Sometimes that is through a linear progression, and sometimes it's through the belief that everything will be okay. But there are some specific steps that you can take to help yourself feel safe.

Probably the best thing that you can do when you feel unsafe about any particular activity is to confront it. The frightening aspects of the search should be acknowledged. After that, go ahead and take this scary thing on. If it is informational interviewing, do more, not less. If it is sending out résumés, send more, not fewer.

Most people are frightened by rejection, so they avoid seeking out new opportunities. Remember high school dances? Why did people watch, but have a hard time asking others to dance? It was the pain of the potential rejection. You need to get comfortable in the search, so take on an attitude that you will get to know the places where you're applying. Visit companies in your area, even if you only make it to a reception area or parking lot. Make it a goal to walk into an office building like you own the place. Make it feel as if you belong here. Some successful career changers have even gone into the company elevators and chimed into a discussion of the company to find out about available opportunities. All of these can help you with safety, because they desensitize you to your own anxiety.

It has been suggested that you may feel safer and more in control if you send out a strong cover letter or broadcast letter. You can also have a friend or colleague send out the letter as a broadcast letter indicating that they expect that you will be a most desirable candidate. With this in mind, try choosing to not send a résumé. That may be provocative but interesting. If a company wants what you have to offer, they will contact you.

Needing to Belong

Self-doubt occurs when you're alone and feeling that you don't belong. You feel that everyone else has a perfect life but there is something wrong with yours, especially now that you are looking for work. The best solution for this is obvious: Don't spend much time alone. If you need to obsess and worry, don't do it alone—use resources like those mentioned earlier. But try for the most part to find a place for yourself that you really belong. You can use the family to fulfill some of that need, but you may find that you feel the strongest sense of belonging in places that need the most. Volunteer organizations seem to be able to give you a special place to belong even if it is for only a few hours a week. So many of these facilities desperately need people with professional skills, and you could find that you'll actually have a sense of belonging for life.

There are probably other times when you feel you don't belong. Maybe you've been in a group interview where you felt that everyone else was more articulate than you were. Or maybe you felt that their credentials were much more desirable than yours were. At these moments, it's important for you to appreciate your individuality. Allow yourself to see your cognitive processing as unique. In any group of people doing the same job, all will have different developmental histories and life experiences. Allow yourself to get a feeling of belonging through your feeling of being able to compete because of your uniqueness.

When Ginger applied for her job in litigation support services, she felt that she didn't have nearly as refined an education as the others who were applying for the same job. She had been a court reporter and had attended court reporting school, while the others had all completed college. She didn't feel that she belonged. Self-doubt ensued and she was not going to apply for the position that she wanted.

I talked with her about finding a way to feel that she belonged to this group of applicants. What could she use as a common experience with the others to show her that she did fit in? She found in talking to the other applicants that she had always had to work under severe deadlines and that many of the others did not. Her lack of a four-year degree didn't matter so much once she had leveled the playing field in her own mind.

When Ginger had her job interview, she emphasized her experience working under pressure and deadlines. She knew that litigators were always going to be under a severe time crunch, and she knew that she could handle that. Others were not nearly as comfortable with that pressure, so even with substantially less education than her competitors, Ginger was able to secure the position. Focusing on strengths rather than weaknesses allowed her to feel as if she belonged.

Needing Self-Esteem

Of all of the needs that you have, this is the one that elicits a lot of self-doubt. When you don't have work, you don't have the sense of familiar personal identity that can lead to the reinforcement of your own sense of self-esteem. Regardless of how successful you've been, that was in the past. In our culture, it is very easy to feel worthless when you're not working.

You begin to become sensitive to experiences that wouldn't have bothered you in the past. You're more self-critical. You'll notice in a discussion that others seem to be more articulate than you. The other job searchers seem to be younger. Applicants that you compete with appear to have had better preparation and education than you. They seem to be more "current" than you. However, this too can be reframed. The greatest sense of self-esteem and self-satisfaction that you may ever have is when you're able to solve the dilemma that you are in while creating a road map for solving it again in the future. Self-esteem is reflected in your capacity to have some sense of control. Knowing that you can survive, be safe, have friends, and solve problems will lead to a greater sense of self-esteem. You will reaffirm your worth. Remember how Jackson (in chapter 2) discovered new interests and skills from a job search that was prompted by his termination on the first day of work? It is quite possible for your search to offer you something that is more satisfying than what you had before.

Realize Your Full Potential

Along with the need to be your best (self-actualization), you have the need to enhance your own experience of living. This need is what allows you to have your own sense of greatness, and unfortunately the career search interrupts it. You might feel a bit like General Patton did when he screamed out in frustration during World War II that the war would be over and he wouldn't have a chance to get in his campaign. While you probably don't think about how you're going to be enhancing yourself during the search, you *are* thinking about what you're not getting. You're not getting ahead and you're not creating a greater sense of cognitive understanding about who you are and what you're going to become.

That is precisely how you can use the career search. If you visualize it as a self-enhancing, problem-solving experience, then it will have the capacity to increase your tendency to become more self-actualized. A good place to start is to see the search as something that is going to add to your life experience rather than detract from it.

There are interesting examples of people who can be actualized both through their careers as well as their avocational pursuits. Take Stanford University physicist Bill Atwood. While Atwood is a particle physicist at the Stanford Linear Accelerator, he is also part of an international team of researchers who are studying mysterious sources of high energy radiation in the universe. He also makes violins. He is the proud member of a group of only hundreds of builders who craft instruments in the $5,000 and above range. He was profiled by Bill Workman (1999) as a woodworking physicist. He is interesting in that he makes his living from particle physics and telescope design. But he is actualized in part by his unusual crafting ability. He says that he has the "luxury of not having to make a living at it." He demonstrates that actualization can come about in an arena that may not be directly related to your career. He has been able to add to his physics career by writing scientific papers on the physics of the violin. While his career was a demanding one, his avocational pursuit made him doubly fascinating. More people will probably know who he is and what he has accomplished as a violin maker and violinist than as a physicist with a linear accelerator.

There is growing evidence that the corporate world wants its employees to be able to achieve some degree of balance between their work lives and their home lives. The job search may end up helping you in the creation of this balance. Make sure that the activities you are pursuing at this time in your life are things you will continue to pursue. More worker profitability is generated by workers who are not continuously frustrated, so creating some balance between work and home life will pay big dividends in the future by making you a desirable employee. This time of reengineering your career is also the best time to reengineer your home life. Try to focus on all your needs and discover for yourself how you can meet them in ways that are different from before. The greater the degree of balance that you have in your life, the more creative and accomplished you will be. You might find that you can create a dual agenda for your life by concentrating on reinventing yourself.

What Can I Do to Finally Eliminate Self-Doubt?

You probably ignite more than a few sparks of self-doubt every day by comparing yourself to others. There are a few final tips for limiting this tendency.

1. Stop comparing yourself to people who are better than you or more articulate than you or wealthier than you or more attractive than you or better dressed than you. If you insist in engaging in a comparison game, then balance it out. For example, if you compare yourself to Bill Gates, then also compare yourself to the homeless person who asks you for money every day.

2. Don't kill ideas and suggestions without gathering loads of evidence. If you have an idea, pursue it and gather data to determine whether it will work or not. Don't kill the ideas of the people around you. Just because they are working and you are not, don't assume they are insensitive boors who don't know what they're talking about. It's crucial to remain flexible and be adaptable to new ideas.

3. Allow yourself to pursue the activities that make you unique. Rather than trying to conform, capitalize on these differences. Remember Elton John, who disliked how he looked as a child. He thought he couldn't fit in, so he created his own unique look. He is clearly an accomplished musician, but he used his outrageous clothing and glasses to differentiate himself.

4. Stay mindful of your self-talk. Listen to the messages that you give yourself. If you need to, keep a record of your negative messages. Regardless of the method, attending to your self-talk allows you to change it to make it more positive.

    Including more positive affirmations in your self-talk will help you to be more upbeat. If you find it difficult to do this, then imagine a mentor or encourager who is instilling confidence in you. If your tendency is to continue to engage in the negative self-talk, then try to determine who it is who is talking to you. You're getting a message that is very unhelpful. But it is coming from somewhere and it would be useful to know its origin.

5. Similarly, stay mindful of the images that you create in your mind. You don't have to recreate *Titanic* to motivate yourself. If you play out particular movies, then be the author, director, editor, and actor. With this kind of creative power, your film can have the kind of outcome that you want.

6. Outplacement consultants suggest that those people who keep their appearance up tend to take less time getting reemployed. If you look better, you're going to feel better about yourself. You can confront self-doubt by paying more attention to your personal grooming. This also follows for the way that you keep your house. If you are comfortable with the way you look, and you feel that your home is a place where you want to entertain, then your self-doubt will diminish. Simple personal hygiene and dress can be very empowering activities.

   Incidentally, for those of you who are fretting about money, take some solace from the actress Janet Leigh. She describes her early movie career, when she had only one dress. To compensate, she learned how to creatively use accessories to keep her appearance different for each reading she attended.

7. You may feel like you're dying inside during your search, but you can lessen your personal doubt by giving the appearance of outward confidence. Again, simple activities like brief, clear, crisp communication will help to empower you, as will the tendency to make and keep eye contact with the people in your life during the search. A well-known high school football coach used to tell his players, "Regardless of the outcome, you will always look like an imposing team, because you'll dress and be equipped like one."

8. The creation of effective habits will give you the greatest degree of success. Healthful habit becomes its own motivator. People who work out regularly mourn the days when they are unable to go to the gym.

9. Remember H. B. Gelatt's truism and put it to your use. "If you think you can, you might. If you think you can't, you're right."

7 | Sorting Out Fears and Anxiety

I have seen the moment of my greatness flicker ...
And in short, I was afraid.

—T. S. Eliot

Fear, Panic, and Performance

Cheryl, a bench scientist and recombinant DNA expert, heard that her company was going to merge with an international biotech firm. The writing was on the wall, and she was advised by colleagues to look for another position. However, she loved her company, and the thought of it being taken over frightened her to death. Suddenly her world had no stability. She tried to put together a résumé, a file of her accomplishments, and a cover letter. But to her the merger meant that she was going to lose the job she loved. Her fears of the change and the impending loss of identity and security paralyzed her from the beginning of her search. Night after night, she lay awake worried and sleepless, unable to do anything about her job search.

C.J. was new on the job search front. Panic attacks prevented her from getting through a job interview. Whenever she attended career fairs, she saw many job postings that she was more than qualified to hold. She walked up to various booths at the fairs, but when employers asked even simple questions about what kind of position she was seeking, she froze. Her heart beat quickly and her pupils dilated. She felt like she was in a bubble. Her hands trembled. She then quietly said, "I'm sorry," and excused herself. But inside her head, her thoughts raced over and over, screaming, "I've got to get out of here. Get me out of here."

Julius was a great musician who had won accolades during his elementary and high school years. In college he was considered to be among the finest flute players in his state. But he began to experience performance anxiety as he moved toward graduation. He was aware of the trembling in his fingers, and it made him very nervous. He sought medical advice to ensure that he was not suffering from a neurological disorder. He was given a clean bill of health and advised to see a counselor at school who could help with performance anxiety. He did not want to see a counselor and take time away from practice. His anxiety worsened, and in the end he was unable to apply to graduate school in music because he couldn't do the requisite auditions.

The majority of job search stories include elements of fear, dread, and loathing about the uncertainties of the search. The job search puts your ego on the line and your vulnerabilities are at their highest. Not only that, but your sense of personal power may be at its lowest. When high vulnerability and low interpersonal power are combined and added to situations that are already uncomfortable, you are likely to experience fear and anxiety. You may not be at your personal best; your interviewing and negotiating skills may seem to fall apart under pressure.

Six Common Areas of Vulnerability

The job search and career change are ripe with circumstances that increase your vulnerability and decrease your feeling of personal power. Even the diagnostic term for fear of open spaces, *agoraphobia*, literally means "fear of the marketplace" in Latin. Issues of anxiety about work have clearly been around for centuries.

First, the most prominent workplace fear is that you don't have the skills for the current marketplace. You've grown too old. You haven't kept up. Or maybe you're a recent graduate, but your grades hover around average. You've been shamelessly upstaged by others who know more than you, or who have a more current education than you do. No matter where you look in your career arena, people seem to be younger, more skilled, brighter, and better educated than you. Everyone else seems to have a better résumé or portfolio, a richer set of job experiences, and a greater impact on their respective organizations than you have. As you watch advertisements in the media, these current employees appear to be attractive, sophisticated, bold, and self-assured. Whether you are reentering the workforce or just beginning, this fear is ubiquitous.

Second, there is the fear that you can't package yourself as well as others can. Your résumés, cover letters, recommendations, and accomplishments don't appear to rival those of others seeking the same position. Maybe you can create a good résumé. But can you create several different, competitive ones to make an impact via snail mail, e-mail, and fax machines?

Third, you fear rejection. You send everything out to the universe, then you wait and wait and wait. Each day you grow more anxious about the prospect of feeling like you've failed. It's reminiscent of the excruciating anticipation of acceptance/rejection letters from schools, camps, or colleges. If you've already gone through the interview process at a new company, you languish and wonder whether or not they want to hire you. You attentively wait for the follow-up phone call. You fear the thin envelope with the one-page form letter wishing you luck in your future endeavors. You feel reduced again to your childhood years, fearful of being left out of the "A" social group or more popular "in crowd." Perhaps you find that you don't have as many contacts or as large a support network as those searchers whom you are competing with.

Fourth, you fear the general judgments of your performance. You present yourself to others in an interview or in a workplace simulation task, and you're evaluated. You may be one of those who experiences the discomfort of performance anxiety. You panic at the image of your self-stammering and stuttering your way through the process. Even worse, you cower with the nightmare that you may faint during the course of a presentation. Perhaps you even fear that you will be so nervous that you will not be able to eat when your prospective employer takes you to lunch or dinner.

Fifth, at times of stress in the job search, old messages about you loom large, haunting you. The message from the family, particularly a jealous sibling or judgmental parent, may elicit feelings that you're not worth very much. How many times do you recall someone in your life describing you as "stupid," "unable to care for yourself," or a "failure"? What about "you're not that good" or "you're not smart enough"? You may, with the stress of the job search, remember these messages and accept them as fact. Perhaps you haven't thought of these judgments for years, but now it seems like these old banners of inadequacy are parading in front of you.

Six, you just don't want to change; it's too anxiety provoking. As addressed in chapter 1, change is difficult, and it forces you to make adjustments that you have no wish to make. It's not unlike being told by your landlord that you need to move, because a member of the landlord's family is going to occupy your space. Your home may not be exactly right for you, but you still don't want to be compelled to leave. It feels unfair and evokes discomforting stress and anxiety. You feel like you can't predict, prepare for, or manage your future.

Is This Fear or Anxiety?

The above feelings of vulnerability fall into two categories: fear and anxiety. While your body may react in remarkably similar ways when you experience these two emotions, there is, in fact, a real difference. Fear, on one hand, is characterized by the presence of a real, available object that can elicit worry, torment, or distress. Anxiety, on the other hand, exists without any sign of a clear and present danger. For example, you are anxious if you seem to be obsessing all the time for no specific reason other than a general feeling that you need to look for a job.

You'll experience normal fear and anxiety in your work life, some of you more often than others. There are plenty of examples of normal fear. There are certainly some jobs that are more dangerous than others. Police officers, firefighters, and cab drivers are in harm's way more frequently than budget analysts and marketing managers. Construction workers take risks daily. So do refinery workers, who are always subjected to the possibility of explosions.

Certain professional responsibilities can alarm you, make you feel tense, and upset you. Confrontation or heightened criticism at work can startle you, cause distress, and keep you uneasy at night. This is normal, reactive behavior that isn't quite the same as fear and anxiety. Make no mistake, however: Feeling constantly stressed is not emotionally or physically healthy for you.

Fear responses are important because they alert you to danger. They help you survive in your environment. Some business executives even use the phrase, "Only the paranoid survive." You may have a fear response if you're called into your employer's office at

3 P.M. on a Friday afternoon and told that you should clean out your desk and not come to work on Monday.

Anxiety, in contrast, is a type of worry and upset that exists without any clear, immediate danger. You may feel anxious and worried if you read in the paper about changes in the economy, even though your company is healthy. Merger mania may keep you upset. So may the roller-coaster fluctuations in the stock market.

When your anxiety is connected to your job search, you're probably worried about a whole host of job-search activities. These can be anything from self-assessment to marketing yourself, from interviewing to negotiating your contract, from worries that you've never worked to worries about entering or reentering the workforce.

If you experience increased muscle tension, fatigue, sleep disorders (too much or too little sleep), general irritability, and restlessness, you're most likely experiencing anxiety. This syndrome of symptoms, if it persists for six months with regularity, is called generalized anxiety disorder (GAD).

Each of your job search activities should be manageable, and should not lead to GAD. Exposure to the job-search process over time can make each of the components of the search more familiar. Help from your support network can validate and relax you and assist in keeping you symptom free. But if the search begins to emotionally overwhelm you and you are worried all the time, then you need to take a more aggressive stance to relieve yourself of some of the tension.

Anxiety can become an even more serious problem if you try to treat it or relieve symptoms through self-medication. For instance, some people try to alleviate anxiety with alcohol. They use the excuse, "I need a little courage." But alcohol is not helpful in treating anxiety—it is quite dangerous and addictive. Remember, you're feeling vulnerable and may look to any kind of quick fix. But self-medication will bring you a host of new problems. You're also, frankly, not very good at it.

You might consider prescription medication, if you feel that your anxiety is overwhelming. But for most people this is no solution. Benzodiazepines like alprazolam (Xanax), clonazepam (Klonopin), and diazepam (Valium) are regularly suggested by many mental health professionals. But these drugs have disagreeable side effects. They can leave you a little fuzzy, numb, and forgetful. They're also addictive in the long term. You'll do best to go through your search being mindful and sharp, rather than dull and sedated. After your search, you'll want to avoid these prescription medicines. In a new position, you should want to continue to be your personal best; substance dependence will only make your new career adjustment even more difficult.

Be on the lookout for some secret passion you have for worry or upset. There are people who actually motivate themselves through worry; they find it helps them stay alert. People who experience worry and anxiety as a self-protective mechanism waste a lot of time. Recall the man on the street in downtown Detroit who sat on the corner snapping his fingers. A woman came up to him and queried, "Why are you snapping your fingers?" The man glowered back with, "I'm keeping the elephants away." The woman suggested, "There aren't any elephants around here now." He replied, "Exactly." He had relinquished much of his time to his obsessive worry and the protective mechanism he had developed. Along these lines, some parents worry obsessively when their adolescent children are out on dates, even though there is little they can do other than monitoring the time they return. Vacationers often worry that their house could be broken into, so they call their neighbors each day to check if everything is all right.

Understanding Your Fears

Fear is the conscious and alarming agitation you experience when you're in the middle of or anticipating real danger. Fear can be sudden, startling, and horrid. It can be short-lived or extended. It causes consternation in four different ways. There can be reactions in your body, brain, behavior, and the manner in which you give interpretive meaning to your emotional experience. You may experience one or more of these different ways of reacting to fear. You may also experience them with different intensity than someone else. You could react more in your body while someone else reacts more in the brain with cognitions about impending doom.

So where does fear come from. For the most part, it has three sources: family judgment, traumatic embarrassment, and life-threatening danger. Fear usually begins in late childhood or early adolescence, just when you're noticing changes in your body. You're more prone to feeling naked, humiliated, or on guard during this period. If you've been told repeatedly that you aren't going to amount to much, then every single opportunity you have to advance yourself will be preceded with thoughts that nothing is going to work out. If you gave a speech or performance in school and you were humiliated by other students, friends, or a teacher, you've probably held on to the humiliation. Over time, you've avoided these aversive situations that can result in physical fear reactions.

Accordingly, the fear has increased and you have become even more clever at avoiding these types of circumstances. At some point you generalized the experience so that any exposure to unfamiliar people and situations became uncomfortable, because you feared that you would act in a way that could be humiliating. Your avoidance of these fear-producing situations (like evaluations) had a deleterious effect on your performance on the job or in school. Now that you are looking for a job again, you must confront the very issues and situations that you had been able to avoid. As noted in chapter 1, you're going to have to get over this, as you will probably be searching again and again through the years.

The experiences that trigger a danger or humiliation response in you may be different from what other people experience. This is somewhat different from the popularized "fear of success" and "fear of failure" described earlier in chapter 2. So what can trigger fear in the job search? Most typically it is some kind of performance issue, such as:

- Describing the type of job you want to an informational interviewer
- Making or receiving phone calls
- Meeting with a headhunter or executive recruiter
- Attending a job club
- Interviewing one-on-one for a position
- Group interviews
- Stress interviews where making you uncomfortable is the intention
- Taking employment tests that measure particular skills
- Engaging in a work performance task or job simulation in front of superiors
- Giving a public lecture or presentation to people who might hire you
- Negotiating a contract

Exercise 7-1   Specific Fears in the Job Search

For this exercise, write down all of the various stimuli that spark a fear response in you as a part of your job search. Try to recall or even anticipate events during the search that cause a reaction similar to those where you were truly frightened for your physical safety. Maybe you remember having a psychophysiological reaction, like severe stomach cramps, when you were called on to give a recitation or performance in a class. Try to recall if you've had similar cramping during job-search events. Are there any events that you anticipate in the future that make you sick to your stomach? It's important to make note of these symptoms, as they can be treated with the steps presented in this chapter. For each of the fears, you can later assess which of the four ways you react to the fear and how you can change your way of reacting.

Now that you've identified what in the job search causes you to experience fear, let's focus on how you experience the fear. As already described, fear can be experienced in four ways: in your body, in your head, in your behavior, and in your interpretation.

Exercise 7-2   Fear in Your Body

Look at the list you just made and recall the experience. Did you feel fear in your body?

People know they're afraid when they have some awareness of a change in their body. They have butterflies in the stomach, tightness in the chest, tension in the face, trembling in the hands, weakness in the knees, a loss of bladder control, or worse, a lapse in sphincter control. Like C.J and Julius, they are having an uncomfortable physical experience. You've probably experienced the most common fear response of stomach butterflies or cramps on any number of different occasions, especially when anticipating an event. Perhaps you've had goose bumps on your arms and thighs. These are the early warnings that you're aware of some kind of danger.

Select at least three of the fears from your list. Where was the fear localized in your body? How did it feel? Is this the way that you usually respond to fear? If you're having trouble with this image, try to recreate the feelings you had when you first asked someone for a date or stood up in front of a class to give a report. What did you feel? Where was the feeling localized in your body?

When you feel changes in your body, you should keep in mind that it is actually readying itself to serve and protect your well-being. Unfortunately, these body reactions usually feel just awful, and they can make you look horrible. Your stomach hurts because your acid flow is shut down, your heart races to get extra blood and oxygen into your system, and you breathe more heavily to bring in extra air. With all this high-level internal effort going on, your body is heated.

So you sweat, tremble, and get a dry mouth while your hands and feet get cold and clammy. It's not a pretty picture.

Exercise 7-3   Fear in Your Mind

While your body is in preparation mode, your head may be analyzing the ongoing experience. You've just described body changes triggered by the fear response. For each of the fears you listed in exercise 7-1, try to remember the messages you gave yourself as you experienced the fear. Write down at least three. Were they negative? These interior statements are immensely powerful; they can adversely affect your expectations and your motivation. Letting fear take over will immobilize you.

Exercise 7-4   Fear in Your Behavior

Now that you feel that your body is out of control and the interpretations in your head have prepared you for getting the worst information of your life, what are you going to do? Well, at this point you have begun to reduce your choices. You can stay on with the experience and fight through the fright, or you can get out quickly.

You have already listed examples of fear in your body and fear in your head. Look at these experiences and, for at least three of them, write down what you did behaviorally when you had the fear response. For example, did you escape by excusing yourself like C.J. at the job fair? Did you avoid making a phone call or back away from the phone when it rang with what you were sure would be bad news? Did you ever cut your experience short because you were afraid?

When you're in the midst of a severe fear reaction, your fighting skills have probably diminished because your thoughts about yourself have reduced you to rubble. If you have a fear response in the middle of a job interview and you want to continue with the interview, you need to muster up some attractive answers to the questions being asked of you.

Some people can't stay in the frightening circumstance, so they escape in some way. Perhaps you have seen performers walk off the stage. Like C.J., people sometimes leave in the middle of interviews because they aren't doing well enough to stay. This is technically called the flight response, while staying in the interview is the fight response. Fear responses are characterized by of the fight-or-flight conflict.

Exercise 7-5   Interpreting Your Fear

Now we come to the summation of this aversive experience, which is where you put words to what just happened. You felt body changes, interpreted them with some words in your head, then made your move. Now you will add the postmortem emotional judgment of the experience. You can talk about the whole package as gruesome, aversive, creepy, horrendous, hideous, dreadful. And then you can give a final summation like, "I never want to feel like that again in my life."

With this last statement, you have completed the cycle of the fear development syndrome. This final verdict is what will impact your search the most. Statements like this will help you prevent any further fight/flight experiences. You will now simply try to avoid the fear itself.

For each of the fears listed earlier in exercise 7-1, write down the final interpretation or evaluation you made of at least three of the incidents.

So what will be the end result of your search if you consistently avoid confronting your fears? First, you'll begin to aim lower. You won't go after the types of positions that make you feel good about yourself. You won't look for congruence between who you think you are and what you hope to become. Instead, your fears will likely reduce you to a second-tier player, so you may not apply for the top positions. If you do, you may find yourself doing some unconsciously destructive things like missing deadlines, not submitting references for positions that you apply for, and showing up late and unprepared for job interviews.

You may act like you're remaining active in the search by going after new ideas, perhaps through your network. But you'll take in the ideas without any action. For example, someone could tell you about a new company to consider, and you'll spend a lot of time researching the company. But you won't make an effort to meet people or apply for and secure a position. You'll be like a frightened basketball player, passing the ball a lot but never going for the winning shot.

You may even consider another career, if your fear is so great about the one you are in. There are fine musicians and actors who could not or would not get over their performance anxieties. They gave up their careers because their fears kept them from work.

Overcoming Your Fears

You have seen the different components of the fear response. Now you can witness how it came into play with C.J., who worked in her family's small bed and breakfast inn to put herself through state college. Her family was from India, and while they had come to the United States with good education but little money, the family had saved over the years. With a substantial amount of sweat equity, they were able to purchase the inn. Her parents wanted her to secure her degree, preferably in computing or business, and then return to the family to work in the inn. They also hoped she would help to expand the family resources and eventually purchase another facility.

C.J. majored in marketing and business data systems, and did well. Her instructors encouraged her to consider different opportunities in the business community aside from the family business. Not surprisingly, the family was very much against this strategy. She agonized over her conflict, because she relished both the support from the faculty and support from the family. Eventually, she decided to pursue new opportunities with faculty recommendations. Interestingly, as graduation approached and she began to submit her résumé to different companies that were interviewing at her career center, she noticed that she became nervous. In fact, if she was called in for an interview and the session went well, she found to her distress that she became even more nervous than before. She had butterflies in her stomach and had trouble sitting still or composing herself.

She discussed her reactions with a career counselor at the career center. The counselor suggested that her behavior might be related to institutional racism or her discomfort in a different cultural experience. C.J. disagreed. She correctly concluded it was due to her apprehension over what her parents would think if she did not bring her educational skills back to work at the inn.

After only a short period of time, C.J. noticed that the thought of applying for any job made her nervous. The better the job, the more the nervousness seemed to increase. She started to have trouble making eye contact with employers. She tried to treat her problem by having more interviews and somehow working through the fear. It didn't help. C.J. became worse and finally could not spend more than five minutes in a job interview.

Let's see what happened to elicit C.J.'s fear response. First of all, in the presence of a new employer, C.J. had a racing heart, high pulse rate, flushed face, clammy hands, and lightheadedness. She felt like she was going to vomit or explode. In her head she said certain things to herself. "Who do you think you are?" "You're not qualified to work here. They don't hire foreigners." "Go to work at the inn." "Don't desert your family." Her stock response was to run away. She wanted to get out of the situation as soon as she could because she was afraid that she was eventually going to have a heart attack. And in her interpretation, she summed up the job search by saying it was simply too difficult for her.

Now in C.J.'s case, we have an obvious psychological conflict that was created by her feelings of being torn between her family's business and the outer work world. She was making a career decision that might go against her family's wishes. She couldn't handle this emotionally, so she unconsciously sabotaged her own search. Even though this might appear obvious to you, it wasn't so apparent to her. How well do you understand the fears that you have in the search? In the list of fears from the earlier exercise, are you aware of where they originate? Did the exercises help you understand?

You might find that you get nervous during interviews, but you don't really know why. What you might believe is that your performance is not very good. Or you might not apply for some of the better jobs or graduate schools. Again, you don't know why; you just tell your friends that you don't feel qualified.

So what can you do to address fear responses, regardless of their origin? Most importantly you need to attack *all* of the components of the fear response that are mentioned here. By attacking all four, you're less likely to allow fear to keep you from seeking out jobs for which you are qualified.

Step 1: Treat Your Body

You're most aware of the fear response in your body, so begin by trying to isolate which parts of your body are affected by a fear or panic attack. Do you notice your heart speeding up? Do you sweat on your upper lip or under your arms? Do parts of your body tremble? What did you learn about your bodily responses to fear from exercise 7-2? If for some reason you didn't have any fear responses to exercise 7-2 or you couldn't isolate fear in your body, write down these bodily changes you would feel if you had a police car flash its lights behind you as you drive home well over the speed limit.

By becoming familiar with how your body reacts under stressful conditions, you can work to slow your body down. One way is through the quieting reflex and the progressive relaxation strategies described in chapter 10. But you'll find that just becoming aware of the body changes gives you some degree of control. As you feel the fear response, stay with it and try to name exactly what is going on rather than creating a global evaluation that says, "I'm uncomfortable."

Then, for each of the statements about your body, go further and visualize creating a body change. Visualize your heart slowing down or your skin being warm and dry. Feel your stomach relaxing. The key to addressing fear is to know in your mind and your body that somehow you are in control again. Don't run from the physiological response. Stay with it. Pay attention to it. It is trying to tell you something. Then try to get control of your bodily response. Practice relaxing your heart rate so it slows. Imagine your hands over a warm fire and feel their temperature rise. Place your hands on your stomach and let their warmth relax your midriff.

There are also other activities that you can do to slow your body down.

Mantras. You can create words or phrases that you say to yourself in times of fear. In the career search, try a mantra like, "Every day in every way, I'm getting closer to my goal."

Theme songs. The popular television show *Ally McBeal* shows a psychiatrist who recommends that all of her patients create theme songs for themselves. As flippant as this technique may appear to be, it can actually work. By changing your thoughts about an experience, you will be able to change the feelings in your body. You can add even further power to this experience. If you do happen to have a theme song, try conducting it as well as singing it, so you get some exercise while your theme song empowers you.

Yoga. Yoga classes can help you stretch you body and increase your awareness of where you store tension. You can draw a picture of your body as well and pinpoint the different areas that feel sore or tense during a fear reaction. It may be useful to do this on a regular basis, not necessarily only in the presence of fear.

Meditation. You can learn to quiet your body with classes in meditation techniques. These allow you to cleanse your mind and your body so that stressful experiences do not elicit unnatural or extreme fear responses.

Breathing. Making diaphragmatic breathing a regular part of your air intake cycle will help you to relax. People who are prone to reacting with fear responses tend to breathe more in their chest than their diaphragm.

Regular exercise. Daily exercise, even if it is only a walk, will help you to release some of the tension in your body. Swimming seems to be especially effective in promoting physical relaxation. It's also crucial to get a good night's sleep so that your body does not need adrenaline rushes to simply get through the day.

Stretching. Stretching exercises, however simple, can be used to relax your body, lower your blood pressure, and reduce the muscle strain that comes from keeping your body tense throughout the day. Animals like dogs and cats are good examples to imitate.

A nice bath. The total immersion of your body into a bathtub, hot tub, or sauna will give you a healing experience while it calms you down.

Dietary changes. You can assist yourself in making your body less reactive by reducing your sugar and alcohol intake while eliminating caffeine.

Step 2: Confront the Messages in Your Head

If the person sitting across from you in your job interview is a prospective employer and you want the job, you may have a fearful reaction. You may feel threatened by the idea of evaluation, and you may feel less than comfortable. This same person could, however, be a sailing friend, a card partner, or a family relative, in which case they would not be perceived as a threat. So it all depends on the context that you're in. Within the interview context, you may be prone to empower the interviewer as you disempower yourself. As the power disparity increases, so does your fear. As the fear increases, the bodily reactions just described begin to take over and the reaction response begins again.

So what can you do to disempower the person who is conducting the job interview? You can be aware of the messages that you are sending yourself before, during, and after the interview. As you sit there, what is coming to mind? Before the interview, how did you assess your chances? If internal messages come to you from other sources like your parents, siblings, or life partner, tell them to shut up (in your head, of course). If you hear yourself saying that you will not do well, confront the message. Give yourself permission to disagree with it.

There is, for the most part, no truth to your internal, obsessive messages. You have created them and you can get rid of them—but it will take confrontational work. The demons that you keep in are messages that you have probably absorbed from others. As discussed earlier, we all get comfortable with messages that are familiar to us. So, if you have heard that you are a nerd most of your life, you will not react negatively to being called a nerd. But during an interview, the thought that a new and unfamiliar person thinks that you're a nerd is most alarming to you. That's why you need to listen to and confront the messages in your head. Focus on getting someone to relate to you. How do you get them to like you? How do you keep a conversation or a meeting interesting? In other words, how do you increase your personal interviewing power?

In addition, use some visualizing devices to help you decrease the power differential between you and the employer or any other fear-provoking stimulus. Instead of seeing the employer as something akin to the great Oz, try to see the interviewer in a different context. Dress the person, in your mind's eye, in a different garment. Imagine what the interviewer looked like just a while ago, getting out of bed. Did the interviewer have on pajamas and was she not as coiffed as she is right now? What if the interviewer had an outrageous haircut or unusual clothing? What if the interviewer had two-foot-long earrings or a wig that was just slightly ajar? Each of these images can make you feel somewhat less threatened than you are currently. You can begin to see how you listen to messages and how you can confront the messages. You can learn to understand how you invest or project a sense of power onto an employer or interviewer that doesn't really need to exist. Remember that people are just people. We are the ones who invest them with authority and responsibility.

How can you empower yourself? First of all, you should have researched the company so you can ask creative or specific questions. To further empower yourself, you also need to ask questions that will give you potential information about your future. This research and the practicing of these questions will help you to feel in control. As you gain more control, you will shrink the power differential between yourself and the interviewer. Answers to the questions will get you good information about the company, but you will be enriched by the creativity of your inquiry. Consider asking questions along these lines to give you a chance to make your interviewer do some creative responding:

- Where do you see the company going?

- Where do you see new business opportunities?

- What new products or services will the company have in the next two years?

- What are my chances for advancement?

- How long do people in my position tend to stay here before being promoted?

- How will I be evaluated? How frequently will this take place?

- How is my salary tied to my evaluation?

- Will I have the opportunity to speak to the person that I am going to replace?

Step 3: Change Your Behavior

It's absolutely crucial that you stay mentally and physically present in the interview or any other activity that scares you. If you run from the interview, you tend to make a bad situation even worse, by creating an avoidance response. Once your body learns to run from different predicaments, it becomes much more difficult to stay in a situation that you find aversive. So how can you do it?

Part of what we know about fears and phobias is that we can systematically confront some of the feared or aversive material by remaining in, and not avoiding, the situation. You can try any one or all of the following activities.

Flooding

Behavioral psychology research has shown that many fears and phobias persist because people run away from the feared stimuli or the situation that may bring about the feared response. If you fear performing poorly, you avoid performing, there by maintaining your fear. If the sight of blood makes you squeamish, you avoid situations where there is blood. More than one prospective premed student has decided not to attend medical school because of the irrational fear of the sight of blood. People who fear riding in planes and elevators don't get on planes or elevators. The fear is never dissipated and even becomes bigger.

In flooding, you force yourself to face your fears: riding on a plane, being shut in an elevator, driving over a bridge, looking at blood while watching an operation. The organization TERRAPP (meaning territorial apprehensiveness) has used this approach for years. It's a method of reality testing that allows you to live the experience. You then discover that the disaster you expected was only in your mind. Or, if a disaster did take place, it was not nearly as bad as you imagined it would be.

Apply this principle to the job search. Your fears about parts of the job search that are frightening you persist because you avoid these activities. When you don't allow yourself to experience what frightens you, then you don't allow the fears to be extinguished.

The crucial aspect of flooding is that you are forced to stay with the experience. To get through the traumatic experience, you can use relaxation exercises and give yourself positive messages. Remember, flooding keeps you from engaging in avoidance activity.

If you need to practice some of your feared job-search situations, friends can help you set up simulated trials. A common and effective flooding technique is to apply for jobs that you may not be interested in, just for practice. If you don't care about the job, then your performance during a job interview shouldn't matter as much and you'll more readily begin to desensitize yourself to the aversive components of the interview. If you happen to not get a job, you won't be upset about it because you didn't want it in the first place. You will be exposed to the irrational aspects of your performance anxiety and this will help you to understand that your fears about the job search may only be in your head.

While some people may want to adopt the flooding experience themselves, others may want the guidance of a professional. A counselor trained in flooding (also known as implosive therapy) can use strongly worded, rapidly presented verbal cues that make you feel as if you are confronting the aversive event. This presentation is made without interruption and can be among the most effective counseling techniques available to treat fears and phobias.

Modeling

In a modeling activity, you watch another person engage in the activity that is aversive to you. For example, people who are afraid of public speaking can attend a variety of public speaking events in order to watch how different speakers perform and handle the stress of the event. If job interviews frighten you, then consider watching another person engage in interviewing activities, either by sitting in an actual interview or by watching appropriate interview techniques on a business video. If you know any human resources professionals, you could ask them to model interview behavior for you. After the experience, you can reflect upon how you might try some of the activities you saw.

New health professionals, counselors, marketing professionals, and human resources types have all been taught with modeling techniques. People who are preparing for different oral professional exams also reduce their fears through modeling. The technique is effective, inexpensive, and allows you to have a nonbookish feel for what an experience will be like.

Applied Tension

As discussed earlier, fear can elicit an increase in blood pressure or heart rate. But for a small percentage of the population, it can reduce blood pressure and heart rate. This is particularly true for people who are afraid of the sight of blood, but it is also true for people who fear passing out while they are in fear-provoking situations. Agoraphobics may have this tendency. Instead of relaxation, these people need to try a technique known as "applied tension." In this procedure, you actually tense the facial muscles, along with others like the muscles in your hands, thighs, feet, and stomach. With this application, your body will begin to feel slightly warmer. As it warms, you can let the tension go. People with a fear of fainting in public places or during a public performance have been helped greatly with this.

In an offshoot of this technique, I have found that apprehensive clients can help reduce their fear by pressing their left or right thumb in the fleshy space between their other thumb and their index finger. You want to apply a quick but strong pressure that causes a slight pain. This can be done quickly and with little notice, so you can do it in an interview or an oral presentation. Fearful job searchers claim that applying pressure like this is almost like getting a whiff of ammonia or "smelling salts." They report feeling more alert, refreshed, and awake; they don't fear passing out.

Systematic Desensitization

This decades-old approach can also work to help job searchers successfully overcome their fears. The constraint to its use is that unlike the others, which may be done without a counselor, this process requires a counselor with a behavioral orientation.

There are three aspects to the process of systematic desensitization. The first is that you must learn some form of deep muscle relaxation similar to that described in chapter 5. Second, you need to build a hierarchy of frightening experiences related to the fear object. These can be exemplified by the following hierarchy that C.J. used. It starts with the least feared experience and ends with the most feared:

- Thinking about the interview a week in advance
- Thinking about the questions I will be asked three days in advance
- The day before the interview
- The morning of the interview
- Driving to the interview
- Walking in the door of the interview
- Greeting the receptionist
- Waiting to be called in
- Entering the room and sitting in the chair
- Getting asked the first question like, "Tell me about yourself."
- Freezing in the interview
- Feeling my heart in the interview
- Not being able to answer a question
- Feeling my brain getting fuzzy

After you create the hierarchy, you then must pair the elements of the hierarchy together with relaxation in what is called counter-conditioning. In this case, the feared stimulus is presented verbally to you by a counselor while you're trying to maintain relaxation. The effort is an attempt to gradually pair increasingly aversive images with relaxation so that the aversive image elicits a new, more relaxed response rather than the old, formerly feared response. Instead of a rapid heartbeat, there will be a slower one. Instead of trembling, there will be a quiet body.

During the course of the presentation of the images, you let the counselor know that a particular scene is uncomfortable, usually by raising an index finger. When that happens, the counselor backs up to earlier, less provocative images and starts over. If these images are now uncomfortable, the counselor moves back to those scenes that don't elicit any fear. Then the counselor begins to state the hierarchy again. You work until the entire hierarchy can be experienced with relaxation responses. This technique is a powerful standard and can be quite useful in preparing for the job search.

Step 4: Modify Your Interpretation

Many of you, when describing a fear response, include negative words like "horror," "dread," and "gruesome." By defining your feared experience in this manner, you set the stage for an aversive job search. Simply by changing the words that you are using to describe your experience, it's quite possible to become more comfortable in your search.

All that is really happening during a fear response is that you experience bodily changes. You could learn to interpret these changes differently. For example, if you get stomach butterflies before a job interview, you could tell yourself they're there to get you psyched up. Athletes, for example, try to get themselves psyched up before a competitive encounter, and the butterflies reflect the fact that they are prepared to compete. Your bodily nervousness can be an indication that you really care and that the job is important to you. That's great because it gives some meaning to your search.

Psychologists have known for some time now that there is a curvilinear relationship between performance and fear about the performance. For example, if you have little or no fear about a particular performance, chances are that you won't do very well. On the other hand, if you have too much fear about your performance, you will also not do very well. What you need to look for is the *optimal* level.

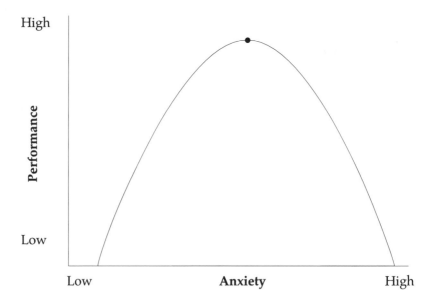

As shown here, you want to get just the right amount of butterflies, stomach acid, tension, and excitement to perform at your personal best. This does not occur when your fear is low or nonexistent. The graph shows the curvilinear relationship and the point of optimal level of fear.

So far the focus has been on fear, and we have used the job interview and performance appraisals as examples of how fear presents itself in the job search. Many of the components of the search can elicit fear so paralyzing that it keeps you from staying active in your search. But what about anxiety? In fear, there is a clear and present danger, which is pretty specific. With anxiety, the same four characteristics exist as they do with fear, but the danger is generalized, not specific. There is a feeling of impending doom without a specific cause.

With your fears, you might say something like, "I don't think that they will like my presentation to the human resources staff at the company." With anxiety you might say, "I don't think anybody is going to like me and I'm probably not going to get any job offers." Your anxiety is nonspecific and keeps you in a state of continuous and uncomfortable agitation. Since anxiety is diffuse, it's sometimes more difficult to treat.

Extreme cases of anxiety are characterized by panic disorder, agoraphobia, and generalized anxiety disorder (GAD). Panic disorder and agoraphobia are more acute problems, while generalized anxiety disorder is more chronic. Agoraphobia is not considered here since it is beyond the scope of the fear and anxiety issues in the job search.

Panic Attacks

Perhaps you've heard of panic attacks. These are attacks which have the same four components as the fear does, but they're usually unexpected. People describe them as resembling what it must be like to have a heart attack. With panic attacks, you feel like you're losing control of your mind, and your body. Sometimes these attacks can be triggered by a particular circumstance, such as giving a speech. As you're being introduced, you might find that your heart is racing and you're starting to sweat profusely. You might be in the middle of a job interview when your heart starts to speed up, your mouth dries out, and your hands tremble as you rapidly fidget in your chair. You try to mask your discomfort, but you believe that everyone knows you're in a state of panic.

Panic attacks begin with a feeling of discomfort and then gradually take over your thoughts and feelings. You may feel like you can't breathe and that your heart is going to blow out of your chest. The attacks can be triggered by particular events or they can be completely unexpected. After having one panic attack, you begin to worry and fret that you're going to have another one. When you begin to worry that another will occur, you mistakenly avoid certain situations. That's harmful to your search, and it's also a potential precursor to agoraphobia. With agoraphobia you become afraid of having a panic attack or fainting in a public arena where no one will come to your rescue. It is a nonspecific fear of fear.

While it is known that some medications can help to alleviate panic attacks, the most effective method is to understand that your panic disorder comes from a terrible misreading of your bodily sensations. You can learn to avoid panic attacks if you can reverse critical internal dialogues using the techniques described in the fear section.

In a stressful job-search situation, there is some tendency for you to imagine that doom is just around the corner. Simply learning how to interpret the symptoms correctly can help to alleviate the panic attack. Knowing, for example, that shortness of breath is related to anxiety rather than a heart attack can help to keep you more relaxed and focused. Learning how to breathe more slowly using you diaphragm can help in a preventative way. The panic symptoms need to be viewed as simply bothersome—not harmful—signals of anxiety.

Generalized Anxiety

Generalized anxiety disorder (GAD) is part panic, part agitation, part obsessive-compulsive thinking, and part heightened worry. It's chronic rather than acute and is very difficult to control. Medication can help to alleviate symptoms, but when you stop taking the medications, there's a tendency to reengage in your worries. GAD is disruptive to your personal life, relationships, work, and job search.

Let's say you have read this far, and while some of what's described in this chapter seems relevant to your experience, none of it seems to apply specifically to you. You don't think you fit any of the categories described so far, yet you still feel very uncomfortable in your job search. In fact, you believe your everyday worry level might be much higher than that of others. In any event, the job search experience feels disempowering. Consider the following checklist about anxiety during the career search.

Exercise 7-6   Checking Your Anxiety Level

The following items can be used to help determine the type of job-search worries you have. Read each item and check whether or not it applies to you.

_____ I blush easily.

_____ I don't feel very happy right now.

_____ I'm afraid of different things happening to me.

_____ I am pretty easily upset by events, circumstances, or people.

_____ I have a lot of trouble sleeping.

_____ I don't feel very secure during my job search.

_____ People think I am a fidgety person.

_____ I think of myself as inadequate during the job search.

_____ I fret about job-search events that I can't control.

_____ My job search keeps me in a great deal of turmoil.

Count up the number of items that you checked. If you have checked off more than half of the items, your anxiety about your search is excessive. It is likely that you're having some trouble honestly relating to people and that you're very self-conscious about your behavior. This makes it difficult for you to flow easily through the process. Instead you may get stiff and have a hard time responding naturally to others. Quite possibly, you tend to watch yourself and try to figure out what other people want rather than to get information and give answers that come from your heart and soul. You may want to seek consultation with someone who understands the anxiety of the career search. Nationally certified career counselors and licensed mental health professionals are good starting points.

Tools for Reducing Anxiety

Try to remember that the job search is a confidence destroyer for most. Even those who seem to be in the very best shape to promote themselves find that their sense of stability and self-assuredness get some severe blows during the search. That's why it's important to take care of yourself to prevent some of the worry and anxiety that is described here. Relaxation exercises, a good diet, restful sleep, fun, laughter, and good relationships can all add to your feeling of well-being during the search. But the most effective confidence builder is your own preparation for the search. You will feel less anxious when you know what you're looking for and how you plan to get it.

Preparation

Like an actor or an actress who goes on stage, you should continue to practice your different roles in the search. Be able to move into search behavior at the drop of a hat. Take advantage of any chance to let people know that you're looking for work. This will increase your network of contacts, give you more exposure, and keep you practicing your job-search role.

Know What You Want

You should be fully aware of what you are looking for and how you can describe it to others. If you don't know what you're looking for, you're probably not going to find it. The idea that you're not going to find it is an anxiety raiser, even if you're not sure what "it" is. Having focused and reachable goals will help to make the search a measurable, clearly articulated experience. Generalized anxiety and worry don't come from specific fears, but from vague generalities. If you can make a move toward different goals, then you will have more specific fears, if any, to address. You can use some of the techniques mentioned earlier for that.

Be Realistic

Accept the reality that many of the résumés that you send out are not going to be read. Instead they'll be opened and scanned onto a computer disk. When a job is to be filled, key words will be typed into the computer program that's accepting the résumés, and only those résumés with specific key words, education, and experience will be moved into a new pool. You may receive a form letter telling you that you weren't selected for an interview. You wonder why they didn't want you; your self-esteem is blown. But what really happened was that the words on your résumé did not match the words that the employer had in mind when they sought to fill their position. There's no reason to let this affect your sense of self-worth or your self-esteem. Give up waiting for a positive response to your résumé. The waiting will produce more anxiety than it's worth.

And a word about electronic postings: It may be shocking to you to realize that with all of the usefulness of the Internet, only about 1 percent of all employers look at any of the résumés. Sure, the chances of winning the lottery are small too, but you need to play anyway if you're going to win. The point is to eliminate unrealistic expectations about some of your search activities. If you post a résumé on the Internet, forget about it. If you don't expect anything, you won't sit around waiting for something to happen when you should be getting on with your search.

Don't Expect the Worst

Try to give up waiting for disasters during the search. This clouds your efforts and causes a great deal of anxiety. People in the Midwest anticipate tornadoes every year, and they do their best to prepare, as you should prepare yourself for disappointments. But that is different from being consumed by a fear of disaster. Several years ago, the Mississippi River flooded upstream. Residents along the river hundreds of miles to the south knew that in two weeks they were going to be swamped, drowned, or destroyed. They prepared as well as they could, but the waiting was what caused the most stress. Many said afterwards that it's easier to respond to a disaster after it happens than to wait for one that you know is coming. Keep that in mind as you search. For the sake of your health, focus your attention on preparation, not on possible doom.

A Few Words about Obsessive-Compulsive Behavior

A final thought pattern that isn't really anxiety but has a base of fear and anxiety is obsessive-compulsive disorder (OCD). Obsessions are the continuous, repetitive thoughts that seem to take over your thinking whenever you have the faintest hint of a threat or a fear. Compulsions are the usually behavioral responses and rituals that you engage in almost as if you were driven to do so.

Cheryl had a lot of fears about the job search. As a scientist, she was an exacting perfectionist. She wanted the very best new position that she could get but began to dread the idea of being rejected. She thought that she was well qualified and should get a new position without much of a hassle. Still, fear of rejection lingered. The more that Cheryl experienced the fear, the more obsessive thoughts entered her brain. She wanted to make her professional résumé perfect. She wanted it to promote her unique skills. She was consumed with making the résumé perfect, current, impressive, and capable of launching her. She obsessed about how people would view her résumé. When I critiqued it for her and suggested seeral minor wording changes, she reworked it for a month.

Cheryl obsessed about being rejected and unable to secure work. Her response to the obsession was to put together a résumé that was perfect. Her compulsive behavior resulted in several months of ritualistically redoing her resume and sending it out for the opinions of her colleagues. When the opinions were offered, she spent more time in this ritual. Another unproductive part of the ritual was to avoid sending out the résumé in order to guard against rejection. She developed very creative excuses for not getting on with marketing the résumé. She also did not do anything else as a part of the search.

Cheryl was certainly not very efficient in her worries. She was also very articulate in explaining why it was important to get the résumé done right. I asked her what it would be like to send out the résumé and then have it rejected via a letter from a prospective employer. She thought it would be horrendous and she had a fear that she might just fall apart right then and there.

There had to be a way to break into the behavior chain that she had created for herself. She was willing to admit that a lot of the fear was in her mind, but that didn't seem to help her get some control over her own behavior. Commonsense reasoning wasn't going to help, so I suggested that she try a couple of different tactics. The first was to send the résumé out to any company that she *didn't* want to work for. That way if she was rejected, then she wouldn't see it as a shot to her self-esteem. Secondly, I suggested that she let me do a very, very critical line-by-line review of the résumé She wasn't sure what I was getting at but thought that we should try anything to get her out of this habitual predicament. I figured that if I could increase my levels of criticism of her work over a few sessions, she would get better at defending her work and ultimately begin to feel better about how she was presenting herself to the world.

By engaging in these two techniques, which had their basis in desensitization through two different types of flooding (expecting rejection and receiving criticism), Cheryl was able to break away from the ritualistic behavior of résumé checking. That didn't necessarily stop the obsessions, which were driven by her fears. But by reducing the behavior she was able to restart her job search and feel some level of control over her response to the fears that elicited the obsessions. Keep in mind that Cheryl engaged in her compulsive behavior because she believed that it was a good response to the obsessions, which suggested that she might be less than adequate to pursue the job she wanted.

Exercise 7-7   Recording Your Obsessive Thoughts and Ritualistic Behaviors

You're all familiar with some ritualistic ideas that you grew up with. "Avoid black cats crossing your path. Don't walk under ladders. And if you step on a crack you'll break your mother's back." The film *As Good As It Gets*, starring Jack Nicholson, told of an adult writer who still compulsively avoided stepping on cracks. Write your answers to the following questions in your journal.

What excessive thoughts and fears do you have about the job search? These are often seen as doubts that you have about yourself or about being successful in the job search.

What ritualistic behaviors have you created to make yourself feel in control? Do you engage in any odd, time-consuming activities? Mostly these will involve checking something related to the job search, like Cheryl checked her résumé. But it could be ritualistically checking whether or not you locked your doors. Some people ritualistically drive by their house to make sure that the garage door is locked. Others ritualistically return to the house after leaving to see if they left the water running or the stove on.

If you have any of the obsessions or the compulsions in this exercise, it is important to do something about your pattern of behavior. You need to do this if for no other reason than that your time and your life are being wasted.

If you have severely negative, obsessive thoughts, you need to confront them by admitting them to people in your support network. Be aware that obsessions are not necessarily uncommon. It is the excessive obsessions that are. So admit what you are doing to some of the potential encouragers in your support network, because it will help to address some of the self-doubt. In addition, if you experience any self-doubt, try to accumulate bona fide evidence that you are correct in your assessment.

What about the rituals? You need to break them. I've found that doing something illogical or flooding yourself with the behavior can help. Applying to companies that don't want you is one technique.

Doing informational interviews in fields you know nothing about is another. With each of the techniques, you are forced to engage in job-seeking behavior in the real world. This can assist you in jump-starting your search.

What Are the Best Strategies for Staying Calm?

1. Don't wait for magic. Keep control of the search. The outcomes will appear with your efforts. There is some serendipity to the search, but don't count on it.

2. Don't believe that the particular technique that worked for someone else will necessarily work for you. Everyone needs to develop an individually driven search. Jobs, companies, and worker personalities are all different. Be an expert on yourself and on your search.

3. Make sure that all of your job-search activities are realistic. Maintain your control in the search by not overextending yourself or your effort.

4. Practice interviews, including informational interviews. The more you practice, the greater the desensitization

5. Research companies on the Internet, which you can access at your local community college career centers or public library. Send for corporate annual reports if you can't get information any other way. Contact the local chamber of commerce for further data. Knowing more about them will help to counteract your fears and prevent interviewing surprises.

6. Attend meetings where members of particular companies might dwell. If they hang out at a particular club, bar, or restaurant, go there. Get into conversation. Find out who they know and compare networks.

7. Find some special place that can serve as your personal sanctuary, an escape from the turmoil of the search.

8. Be prepared. Be aware of the trends in your industry. Good research and knowledge will keep you from any blind-side assaults.

9. Don't invent new fears. Just because one bad thing happened does not mean it will be this bad again. Stay present.

10. Learn to let go of anxiety. Don't let your anxiety become too familiar—and don't let it become your friend.

11. Identify your specific fears and worries. If you need them, then control them by keeping them on a tight schedule.

12. Keep your fears and worries in a separate room. Call it a "fret room." You can have all the fear and anxiety you want, but only in that room. If you can't sleep at night, create an insomnia room where you can go to have your insomnia.

13. Form a fear group with your friends and colleagues to avoid being alone with your fears.

14. Keep the language of your search filled with positive words and images. Don't feel that you will receive more attention from your negativity.

15. Don't engage in self-flagellation. Describe yourself only in the most positive of terms.

16. Listen to music that you find personally soothing. Let it be whatever is relaxing to you. If rap or hip-hop relaxes you, then so be it. You will become even more relaxed if you try dance lessons with your favorite music.

17. Find some free pleasurable moments each day. For example, department stores often have free or complimentary facials that you can take advantage of. Finding bargains for yourself at this time will be a treat.

18. Visit art museums on the days when they are open free of charge. Take advantage of these, as they keep you relaxed and open up new opportunities for learning and networking.

19. Attend the open rehearsals of symphonies, dance companies, and other performing arts groups. These are more readily available than you might think and can be free or low cost.

20. Treat yourself to a nice lunch at least once a week. You will find that it is healthier to have a large meal in the middle of the day, and it will also remind you of your own importance.

8 | Managing Rage and Anger

I'm mad as hell, and I'm not going to take it anymore.

—Peter Finch in *Network*

Where Does Your Anger Come From?

Perhaps you've heard the story of the man who had a flat tire on the highway. He went to change his tire and found that the tire iron was missing from his trunk. So he went traipsing toward a service station to secure a tire iron. He talked to himself along the way. "They probably don't have a tire iron. Stupid station. Or, if they do have one, they won't let me use it. Idiots. They probably think I'm not mechanical. I could offer them money, but they will probably over-charge me. I bet they won't even give me a ride back to change the tire. So, I'll be overcharged and I'll have to walk back and change my own tire and my clothes will be filthy." After this intense obsessing, the man reaches the service station, walks up to an attendant, and slugs him, screaming, "I don't want your ugly, damned, no-good tire iron."

You feel enraged when you can't change or control a situation. You're angry over your impotence, so you may express anger or rage simply to feel as if you're doing something. Sometimes you want people to know that you're upset, so you allow your anger to become a visible representation of your internal feelings.

In counseling many angry people claim that they actually prosper emotionally through their anger and rage. To be fair, even Aristotle mused that anger was a creative force. In contrast, the Bible considers anger one of the seven deadly sins. Recent tragedies in our nation's schools that seem to stem from rage over individual impotence have brought more attention to this topic.

Chances are that the career search has made you angry. You've prepared so well and worked so hard. Why then is it so difficult to get the job you want? You feel frustrated, impatient, argumentative, alone, and maybe even depressed. But why?

The emotional roots of anger stem from a number of personally loathsome feelings, according to Tolchin (1996). She suggests that betrayal, confusion, deprivation, and injustice are powerful feelings that can lead you to act out. These feelings are often experienced in the job search, as are others like frustration and sense of entitlement.

By its very nature, the job search is practically guaranteed to elicit virtually all of these emotions. You experience betrayal when promises are not kept or information is not provided. The changing work world can leave you bewildered. You feel personally deprived when others have a job and you don't. This stimulates your sense of entitlement; after all, you and other Americans expect to be able to work. Meanwhile, when others have jobs and you don't, you may experience a sense of injustice. You don't feel that you're the right gender, age, or ethnic group.

These are the psychological roots. Now let's explore how anger is triggered in different phases of the job search.

The ABCs of Anger

The career search is filled with many circumstances and events that are beyond your control. The job market; salary schedules; responsiveness to your mail, e-mail, résumé, and phone inquiries; employer attitudes and selection strategies are all external to you. You feel dependent on any number of people or situations. And you'd love to have more influence. So, you create certain distortions that are sometimes subtle but are almost always irrational in order to "explain" what is really happening. This process helps you gain some control. Then you react to your own distortions.

It works like this:

A. There is an external event that is out of your control.

B. You react emotionally and develop a distorted belief about the event in order to capture some control. The control is usually of your own making and may be unrelated to reality.

C. You then have an emotional reaction to your own distortion, not the external event.

D. You create a circular obsession between your distortion and your emotional reaction so that your reaction becomes intensified. With increased obsessing, you trigger your anger. Your anger grows with further obsessing, as it did with the man who needed the tire iron.

E. You finally displace your intensified anger onto someone else, often someone you're familiar with.

Erin had excellent career prospects. She was well educated, with master's degrees in both finance and international relations. She was looking for a position in the federal government, preferably in the Washington, D.C. area. She received many responses to her résumé, but she found that she wasn't getting called back for further interviews subsequent to the initial screening process. The longer she waited, the more frustrated and angry she became. Her ABCs looked like this:

A. External event: Government recruiter would not return her phone calls.

B. Distortion: After they meet me, they decide I'm not qualified. They also don't like me or my style.

C. Emotional reaction: How can they believe that I'm not qualified? I have more education than any of the people in that office. I'm also a better dresser and communicate more clearly. I'm smarter too.

D. Intensification: I know what it is, even though they won't tell me. I'm not the right ethnicity for what they have in mind. I don't know the right people. I don't have the connections to be part of their world. Maybe they don't want anyone Irish.

E. Displacement: I'm sick of the government clique. I'm tired of hearing about my boyfriend's political beliefs. He thinks that the government is fair in its hiring policies. Bull. I'm so angry at him for his attitude that I pick fights with him about everything. He is such an ass and in so much denial.

After exploring the ABCs, Erin began to see how her cognitive distortions and irrational thinking took energy away from her job search. She was creating self-sabotaging thoughts. Her words and aggressive moods also adversely affected her relationship with her boyfriend, so she was headed for a double loss. She would not get a job in the area she wanted and she might lose her relationship. She would also develop a distasteful reputation around town for her focus on ethnicity, a potential outcome that shocked her once she paid attention to it.

Exercise 8-1   Documenting Your ABCs

In this exercise, follow the ABC paradigm that has just been outlined. Try to recall one recent event during this career search that made you very angry—so angry that you had to displace your anger onto something or someone else. It can be an event as simple as not having a phone call returned. This exercise will help you realize that it's not the event itself, but rather the irrational beliefs or distortions that you had about the event that caused most of your anger. In your notebook, finish the following sentences.

A. The external event that I remember upsetting me was . . .

B. The distorted idea I developed about the event was . . .

C. The words that I used as the emotional reaction to my own distortion were . . .

D. My reaction intensified with the following words or actions . . .

E. I displaced my feelings on to . . .

What you may be able to learn from this exercise is how your anger evolves with your own creative cognitive distortions. The key to preventing your anger response is to be aware of the types of events you react to and the deeper feelings related to the events. With this understanding, you may be able to control the intensity of your anger.

Righteous Indignation

There are two terribly unfortunate aspects to the anger process. First, something happens, not even necessarily to you, and you create distortions or irrational ideas about its effect on you. When you combine your self-absorption with your search and your need for control, success, and recognition, you end up misinterpreting the facts. The event is not nearly as important as your new, distorted idea. Second, your distortion gives you permission to perceive different feelings. Let's say that your sense of entitlement has been trespassed upon. You have the "I was robbed" feeling, and that makes you angry. But you weren't really robbed. You felt that something should have been done for you and it wasn't. That's all.

There are many "unfair," "I was robbed" messages you can latch onto during your job search. You know you've tried so very diligently to get a job, so it's unfair that nothing is working out. Or, you know how hard you worked for your last company, so it's not fair that they let you go. Or, you're fifty thousand dollars in debt from your education, so it's not fair that you still have to work as a cocktail server even though you just received your master's degree. With all of this negative, irrational processing, your frustration builds until you get so angry that you feel you just can't take it anymore. Then you explode at events that aren't even remotely related to your predicament, and you begin to say inappropriate and hurtful things to people. You may burn a lot of bridges if you engage in this process.

When Is Anger Justified?

Appropriate, timely emotional reactions are important to your mental health and physical survival. If you were in a bookstore and suddenly you saw a person jump over the counter, put a weapon to the head of the cashier, and shout, "Freeze," you would have a very strong emotional reaction. Your heart would race, your breathing would be shallow and intense, your pupils would dilate, and you would be physiologically energized to run. On the other hand, if you were purchasing a book, and you were outrageously overcharged by double the purchase price, you would also have an emotional reaction, undoubtedly not as intense as the first, but a reaction nevertheless.

Physiologically your body responds to all intrusive events in remarkably similar ways. The robbery reaction is called a fight-or-flight response. The overcharge reaction is called an anger response. Anger is certainly appropriate when there's a bona fide and tangible intrusion into your personal space. Both of these emotional reactions are designed to keep you alert and protected. They're appropriate for the circumstances that elicited them.

But what if you live with heightened vigilance regardless of the circumstances? If you're anxious and hypervigilant most of the time, you probably have an emotional problem called generalized anxiety disorder (GAD), which is discussed in chapter 7.

Similarly, if you noticed that you were overcharged in the bookstore, and you had to have a confrontation with the store clerk, it would be normal to experience displeasure over the conflict. If the matter were not settled, you would probably prepare to retaliate with clever verbal combat or try another intervention like seeing the manager or store owner. However, if you find that you react as if you are being overcharged most of the time, and if you frequently mistrust people's motives and you're regularly poised to attack, then you most likely have dysfunctional reaction syndrome. In short, you need to learn to manage your anger better.

Anger and anxiety aren't always bad. Most of the time they work to protect you. But if they become your standard way of responding to people in your environment, especially during the job search, then you could have a more serious problem.

Exercise 8-2   Evaluating Your Anger

Since anger is such a common experience in the job search, you need to keep it contained. Many typical events, like waiting for letters or e-mail responses, lend themselves to frustration. You need to prevent discouraging and unfortunate events from disrupting your search process. You need to be able to appropriately manage any rage, hostility, cynicism, aggressiveness, or anger that comes up in your search. That's not easy. Being aware of the ABC anger paradigm can help.

Let's see how well you are managing your anger right now. You can do this by completing my Intelligent Anger Management (IAM) questionnaire. This will serve as a barometer of your anger. Read each of the items in the questionnaire, then put a check next to each thought, feeling, or behavior that you have experienced in the past week. The questionnaire results are a good place to begin to examine to what extent anger might be distracting you from a successful career search.

Intelligent Anger Management Questionnaire

_____ I argue with others, even those who try to help me with my search.

_____ I blame others for my career-search problems.

_____ I brag about myself, trying to sell myself.

_____ I demand attention from those around me, especially when I talk about work.

_____ I have jealous feelings, especially toward those who are content at work.

_____ My mood is irritable when thinking about or discussing my career.

_____ I have temper tantrums when events do not go the way I had hoped.

_____ I worry excessively about my career search.

_____ I break rules, like traffic laws.

_____ I am easily frustrated when I do not get my way.

_____ I feel like I want to explode.

_____ I have thoughts of harming someone, especially someone I know.

_____ I have thoughts of destroying property I am familiar with.

_____ I show off.

_____ I lie about my career and life circumstances.

_____ I swear excessively.

_____ I drink alcohol every day.

_____ I am late to events, even those that have to do with my search.

_____ I self-medicate with the drugs of my choice at least once a week.

_____ I am loud so that people know I am present.

_____ I tease other people.

_____ I resent sending out my résumé and cover letter.

_____ I feel like I am entitled to more than I am getting.

_____ I think a lot about my financial situation and where I will earn a living.

_____ I feel like I am isolated from others, especially workers.

_____ I make harassing phone calls about my predicament.

_____ I think about sabotaging companies that don't want me.

_____ I consider slashing the tires of headhunters and recruiters.

_____ I am obsessed with weapons and gun magazines.

_____ I feel panicky.

_____ I question whether anyone really wants to help me with my search.

_____ My thoughts about work are mostly hostile and negative.

_____ I feel like I am not receiving due consideration by people who can hire me.

_____ I negatively compare myself to others.

_____ I feel disconnected.

_____ I think of myself as a loser.

_____ My energy level is low when it comes to working on my search.

_____ I think I try to prevent any real change in my career goals.

_____ My language is spiteful.

_____ Everything about my search seems hopeless.

Now calculate your score by adding up the number of checks. The lowest score is 0 and the highest is 40. If you scored 0, chances are pretty good that you didn't take this seriously, or else you're having trouble with the truth. If you scored 40, you also probably did not take the measure seriously, or else you are positively out of control with your anger and are a danger to society. For the rest of you, interpret the scale with the following numbers

1-5   You seem to have your anger management under control.

6-10   Your anger management is loosely controlled but could become problematic during the job search.

11-15 You have definite problems with your anger and need to address these now, as they are seriously interfering with your search.

16-20   Your anger is sabotaging your job search.

21-40   Your anger is clearly out of your control. It is beyond
the boiling point and you are undoubtedly abusive to
yourself and to others. It would not be surprising to
hear that you're hypertensive, have gastrointestinal
problems, and are unstable in your relationships.

So why is anger so difficult to manage? Anger is reactive and
retaliatory. It can be provoked by a number of different factors. It has
psychological roots that are singularly different from each other. It
may make you feel good or bad.

Reread the statements in the IAM and think about the different
stimuli that can elicit anger. Items one and two indicate frustration.
Items thirty-five to forty show deprivation. Items like twenty-three
indicate entitlement while items twenty-six through twenty-eight
measure feelings of betrayal. Thirty-three and thirty-four relate to
injustice. Items fifteen and twenty-five illustrate confusion. Or you
can numb yourself by self-medicating with drugs and alcohol.

Anger can also be turned against yourself, as exemplified by
items six and eight. In fact, early psychodynamic therapists like
Freud treated anger against the self as one of the causes of depression.
Some modern therapists believe that anger is the outward mani-
festation of depression. Medically, both anger and depression may be
treated with similar types of prescriptions, namely serotonin reup-
take inhibitors. Like depression, excess, chronic anger can be debilitating. Committing suicide is often viewed as a violent, angry
reaction against the self, precipitated by depression.

Looking for work and getting rejected in the process feels
insulting, like your soul has been intruded upon. You have lost your
entitlement. It's similar to the humiliation people feel when they are
chewed out publicly for poor performance. Sometimes we refer to
this experience as a narcissistic injury. It can be caused either by criticism or indifference of others to your actions. In initially defending
and protecting yourself from narcissistic wounding, you choose not
to get angry at yourself. Instead, you get angry at someone else, often
a loved one, especially an authority figure like a parent. But your
anger can also be a directed at person who is close to you on the job,
like your boss or a co-worker you feel competitive with. The work
world is full of examples of anger, rage, shame, and humiliation. You
can usually expect it in the job search.

You're probably surprised by how terribly angry you can
become at different stages of the search. It's like road rage. The event
is inconsequential, but the injury seems so great, because your ego is

so fragile. You probably find it ironic that you may actually feel good when you get angry, because at least for a few moments, you feel as if you are in some kind of control. Your rage is the result of injury you feel, distorted or real.

Anger is not only dysfunctional and paralyzing, it's not particularly beneficial to your physical well-being. Anger is, in fact, known to be lethal. It has been related to heart disease, as well as other often life-threatening illnesses.

Deciphering Your Irrational Thoughts

Rage is triggered by your cognitive distortions. In reacting to different events, you should become aware of the manner in which you distort information and create irrational ideas. The ten distortions described here are the backbone of your anger. Remember, you're in a sensitive and vulnerable position, and your heightened sensitivity has you more potentially irrational and reactive than ever. Examine the list and use it to help you refrain from distorting job-search events. These are guaranteed ways to reduce your anger.

It's All or Nothing

This is the tendency to evaluate events or facts in an all-or-nothing kind of way. "Since the labor market is sluggish, I'll never get hired." "Since my Scholastic Aptitude Test scores were low, I will be a failure because I will not be admitted to the college I want." "I'm a people person, so I need a job helping people." "I screwed off in college, so I'll always be a failure."

If you're reacting in polarized ways, you need to challenge your thinking. For example, ask questions that confront your polarizations. "What is the evidence that you will not get hired?" "How are going to a specific college and your personal or career success related to each other?" "What job anywhere is not going to involve people at some level?"

Jumping to Conclusions

When you experience a single life event and then make a rule for living or a philosophy of life from the event, you're overgeneralizing. If after a first interview, for instance, you don't get called back, and then conclude on this basis that you are a lousy interviewee, you're overgeneralizing. Overgeneralizing is probably the most pernicious distortion you can make when you have to address the pain and discomfort of not getting recognized. You send out a set of résumés and no one calls. You conclude, "No one will ever call me." You don't get chosen after your first job interview and comment, "I'll never get work." Or you say, "I'm a crappy interviewee."

To avoid distortions like this, you need to be more like a scientist in drawing your conclusions. Each negative hiring experience needs to be viewed as a temporary setback, not a statement about your worth as an employee or human being.

Another helpful way to stop overgeneralizing is to discontinue using words that are "universal qualifiers." If you use words like "all, always, ever, every, everybody, never, nobody, all," try to decrease the frequency of their use. You'll naturally reduce your tendency to overgeneralize.

Obsessing about Details

People who are under the stress of the job search find that they obsess on one or two negative details of a particular event. You might be asked fifty questions in a job interview, answering forty-nine with alacrity and brilliance. But you remember only the question you missed. You might give a memorable speech to a thousand people, but you remember the two who walked out. The standing ovation or applause you received at the conclusion of the experience is irrelevant to you. Instead, you wonder why those two people left and whether or not they were dissatisfied with what you had to say.

This process is called mental filtration. You're unaware that you are doing it, but you are ensuring that you end up in a very bad place with a depressed attitude.

You can use the filter, but let it filter out the bad, negative, irrational thoughts. Begin to better reward yourself for your accomplishments and the job-search activities that you do well. If you filter out all of the good experiences, you will not be the energetic, positive person that people want to associate with.

Ignoring the Good Stuff

When someone tells you what a good job you've done, do you say, "Oh, they're just trying to make me feel good"? Disqualifying positive reinforcement is a cruel distortion of a positive experience. You're making a negative out of a positive. As before, examine the evidence and accept positive reinforcement at its face value.

Assuming the Worst

Mental catastrophizing is kind of the opposite of disqualification. In mental catastrophizing, you convince yourself that an error you made in the search will have absolutely dire consequences. "I didn't respond to the ad quickly enough." Because of this act, your job search, career reputation, and capacity for employment will end. To be sure, certain mistakes can be costly. But even those that are most costly become much less important after a while. Few of your decisions or behaviors are going to unilaterally destroy your search. Inaction is a more threatening culprit. Mental catastrophizing can be a problem if it puts brakes on your search.

Feeling, Not Thinking

A truism in philosophy once was, "I think, therefore I am." We have graduated to a common cognitive distortion, "What I feel, must be real." In the job search, you might feel that you performed like an idiot in an office quiz demonstrating your management skills. But that doesn't mean you are an idiot. During the search, you may feel hopelessness and helplessness, but that doesn't qualify you as hopeless or helpless. You may feel that nobody wants to hire you, but that doesn't mean nobody will hire you. You should be in touch with your feelings—but keep in mind that your feelings aren't necessarily purveyors of truth. Take an empirical, hard-line approach, and consider the data, not just your feelings.

Shoulda, Woulda, Coulda

These three insidious words are used to make blanket distortions. Shoulds are used to motivate your behavior through guilt and past judgment. "I should do this. I should do that." Woulds and coulds are used to predict what an event will do to you in your own mind, not necessarily in reality. "That would ruin me." "My poor performance could cost me this job." It's probably impossible at this point to stop you from using these words regularly. But if you try to refrain from the shoulds, woulds, and coulds, you will find that your thinking will be less distorted, and you won't feel so guilty. This in turn will reduce your propensity for anger.

Taking It Personally

Anger begins with an event. It's not a crapshoot. But personalization leads you to believe that you are in some way responsible for the event taking place. Personalization is disabling because it causes you to think that every conversation, criticism, or comparison is about you. Remember that in your search, you're already feeling vulnerable. You're incredibly self-involved and expecting comparative evaluations from others. Personalizing events will just add stress to the search because it can be so disabling, alienating, and guilt producing.

Biting Off More Than You Can Chew

If you look at a particular project and can't break it up into smaller parts, you create a distortion about how demanding it is. Job searchers can become overwhelmed because they look at the whole process, not the smaller parts. Engaging in fractionalizing allows you to see that situations are made up of smaller components. Break up the search into manageable tasks that you know you can accomplish. Focus on the steps, and be sure to reward yourself for completing the steps successfully.

Grasping for Control

People like to believe that they have control. Control is the mother of all cognitive distortions, but clearly, all you can ever control is yourself. You certainly can't control the people and events in your life. The more that you accept this notion, the less angry you'll eventually become because you'll give up the belief that you have overriding influence. As you give up your need to control, you will begin to accept the search process and some of its randomness.

The Many Stages of Anger

The job search is exemplified by different stages, each with an endless array of potential events and therefore an endless array of potential irrational beliefs. Here are some examples of places where you may be prone to distort your assessment of your experience.

Anger at Job Loss

Psychologist Tom Cottle (1992) has written about two types of anger among workers who have been laid off. Early in the unemployment process, they are angry at their employers, supervisors, or other co-workers. That's the time you often hear about workplace violence or acting out against former employers.

According to the Department of Justice, workplace violence is the leading cause of death on the job for women and the number-two killer for men. From 1992 to 1996, workplace homicides averaged 1,023 a year, rapes 50,500, robberies 83,700, and aggravated assaults 395,500. Twenty-five out of every 1,000 workers are physically attacked on the job, resulting in fifty-five million dollars in lost wages each year. For companies, workplace violence can cost over four billion dollars a year, according to a business insurance study. Companies now employ "threat management teams," "rapid response teams," and "trauma teams" to enable them to handle problems with acting out at work. Outplacement consultants are often hired to assist with a firing and to offer psychological counseling immediately after an employee is let go. They're waiting in the wings to adjust any missteps that the firing manager makes.

Some former employees act out in unusual ways—occasionally even high-tech ones. At the end of 1998, after losing a worker's compensation battle, a disgruntled former employee of the Intel Corporation began to send thousands of e-mail letters to Intel employees on their Intel office computers. At one time 29,000 employees received his e-mail with his personal spin on the company's personnel policies. He told employees that they were lied to about their job security, and that his situation was proof of the company's lies. He set up his own Web exposé in an attempt to get a response from Intel. His anger has made him famous in the courts and in the press. But it probably won't make him more employable. He expended a great deal of time and energy at retaliating, but his rage only subverted his work potential.

If you're angry at a former employer, then you need to address your old employer in a systematic way. Most employers cannot legally hurt you, and it's not in their best interest to do so. Your old employer has no obligation to say anything one way or another about what happened to you. The former company is allowed to avoid comment. Many, in fact, give out no information about your job performance, out of fear that they will be exposed to a liability action suggesting that they defamed you. They also don't want the exposure generated should you be hired by a company on the basis of their recommendation and you perform poorly. Frankly, they don't want the responsibility for withholding negative information, especially if you get involved in a hassle on the new job. Some companies have gone so far as to establish phone banks and call centers that give out computerized messages about you that verify employment dates and job title only.

So what should you do if you find that you're furious at your old company or employer? Most of the time this is pent-up anger that you can begin to dissipate.

Five Steps to an Anger-Free Termination

Being terminated is never easy. It's disconcerting, it elicits feelings of resentment and unfairness, and it provokes an angry reaction. Still, there are activities that allow you to prepare for any institutional changes that might affect your work life. These strategies will keep you from becoming enraged during your search for a new position.

First, when you are angriest, write a letter to your old company or your former boss. Write everything that you need to, then store the letter somewhere and read it a week later. Don't send it. Some of the parts of the letter will appear to be rational, but you'll also notice parts that seem angry, obsessive, and somewhat crazed. Saving the letter and reading it when you're more subdued and articulate will allow you to focus your energy and feelings on actions that are more productive for you.

A variation on this theme is to make a tape recording of everything you want to say to your old boss, human resources professionals, and co-workers. Get all of your thoughts and feelings out there. Therapists have known for some time that simply ventilating feelings is not very useful in and of itself. However, by expressing your thoughts in a reactive way, you can ferret out that which is truthful from that which is, well, loony.

When Laura made her tape recording of her feelings toward her company's exit interviewer, she realized that what was making her angriest was that the exit interviewer didn't seem to care about her or anyone else at her company. The exit interviewer seemed only to want her to sign off on a severance and benefits package. She felt like erupting during the session. Instead, she made a recording of her thoughts and feelings afterward. She discovered that her words would be of no consequence to the exit interviewer. He had a job to do and couldn't express his feelings. He was only sorry because he had to process over thirty severances. Still, Laura wanted her pound of flesh. When she replayed her tape, she realized that she could make some useful points in a brief note, which she sent. The rest of the material made her sound nutty.

Second, you should consider writing a lucid letter to your old company outlining your plans and letting them know what types of positions you are pursuing. Some people will be interested in your future, so don't burn your bridges. You can also suggest in the letter what you would like your old company to say if a new or prospective employer calls. This may help you determine what, if anything, will be said.

Further, you are certainly entitled to write a rebuttal letter about your termination. Just make sure to write a rational letter, not one filled with angry expletives. Have a trusted friend or mentor read the letter and give you feedback. If the company doesn't offer an exit interview, certainly ask for one so that you have an understanding of their opinion and they have an understanding of yours. Remember that in the end this is not going to save a position for you, but it will help to keep you focused during your new job search, and it will reduce your anger.

Third, if you fear being laid off or if you think that there is to be some kind of merger or acquisition, ask individuals in your unit to supply you with some general letters of recommendation. These letters should outline what you have accomplished at the company. Often when you're in a rage, you won't remember all that you have done, and you may exaggerate lesser accomplishments. But if you try to document your work accomplishments before you're in a rage, people will be friendlier and more helpful. By the way, if you have copies of letters of commendation or old performance evaluations, be sure to keep them for future reference. If you can't get a letter from your former company, these documents can serve as testimonials.

It's also appropriate to get letters of support from people who are no longer at your former place of employment. Former partners and bosses can be useful resources and can also be used as a part of your network of contacts. You never can tell when these may come in handy.

Lee had a dicey relationship with his boss because she thought that he did not bring in enough new business to the consulting firm. She was very aggressive, demanding, and difficult for him to relate to. When she took over his unit, he knew that unless he landed several hundred thousand dollars' worth of new business, he would be gone. Sure enough, in just three months, she gave him his walking papers. But Lee had maintained good relationships with his colleagues and never tried to rally the troops against his supervisor. Two months after he was let go, another colleague at the firm contacted Lee and said that they needed him to return on a consultative basis. It turns out that while he couldn't generate the rain that his boss wanted, no one else at the firm had so many excellent relationships with the firm's clients. Lee now commands a handsome consulting fee. And he still does not bad-mouth the old boss.

Fourth, for those of you who fear termination but are still working, begin to create a self-contained personnel action file. Keep all of your old pay stubs as evidence that you worked at the company. In the case of a merger, no one is too sure what happens to this stuff. Keep examples of your work. If you write regular reports or prepare spreadsheets, keep them so that you can describe to others what you have been doing. These data can also be used to reflect back on your work performance when you feel as if no one believes in your skills. You'll be creating a job portfolio, much as an artist arranges a portfolio of creative works. It's best to do it while you are still on the job. Your portfolio will help you feel good about yourself.

Try to get a copy of the company's termination policies. Take your human resources manager to lunch. Find out exactly what information they're going to give out on you and what their written policy is on letters of recommendation. By doing this you will ensure yourself that you have covered all of your bases and that your former employer can't do anything that is going to hurt you.

Fifth, if you believe that your former employer is blackballing you in some way, contact a labor attorney to get an explanation of your rights. This will keep you from obsessing on the company and will put you into the mind-set that you're doing something about your circumstances. Labor attorneys can give you an idea as to whether you should get a restraining order against the company or file a claim for anything from wrongful termination to sexual harassment. However, bear in mind that suits are often expensive and difficult to win unless you have very strong evidence.

Tips for Preparing to Quit

If you're going to quit, for whatever reason, it's wise to develop a summary exit strategy for yourself. Keep a diary of your likes and dislikes about your place of business. At the end of your job tenure, you'll have a tendency to focus on negatives rather than positives, so try to maintain some balance in your feelings. You're going to remember this experience for the rest of your life, and a positive ending will sit more pleasantly with you.

You should also consider recording the reasons that you're leaving. You can then decide whether you want to share this with your employer. It will help you to gain some perspective on the variables that drove you away, and can even help you make suggestions to a new employer. If you have friends and acquaintances at your old place of work, sharing this information can help to cement a relationship for some years to come. In every business or profession, you will find yourself meeting people from your work history over and over again.

Current opinions differ as to whether you should tell your employer that you're planning to quit a long time before you actually leave. Many employers will not want you around, because they fear your presence will hurt morale. Others are afraid that you might steal secrets or be spying for a new company. If you give notice too early, you risk making an easy job transition much more difficult.

The best approach is to give notice when you're sure that you're going to leave. Try to be fair with the company, but be aware that the company may not want you there as long as you want. If it helps, fantasize that they may want you to leave that very day. With that in mind, you can prepare or brace yourself accordingly.

Anger at Yourself

According to Cottle, after a period of six months to a year, unemployed people turn their anger inward and blame themselves rather than others for their circumstances. When their loss and rage turn inward, they shy away from help from families or intimates. They also give up hope and act out against themselves. They feel expendable and lacking in relevance. They seem to parallel some of the stages that Elisabeth Kübler-Ross (1969) spelled out in describing the process of dying: denial, anger, bargaining, depression, anticipation, hope. Anger surfaces from denial.

What people at this stage appear to be experiencing is the creation of distorted ideas reflecting that they will never work again. Or, they believe that if they do find work, it will not be in their desired arenas. Their distorted ideas become powerful and painful, and they begin to act out more against themselves, often numbing themselves with drugs and alcohol.

Watch out for signs that you're beginning to act out against yourself, or that you're engaging in self-hatred or self-loathing. This may feel like depression: if you think that it is depression, you should consult a mental health therapist or a physician.

What are some of the signs of depression? Well, if you're frequently sad or down in the dumps, and you have lost your ability to experience any pleasure, you have noteworthy signs of depression. Pay attention to whether or not you have become more angry, irritable, or whiny. If this mood has lasted for six months or so, you could be experiencing depression. If, in addition to your mood, you find that you are either not eating or eating too much, your energy is low, your sleep is disturbed (you cannot fall asleep, you sleep all the time, or you awaken early), your thinking is slowed, and you're easily distracted, you have strong evidence of depression. Also look at whether you have lost interest in your friends, sports, or other activities that used to give you pleasure. Depression is also linked to self-deprecating statements that you might make toward yourself. If you also have thoughts of hurting yourself or killing yourself, then you have strong evidence of a major depressive episode. Depression is certainly not an uncommon reaction to the type of life change that you're experiencing. But, if you have many of the symptoms just described, you should seek intervention. Don't medicate yourself with drugs and alcohol—get professional help.

Learn to Stop Blaming Yourself

It's possible to elevate your mood by assessing and then reducing your automatic thoughts. Automatic thoughts are cognitive distortions that have been well rehearsed and practiced over the course of a lifetime. When people are depressed they tend to use automatic thinking regularly and frequently. Assessments include: "I'm a loser." "I'll never be any good." "I'll never get a job." The thoughts, by the way, tend to vary little from situation to situation. If you find that you create these thoughts, reducing or eliminating them will make you feel better about yourself. You will be less depressed, less angry, and more upbeat. Since your language mirrors your thoughts and feelings, changing your words changes your attitude.

Feelings of Self-Loathing

If you have not had symptoms of depression, but you feel lousy about yourself, chances are that you are experiencing self-loathing, not depression. This self-loathing needs to be confronted regularly during your search, because it's so easy to get into a regular pattern of self-critical behavior. Below is a checklist of thoughts that you may have had during your career search. Simply put a check next to those statements that describe a self-loathing remark that you have made during the search. Later you'll learn how to fight back against the self-loathing impulse.

Exercise 8-3   The Self-Loathing Checklist

_____ I am disgruntled most of the time because of the demands of the career search.

_____ I hate my life because I don't have a job.

_____ I hate my résumé and can't make it any better.

_____ I cannot seem to market myself effectively.

_____ I feel like a fraud and an idiot in a job interview.

_____ I find that I am less attractive than people who seem to be working.

_____ After receiving my résumé and cover letter, personnel officials laugh.

_____ I'll never get the job that I want.

_____ I'm not stylish like those who are working.

_____ Nobody wants to be around me because I am not working.

_____ I am not computer literate, so no one will hire me.

_____ I can't correct any of my presentation issues because I have no money to spend.

_____ I won't get hired without more education.

_____ I am basically unattractive.

_____ I am basically boring.

_____ I can't make appropriate decisions

_____ I am isolated without work.

_____ No job looks good to me.

_____ I can't find anything nice to say about my job skills.

_____ All I really have is my anger.

_____ Most of my career decisions have been wrong for me.

_____ In my career campaigns, I am never a finalist for the jobs I want.

_____ My career record seems spotty and inconsistent.

_____ Personal and family issues keep me from being my best.

_____ I have ruined a stellar career path.

If you have other self-loathing messages that are not on this list, write them in your journal.

As you explore the items that you checked off, reflect for a moment on why that particular statement is a useful one for you. Since you engage in negative self-loathing frequently, it must have some reinforced usefulness to you. For each of the items, write in you journal why it is a useful description of yourself or your behavior. You could say something as simple as "It's a habit" or "It motivates me." But in order to resist using these statements, you need to determine why they benefit you.

Now let's contrast the usefulness exercise. Indicate how these same items serve a self-destructive component and are not useful to you. Write down the same items again and describe how they are destructive to you. Label each of the statements with one of the cognitive distortions listed in the "Deciphering Your Irrational Thoughts" section earlier in this chapter.

When Erin completed the checklist, she identified the following items: 1, 2, 5, 6, 14, 16, 25. She found that there were several themes that were actually helpful to her as she engaged in self-loathing. First, she noted that her boyfriend, as well as others, would try to rescue her and reassure her if she engaged in this pattern of behavior. Second, by complaining and loathing herself, she actually found that she was more motivated. Her self-loathing also helped her to feel some control. Finally, if she hated herself, she found that her career expectations were lower, so she did not put so much pressure on herself.

Erin was also able to describe a destructive component to her self-loathing. First, she found that she cried more often than usual. She also found that her friends and even her boyfriend did not want to be around her so much when she was complaining. They wanted her to be more successful, but they found her negative self-talk was destroying their relationship with her. She often became angry with her friends as well, distancing them at times when she needed help. Reviewing her checklist gave her a sense of her own strategy and how unproductive and enervating it was.

Erin needed to begin to confront the statements that she made about herself so that she would be able to reject them. The first step in the process was to get Erin to be aware of how frequently she engaged in self-loathing attacks. She was asked to wear a rubber band around her wrist for a week. Each time she had a self-loathing thought, she was to snap the rubber band on her wrist just enough so that it hurt a little. This made her conscious of her internal messages. Erin noticed that her self-loathing comments decreased by over 40 percent in just two weeks.

After becoming conscious of her self-loathing behavior, Erin was told to confront the self-loathing thought. For example, if she said she had ruined a stellar career path, she had to also develop a confrontation to that statement. She had to answer the question, "How have you ruined a stellar career path today?" If she said that she hated her life because she did not have a job, then she had to answer another question about what part of her life she hated. For each of the items, she had to confront the thought whenever it popped up. She was now creating her own new reality about the career search. She began to engage in less self-destructive thought processing and felt more energized in an appropriate way.

Anger at the Interview Process

You may set the stage yourself for a distressing interview process. In the beginning of the job search, if you're not getting responses to your inquiries, you're probably frightened that your skill level is not competitive. But you may turn fright into anger and frustration because of your cognitive beliefs and distortions. Alternatively, if you have received an offer of an interview, you may be terrified by the radical changes that have taken place in the workforce and wonder whether you have what it takes to keep up with their questions. You convince yourself that you will fail the interview.

The interview process offers a mixed experience. At first, it's a reflection of how you're perceived by the community of people who can hire you. They have scanned your résumé, screened you in over others, and decided to invest some time and energy by inviting you to meet with them. So at least you know that your résumé and cover letters are effective. Unfortunately, if you're lucky enough to get job interviews, you find that, like most people, you despise being evaluated. And you're evaluated all the time, by lots of different individuals. What a conundrum. It makes you feel out of control. The result is that you may create a variety of distortions about being out of control, which can eventually lead to anger.

The event that you detest is really just an interview, but you react to it with your own unique perceptions. After the interview, you engage in high-end, creative thought distortion about what must have happened. You expand upon your distortions with every friend and colleague you talk to. Since they're usually sympathetic to you, you tend to go on and on about how the process went. Then you talk about what you should and should not have done, and you reflect on how you talked too much or too little. Your polarizing and mental filtering have worked wonders. You expect the worse, and you're mad as hell. Remember how Erin was so disenchanted with her experience that she wound up blaming ethnic bias for her lack of job offers?

If you have not been contacted immediately after the interview, you become convinced that you're being rejected. As a result, you label the interviewers with words that show you have little or no respect for them. You keep yourself in a state of anger and turmoil.

You begin to mistrust all interviewers, and you start to mistrust yourself. You lose your grip on the process, which sabotages your own search. You believe that you need to guard against people you can't trust. You're no longer able to flow smoothly through the interview process. And to add insult to your injuries, you feel you may be forced to pursue back-up positions that are undoubtedly below you. Here you are enraged by the sense of injustice that you feel.

Managing Interview Anger

So what can you do to manage your anger at the interview process? There are several positive steps that you can take to keep yourself from distorting events.

1. Create a post-interview worksheet. The worksheet should include the following:

   a. The date you had the interview

   b. How well you prepared for the interview

   c. Questions you remember being asked

   d. Your evaluation of your interview performance

   e. A list of what you should and should not have done during the interview

   f. What you can do to improve your interview skills

   g. The date you sent a thank-you letter to the interviewer

   h. Your perception of whether or not you really wanted the job

2. Review your interview with a mentor or someone who is familiar with the line of work or the company you are pursuing. This gives you a partial reality check and some unbiased feedback.

3. Prepare an ABC list for any events that you suspect you might distort. Label the distortions that you're using according to the ten patterns described in "Deciphering Your Irrational Thoughts" earlier in this chapter.

4. Make a final follow-up phone call to express your continuing interest in the job.

5. Let go of the experience. You can't control the behavior of others, so don't fret about what happened. Continue to review your list of distortions. That will help you to understand your own process.

Anger at Being Betrayed

A common myth people have is that the workplace is like a family. It provides a diversion from your own family, and your co-workers may be your best friends. While some of that may be true, the fact of the matter is that the workplace is just that: a place where you work.

But employees view the workplace as a family, and they gravitate to the idea that they are respected for something. Take this away and rage can erupt. It is not the loss of the job, but the loss of the perceived family experience that prompts the rage. If you lose the work family you may feel that loneliness is your only alternative.

Further, pride as well as self-esteem get linked to the belief that you're contributing to a common good, regardless of what you do. When you lose your job, for whatever reason, you create a belief that you were betrayed. It's easy to forget that you were in a contractual arrangement with an organization that could do whatever it wanted. To those of you in this predicament, it feels like your friends turned on you. You feel you were betrayed because the people you loved turned on you.

Anger at Loss of Livelihood

Another difficulty with being unemployed—and something that can draw out your inner rage—is that you're being left out of one of the key mythical elements of being an American. Americans, unlike those in some other cultures, define and value themselves by their work.

Developmentally, you've been asked for years about what you're going to be when you grow up. The idea that you can pay your own way or pull yourself up by your bootstraps is so ingrained in your notions of success that job loss or difficulty in getting a job hit at the core of your self-worth. Lack of work leads to plummeting self-esteem and feelings of worthlessness. It is not the unemployment that causes this, but the belief that you are not participating in the dream.

Psychologist Tom Cottle (1992) has chronicled that the consistently unemployed experience psychological symptoms that are similar to those of people who are experiencing death. Why not? If the beliefs that you have about work are related to the feeling of being alive, then one would expect that unemployment could feel like a death. For some, work is the breath of life. You can begin to remedy this experience of anger by valuing who you are, independent of the work experience. You can create your own myths about what is important for you, even if it does go against the grain of your upbringing and culture.

To create your own myths, try the following steps.

1. Reevaluate your effort.

The job search process has a clearly defined outcome: Either you're getting an offer of employment or you're not. But it's healthier to set aside the all-or-nothing perspective. You're putting a great deal of energy into the process. Just make sure to value the effort, rather than the outcome.

Keep a record of your job-search activities in your daily calendar, and be sure to give appropriate praise to yourself while acknowledging the support of others. Life is made up of good times and bad ones, and so is the job search. Just like days at work, there will be some activities that go more smoothly than others and some specific parts of it that are easier on some days than others.

2. Reevaluate your concept of success and failure.

In the process of your search, you might have produced four excellent résumés, learned about three new fields, and studied fifteen new companies. That's successful. As a society we tend to look on successes without noticing the failures. Think about current home run star Mark McGwire. We focus on his home runs, but not on his strikeouts and the earlier foot injuries that kept him out of so many games. And what about Sammy Sosa? Is he unsuccessful because he wasn't number one? He too broke a record that had stood for thirty-seven years.

3. Explore your sense of entitlement.

Reexamine your expectations about fairness. Your anger comes from the distorted feeling that you are being treated unfairly. But what is really fair? In the work world, companies merge or go bankrupt, or they grow and make their employees wealthy. Why do you bother to question whether this is fair or not?

Job searchers become angry when they perceive that they are treated unfairly. But fair treatment, aside from obeying particular employment laws, has no universal standard. What is fair to you may not be fair to someone else. It's a zero-sum game. The fact that you attended a particular school or have a degree in a competitive area or have job skills that are in great demand has nothing to do with the fairness of the search. You can only play out your behavior against the behavior of others. There is a tendency among all job searchers to view themselves as the have-nots, which simply can't be true.

Jeffrey had been a successful marketing manager at a large international detergent company. The division that he had proudly led for seven years was spun off to another company. He was not a part of the spin-off and was let go. Afterwards, he drove each night into the hills above the city and sat in his car by himself. He looked at all the nice houses and the people in them as the haves. He sat in his car and felt that he was a have-not. When he was asked about this, he exclaimed that he had done all the right things. He had a good undergraduate degree from Indiana University and an MBA from the Haas School of Business in California. He thought that he deserved better in the career world. He expected to be a partner or an owner or a person with large stock holdings by this stage of his career. He did not expect that he would be looking for a job. He identified have-not as his life path.

His whole career focus was filled with distortions, even though he was a successful businessperson. He had been through many mergers and acquisitions, but he didn't think losing a job would ever happen to him. He had the added problem of being over fifty, so he felt that the reason people didn't respond to him was that they thought he was too old to contribute to their enterprise.

He didn't believe that any career search strategies could work for him. As he became more and more angry at his old company, he began to think that they were giving out bad references on him. His search soon proved to be so difficult that he became obsessed that his old boss was trying to hurt his career. The obsessions took time and energy away from his search and also began to alienate those who could help him. He seemed to be volatile and crazy toward those who did not agree with his point of view. Friends became concerned.

It was finally recommended that he take some courses in philosophy and business ethics. With that he started to understand the concept of entitlement and saw that his sense of privilege was flawed. As he began to slowly rid himself of the sense of entitlement, he was able to resume a more successful search.

Don't Look for Justice

The United States inculcates a sense of justice into its citizens. That's an unfortunate distortion to hold on to during the search, because there is no justice in the career world. That is perhaps among the most important facts about the search to keep in mind. Think about the two classmates who graduated from the same business school on the same day. They both joined computer companies. One was at Osborne and the other went to Apple. Since you have probably never heard of Osborne, you can probably guess that one was able to obtain a measure of success more easily than the other. Stories like this are legion in the career world. The best you can do is to accept it and give yourself maximum control by doing the best research that you can.

Don't be angry if some people have an easier time of it than you. Learn to appreciate your own effort, and take pride in the fact that the work did not come so easily.

How Can You Be Less Angry Overall?

1. Control your impulsivity and reactivity. If you react slowly and methodically to different stressors, you will be less inclined to create distortions. Take your birthday, for example. Many clients with a consciousness of time fear the limitations of the aging process. The day before their birthday they may say, "I'm getting so old." But in reality, they're only a day older than they were the day before.

2. Suspend judgment about events. When you read something, don't necessarily apply it to your set of circumstances. Not everything has to be about you. Ask "Why?" more often.

3. Make alternative interpretations of all information. Evaluate your facts and use them creatively. Use only what applies to you. There is always more than one interpretation of information.

4. Stop blaming others. It makes you unaccountable for your own behavior and is distracting.

5. Help others daily and be ready to pay compliments. It's hard to be angry when you are helping someone else or saying friendly words. In addition, try not to be critical of others. When you criticize others, there's a tendency to criticize yourself, and then you lose your own power. Try this with co-workers or a supervisor you disdain and consider the results.

6. Do what you plan to do, especially regarding the meeting of your goals. It will allow you to trust and empower yourself.

7. While anger may seem to drive you, personal self-motivation is a better chauffeur. When you move through your search with anger, you make it easy for others to pick on you. You certainly won't engender much support, and you might even get laughed at.

8. Getting turned down may be shattering, but it also gets you closer to your perfect job. A teenage boy I counseled taught me that. When he tried to get a date for his junior prom, he was regularly unsuccessful. But he finished each phone call with the mantra, "I'm closer than ever to getting a date." Eventually, he got a date.

9. The career search has ups and downs. Don't let yourself get either too high or too low. Get back to the middle and maintain your balance.

10. Remember, when you're angry, your communication skills disappear. You also end up saying things that you'll regret later. If you want to hear what an idiot you sound like when you're angry, record some of your most precious words and play them back a week later.

11. Differentiate sadness from anger. Sadness is over your loss. Anger is over threats that can result in loss.

12. Remember that anger destroys your creativity. It will prevent you from a unique job search.

13. Don't compare yourself to others. Everybody's assets are relative to their life circumstances.

14. Begin to keep a log of how much time you spend being angry. Determine the times and circumstances and relate them to the root causes described earlier.

15. Minimize suspicious thoughts. Not everyone is trying to keep you from working.

16. Remember, learned optimism has a beneficial effect. There is some evidence that high hopes lead to elevations in your T-cell (immune system cell directors) count.

9 | Overcoming Career Barriers

I'm sick and tired of being sick and tired.

—Welfare to Work client

Barriers Are Everywhere

Face it: You all have barriers that will reduce your chances of getting what you want in the career marketplace. Accept that as a given. Those stubborn, omnipresent barriers arrive to inhibit you just when you're starting to get a handle on what you hope to do. They're like the restraining forces discussed in the goal-setting chapter, although they tend to be longer term. But there *is* hope, and more than a few ways to cope.

You can confront and perhaps even overcome your career search barriers by attending to three variables. First is knowing and consciously understanding what the particular barriers are. Second is finding a repertoire of techniques to get them out of your way. Third is finding a way of taking a positive experience from knowing about and overcoming the barrier. When you're able to take some satisfaction from identifying, owning, and hurdling a barrier, you become a more valuable candidate and employee. You'll feel more empowered to confront other barriers. In this chapter you'll learn just how to do that.

Brenda had been on welfare for six years, since she was nineteen. She had an eleventh-grade education and had been a student in the California Teen Age Parent and Pregnancy Program. She now had two children and only spotty work experience. Her dream at one point had been to be a cardiovascular surgeon, but school proved to be very difficult and confining for her. By the end of the tenth grade, she had started to skip classes or hang out in the schoolyard with the "bass heads." She was disheartened to realize that she might not have the educational interest, perseverance, or skills to pursue a career in medicine. Brenda became quite discouraged, depressed really, after deciding to relinquish her dream. Slowly, class by class, she started to drop out of her high school program. She became pregnant in the eleventh grade; by then she was only taking a partial class load. Even though she was admitted to the teen parenting program, where she could take classes for credit while pregnant and after her child's birth, she eventually dropped out of high school altogether.

Brenda had a difficult time imagining how she could enter the work world at age twenty-five. She had made some movement on the career front by completing her high school equivalency diploma three years before, but the thought of going back to work seemed full of barriers. Her work experience consisted of only two part-time jobs, neither of which she performed at her personal best. The cost of sending her children to child care meant she needed a good salary. Furthermore, she didn't seem to be able to maintain a stable relationship with a life partner; she felt very much on her own. Meanwhile, she received little, if any financial or emotional support from her family, as her father was in prison and her mother had a degenerative muscle disorder that kept her housebound. Her siblings had moved to other states.

Brenda was asked to meet with her welfare eligibility worker and an intake officer in the new Welfare to Work program. At the meeting, it was clearly difficult for the staff to assist Brenda in overcoming her career barriers. She used real-life barriers and some convoluted explanations to keep her options open, to stay on welfare for as long as possible. She was no fool. She knew that the intake officer and eligibility worker were aware that she used her numerous barriers as excuses. But that didn't stop her from also truly believing that it would be incredibly difficult for her to find rich, meaningful, financially beneficial work. The intake worker had some empathy for that position. Brenda would net about the same income from working at minimum wage as she did by remaining on welfare.

A Welfare to Work counselor was assigned to Brenda. She wanted to assist Brenda in finding a career field that was substantially more rewarding and exciting than the welfare world that she was dependent on. The counselor capitalized on Brenda's interests and experience in helping people, especially helping people with health-care problems, which had been Brenda's childhood and adolescent fantasy.

Brenda had raised her children alone and tried to offer what she could to her mother. Her father's legal troubles had given her some exposure to the criminal justice system and the county probation offices. And she had the experience of witnessing both parents struggle with health care and county social services.

The counselor wondered along with Brenda whether she could find a career that had some excitement, was similar to medicine, and helped people in predicaments similar to hers. The counselor thought of positions in allied health and, in particular, as an emergency medical technician (EMT), or ambulance assistant. Brenda thought that the opportunity was questionable but worth considering. Career testing supported the counselor's idea.

Brenda was most concerned that few, if any, companies would want to hire her, because of her spotty work record. But she decided to give the training program a chance. She enrolled in a community college, took advantage of the school's subsidized day-care program, and completed her work with satisfactory grades.

Now that she's had some real-world apprenticeship exposure to serving as an EMT, Brenda has become excited about the opportunity for herself in emergency medical and allied health work. She has not only passed her training program, but she has learned to tell a pretty interesting and engaging story about herself and her life circumstances.

Most importantly, employers have become interested in Brenda because of her background. She has lived among the disenfranchised, has a firsthand knowledge of public health, and is aware of the issues that people have with social services, medical services, and law enforcement. Brenda is now perceived by the community she serves as an extraordinarily valuable resource in inner-city emergencies. In her apprenticeship, she demonstrated that she can mollify angry people. She can remain composed and work amidst the chaos of a crisis. She relates to what her patients are feeling.

In addition to handling crises, Brenda's own experience with personal frustration over public services has given her a thorough knowledge of the public service and policy systems that her patients use. Through her own direct experience, she can help patients navigate through the public emergency health-care system. She still has financial problems and certainly, relationship problems, but she has learned how to use the purported life barriers to her career plans to enable her to become a more socially sensitive and proficient medical technician than others with similar training.

Brenda now believes she is one of the more valuable trainees in her company. She has received lots of encouragement, and as she learns to market herself, the future appears somewhat brighter. The EMT job pays reasonably well. It has eight-hour shifts that fit with her parenting responsibilities. And her counselor has arranged for her to receive a stipend to help with child-care costs. It took time and perseverance for Brenda to come so far; now she serves a a model for overcoming career and life barriers.

Like Brenda, you have probably created a number of barriers for yourself. Before completing the next exercise, write in your journal about the personal and life barriers to your having a satisfying career path. Then complete the checklist below, which will help you become even more aware of the circumstances that seem to get in the way of opportunities that you hope for.

Exercise 9-1
Determining Your Personal Barriers

_____ History of poverty

_____ Health problems that prevent full-time work or need specific accommodations

_____ Health insurance needs

_____ Preexisting medical condition

_____ Pharmaceutical needs, effects of medication on work productivity

_____ Visible physical disability (blindness, confinement to a wheelchair)

_____ Invisible physical disability (AIDS, chronic fatigue syndrome, environmental sensitivity, attention deficit disorder with hyperactivity, etc.)

_____ Learning disability

_____ Little or no work experience

_____ Difficulty making changes

_____ Poor interpersonal skills

_____ Lack of feelings of equity; feeling you're not paid what you're worth

_____ Conviction record

    _____ Jail-term record

_____ Arrest record, especially for drunken driving (in fact, you never have to admit any arrests on job applications, only convictions. But job seekers fear this as they might show up on a driver's license check)

_____ Personal rigidity barriers

    _____ Undercommittment or overcommittment to the job search

    _____ Perfectionism, especially when it is not called for

    _____ Pessimism in the face of opposing evidence

    _____ Optimism in the face of opposing evidence

    _____ Workaholic behavior

    _____ Victim and martyr behavior, especially that which draws attention to you

    _____ Spiritual barriers (religious or spiritual conviction stops you from a particular kind of work)

        _____ Family influence

        _____ Demands of parents

        _____ Demands of spouse/partner

        _____ Demands of children

    _____ Demands of siblings

    _____ Poor decision-making skills

    _____ Other psychological blocks

_____ Emotional self-awareness barriers

    _____ Lack of feeling empowered

    _____ Fear of new situation

_____ Fear of making wrong decisions

_____ Poor interpersonal relationships; social insensitivity

_____ Lack of flexibility (rigidity)

_____ Poor impulse control

_____ Problems with assertiveness

_____ Problems with independence

_____ Feelings of social and moral responsibility constrict your choices

_____ Poor reality testing

_____ Inflated self-regard

_____ Inappropriate empathy

_____ Poor problem-solving skills

_____ Need for reassurance

_____ Changing interests

_____ Changes in self-knowledge

_____ Nihilism; nothing about the work world feels appealing

_____ Uncooperative

_____ Not socially confident; nervous and jittery

_____ Intolerant

_____ Risk averse

_____ Too impulsive

_____ Too dominating

_____ Alienated

_____ Education not consistent with requirements for a particular position

_____ Salary does not make it worthwhile to consider position

_____ Poor salary affects self-worth

_____ Poor salary is not enough to make ends meet

_____ Time appears to be unavailable

_____ Child care is unavailable or is too costly to make working justifiable

_____ Children need too much time

_____ Relationships need too much time to nurture or develop

_____ Not enough vacation time

_____ Language skills are limited

_____ Poor English usage skills

_____ Poor communication skills

_____ Unable to speak another language

_____ Commuting and transportation problems; no driver's license

_____ Current legal problems

_____ Child support or spousal support issues

_____ What to say about chronic unemployment, prior layoffs, or firings

_____ Sexual orientation: gay, lesbian, or bisexual

_____ Sex roles

_____ Mommy track; not competitive with others due to raising of children

_____ Dual pay schedules

_____ Sexism

_____ Sexual harassment

_____ Ethnicity and culture

_____ Racism

_____ Ageism: too old or too young

_____ Classism: too poor or too affluent

_____ Affirmative action

Look at your checklist results. What are the kinds of issues that have emerged for you? Are you surprised that there are so many different barriers to your completing a successful career search? Most people know that there is some kind of problem with their search efficiency or effectiveness—they just don't know what the problem is.

From the checklist of problems, let's select a few barriers to explore how you might try, like Brenda did, to turn the barrier into something that makes you more employable.

A Disability Doesn't Have to Be a Disadvantage

Over the years, one of the most striking barriers that I have had to address as a psychologist is how to help people with physical and emotional disabilities become competitive in the job search. Instead of focusing on how a particular disability is a hindrance to being competitive, I have always believed that it is quite plausible to consider the unique qualities disabled people can offer an employer.

If you're feeling somewhat uncompetitive due to learning, physical, or emotional disabilities, what you can promote as part of your knowledge base is experiential information that most people aren't aware of. Because of your life circumstances, you can, as a first step, become an expert in the Americans with Disabilities Act (ADA). You can stay tuned to the politics of the Act and stay abreast of all of the ever-changing amendments. You can do this out of commitment to yourself and your employability, as well as to ensure that others who are disabled are also able to get a fair shake.

In addition to developing an expertise in the ADA, you may already have some experience as a liaison with the Equal Employment Opportunity Commission (EEOC), the federal government body that is charged with handling complaints about employer compliance with the ADA. In addition, you can also become more knowledgeable about the different needs and contributing abilities of people with different types of disabilities. That could include, but not be limited to, disabilities like deafness, blindness, paraplegia, and quadriplegia, along with other sensory and mobility disabilities. As an informed disabled worker, you can offer additional support and information to all of the individual employees of a potential employer.

To the organization, you can serve not only as an internal consultant, but you can significantly affect the company's bottom line. You can become an expert in the technological aids or assistive devices that different workers might try to use on the job. You can pledge to stay current with the growing trends in the evolving field of rehabilitation engineering.

People who are disabled are consumers too, so you become the watchdog for changes that might be worth considering in the organization. Keep in mind that the first banks to lower their ATM machines and make them wheelchair accessible were able to corner the market on the wheelchair-using community. That move resulted in the capture of millions of dollars of business as more and more

disabled clients supported these banks. So your disability management expertise can be a money maker and an emotional winner.

When to Discuss Your Disability in the Interview

As a disabled worker, you can also confront the notion that
you'll never get a fair shake. Stay with the facts as you know them. A
good employer probably won't ask illegal questions. But you can
bring up your past work history, demonstrating how different aids
and assistive devices in the workplace can actually give you an advantage. (People who can't use their arms or hands can be extremely fast
in writing on the computer using voice-activated systems.)

The point of this discussion is to bring up the barrier and use it
to give you an advantage. Put it out to the employer. Then, discuss
your needs rather than staying quiet about them. They don't need to
fester within you. Let the hiring managers know that you've
addressed issues that they may be contemplating. Let them know
that you've solved transportation issues and workplace accommodations. Talk about telecommuting and job sharing as an innovative
possibility. If the company can qualify for certain tax credits or other
economic advantages, it's in your interest to know them and promote
them. Look to places where the disability is an advantage. New companies trying to capture market share could be among the best places
to begin to look.

Since the interviewer may be uncomfortable talking to a disabled candidate, talk about how you have addressed issues of
employee discomfort in the past. Remember that most interviewers
are inept at asking the more in-depth questions that could be helpful
to them, the company, and the disabled candidate.

My own rehabilitation clients usually ask me when they should
disclose the fact that they are disabled. A number found out that letting an employer discover that you're disabled when you come in for
an interview works against you. Employers are usually uncomfortable, may feel duped or set up, and are fearful of legal ramifications.
You can avoid this.

It may be wisest to disclose the disability in a somewhat indi-
rect way after the interview is arranged. Someone who is frightened
or uncomfortable about your condition is not going to hire you or
even hear you. So keep in mind that your goal is to get a job, and
focus on the outcome you want to have at the end of the interview.

Rebounding after Prison

For a number of years I worked in the probation and juvenile justice systems. In those systems, even very young offenders find themselves on the verge of giving up. There's no doubt that if you hope to reenter the job market after conviction, you will need some kind of assistance while on probation or parole, especially regarding interviewing techniques and appropriate job-search skills.

But there are events that take place in a prison that you can use to make yourself interesting and to bolster your credentials. First of all, there are the coping and survival skills that you learned. You had to break into a rough, threatening peer group, which probably helped you become a very good talker and seller. In addition, you may have continued to amass work experience and continuing education while in prison. This experience can demonstrate several important points for a prospective employer. You had to have been on good behavior and nonthreatening to make this work, so that is certainly a plus. You can obtain a letter from the prison detailing your work roles, what was accomplished, what new skills you learned, and what "soft" work skills were developed. (These are skills like good communication, arriving on time, and getting along with cohorts.)

Prisoners, probationers, and parolees—or anyone else who is away from the job market for an extended time—need to remember to always stay in touch with the changes in the work world. You can talk to prison staff, read papers, and listen to the stories of the others, then use that information to show prospective employers that you're still tuned in. New ideas can come from other inmates.

Prison can also be a place to learn or further hone persuasive skills. If you want to learn to sell your ideas and improve your communication skills, you can practice with other inmates. In all of my time in this type of institution, I found the inmate population to be one that could, under the right circumstances, be an enormously supportive group. They were also a group that was tuned into the politics of an institution, the power base of different individuals, and how to mediate through different conflicts. They were, for the most part, good talkers, and that was the skill that was capitalized upon the most.

At San Francisco State University, the Rebound Program was set up to help ex-convicts from the state and county prison systems to enter or reenter the university system. Through this program, ex-convicts provided a lot of support for each other in determining which organizations were most willing to hire ex-offenders for part-time work, where the best prospects were, and how to sell yourself.

There is a lot of latent learning and useful information about the behavior of others that can be learned in a prison, in a way that is not dissimilar to learning in other large, confined situations like battle-ships or aircraft carriers. Everyone is confined to a limited space, so you have to learn different methods of getting along with each other.

If you happen to have had military experience, try to think of the human or "soft" skills that you learned from the experience. Even if you have not thought of them, these need to be considered as part of your employment skill base, along with your technical skills.

What you learn from these two examples (disability and imprisonment) of confronting barriers is that it is possible to reframe the barrier and take advantage of it. It's also important to gather information from others with similar barrier problems to determine how they handled it. Peer advocates can be very useful here, as we found in the Rebound Program and the Veterans Reentry Program at San Francisco State. Confronting the barrier will help you to build skills in advocating for yourself. If one of the barriers you experience is such that you feel that you may have been discriminated against, then you can consider contacting a watchdog or other appropriate agency for help or to argue your case.

Can Barriers Work in Your Favor?

You need to see that new opportunities can come from different barriers. A whole industry of rehabilitation engineering wouldn't exist unless there were people with disabilities. Even concepts like the highly criticized "mommy track" wouldn't have existed unless there were mothers who felt that they couldn't compete with other women and men who did not have children or the responsibility to care for them. Whatever your personal barriers, there are gifts that they give you that are exemplified by some of the following categories.

Openness to New Ideas

People rarely think that there can be an advantage to not receiving what you thought you might deserve. However, some of the most creative people in the work world got there because they were denied access to the career that they had hoped for. Brenda didn't go to medical school, but she has a job that, in the end, might let her make as good or better a contribution to society. Sure, if you don't have certain advantages, you'll have to be somewhat more clever at getting what you want. The key to success in such situations is perseverance. The unfortunate part is that it's natural to become terribly discouraged when you are turned down. Try to see being turned down as you a chance to reassess and change directions.

If your barriers make it difficult for you to move forward, contact people in your network and put together a focus group to assist with what you need to do. By actively seeking new ideas, you put yourself in the right mind-set to listen to the suggestions of others. Trying something new is the best way to get out of a rut.

In California, we have far too many therapists to make the profession economically worthwhile for most new counselors. Yet students continue to flock to the graduate programs in counseling, psychology, and social work and to put in their thousands of hours of work to become licensed. While most will never make a living practicing psychotherapy full time, they do start some interesting projects in the meantime. One SFSU graduate started a company called Theraplay that built high-quality sand trays. Another of our graduates became a writer. Still another used his newfound communication skills to become a wine company marketing manger. At least two became hostage negotiators, and one became a stand-up comic. A rehabilitation counseling student designed clothing for disabled people. None of these careers would have developed if the students had been able to follow their initial dreams. In the end they found career paths that were even more intriguing.

Sometimes the "coolest" jobs are held by people who had to create a new path when the one they wanted to follow was blocked. Many actors and actresses are painfully shy, but they can express themselves to huge audiences even if they can't easily communicate in casual conversation in a small room.

Stand-up comedians function well in that venue because many are hyperactive and can't pay attention to details. But they can learn a routine and respond quickly to audience quips—and their work day is over in an hour. Some physicians become great pathologists after being told they didn't have enough patience or the clinical skills to work with sick people. Patent attorneys will tell you that many ingenious inventors have a difficult time working in any organization with a rigid structure.

A Flexible Approach

Even though I have been an advocate of the portfolio career for some time, I find that these have been developed almost exclusively by people who were not getting what they wanted. For most, the presence of barriers forces them into these careers. That doesn't mean that they should be viewed as second choices; they are simply a different way of being successful. The most important component of this approach is to know your skills and the market niche where they can be used.

The portfolio approach is also useful when you are confronting health barriers. If you have health concerns like Epstein-Barr syndrome, cancer, or HIV, it may be that you don't have the stamina for forty to forty-seven hours of work per week. Other income streams generated in ten to twenty hours per week at different locations may keep your career path open and exciting and give you the feeling of continuous empowerment. Portfolio careers can also be very beneficial if you have retired from your "traditional" career and want to do several part-time activities.

A Sense of Fairness and Goodwill

People who had to work diligently to get where they are—without psychologically perishing in the process—often have a keen sense of fairness. They also have respect for hard work and they know that struggles are a part of achieving their goals. Whatever barriers you have and the way that you or others about you deal with them will help to socialize a sense of fairness in you. The struggles can make you a better manager of people and their problems, allow you to impart your unique knowledge, or help you make special contributions.

Unique Methods of Problem Solving

Keep in mind that the best athletic coaches are not often the best players (although Larry Bird and his Indiana Pacers tempt me to rethink this thesis). Usually, great coaches are the ones who had to struggle to hone their skills and excel. Because they had to be clever, they are often better coaches. They can offer a unique perspective and demonstrate innovative methods.

When the nation's fire-fighting forces expanded to include more women, there were vehement critics who said that women did not have the strength or stamina to do this work. There was a lot of criticism of their employment, and in San Francisco it took a federal judge to deliver a decree demanding that more women be hired.

Through this experience, female firefighters learned to stick together; at times they had to figure out how to do things that may have been different from traditional training. They did the work in teams and suggested many alternative ways of operating the equipment. New procedures like dragging people out of fires rather than trying to carry them out exemplify new approaches that are simple and more efficient than those that had been taught earlier.

Willingness to Ask for Support

The women firefighters demonstrate how life barriers can help you learn to enlist the support of others. By doing this, you gain firsthand experience in watching—and then perhaps modeling—what that person does.

At San Francisco State, we ask students in the introductory counseling course how they decided to become counselors. Almost 80 percent of them have attributed it to a growth-enhancing experience as a therapy client. So if they hadn't had the particular problem or drawback that drove them to counseling in the first place, they probably wouldn't have considered the career at all. The barrier forced them to seek the support of others. They learn how others can be supportive, which gives them a model for considering a change in their own life path.

In addition, having barriers and getting the support of others allows you to recognize that it is okay to enlist the help of others in solving problems. Many managers have said that they grew up expecting to solve problems on their own, so they have not been very good at delegating, a quality that has caused them to be inefficient in their approaches to their work. By experiencing how others play a role in helping you hurdle a barrier, you develop a greater degree of freedom to ask for assistance each time you have a burden that you can't handle alone.

Motivation to Learn

Often the presence of a particular barrier will help you to become interested in gathering information about that barrier. A few years ago, I consulted on the career development case of a person who had an illness called scleroderma. At the time I knew virtually nothing about the condition, although I had heard that a made-for-television movie was in the works. So, as a novice Web surfer, I went to my computer and typed in the term. I was taken aback to find that there were thirty different Web sites that had information about scleroderma. In addition, there were networks of information to help people with scleroderma receive local support.

This experience was the key to fully understanding the power information gives us. Having the barrier forces you to seek out knowledge. The Internet has become a remarkably handy tool for getting information about problems.

This experience also changed my teaching style. As a clinical supervisor, I listened to the work of my students, read their counseling process notes, and made what I thought at the time were pithy comments. I am now much more scientific in my supervision, and when a question comes up that I can't immediately answer, I try to guide the student to appropriate resources on the Web that can answer the question.

Personal Expertise

With whatever barrier you have to hurdle, you are the authoritative expert in that arena. For example, over the years our multiethnic, multicultural, and diversified citizenry has been beset with different prejudices that have excluded certain people from opportunities. The times have changed, however. As our highly diversified population demands more goods and services, the need has grown for the providers of those goods and services to learn something about our multicultural society.

That has resulted in a new field, and for some a new career, called diversity training. People who were among the excluded and disenfranchised are now offered additional training to become experts and trainers in marketplace diversity. Since companies are in the business of making money from customers, they want to be able to communicate easily with customers and ensure their satisfaction. Knowing the history of exclusion, many companies are hiring people of diverse backgrounds to make a new contribution. At another time in our history, they would have been excluded from certain consulting posts; now they are able to impart their expertise in a place that would have at one time been seen as a barrier. For example, if being a nonnative English speaker was once seen as a barrier, today the ability to speak another language fluently can be seen as a real strength that adds to your employability.

As you go through your search, remember that whatever your difficulty, you have unique firsthand experience that no one else has.

Decision-Making Skills

The barriers to the opportunity of your dreams also force you to explore the way you make decisions. From the time you were little, people had expectations for you. You probably responded to this by saying, at quite an early age, what your career and educational plans were. These early decisions don't usually pan out, which might be just as well since they are generally based upon the expectations of others instead of what you wanted to do for yourself.

For those of you who still don't know how to make decisions, it's a crucial skill to learn. If you have had to confront real barriers, as Brenda did, you need to take the time to understand yourself and the decision-making process. Brenda was lucky. She pulled herself out of the medical school competition long before she might have been told that she didn't have the intellectual capacity to make it. When she was able to reenter the workforce, allied health was not aversive to her. She saw the field as a genuine possibility.

When you choose your career early on, based mostly upon the expectations of others, you run the risk of feeling like you've failed. But if you have the barriers in front of you early on, and you find creative and persevering ways to overcome them, then you have learned new ways to cope. Along with this you also learn how to make career decisions. Tugboat drivers, sail makers, train engineers, harbormasters, large crane operators, submarine repairmen, and painters of the Golden Gate bridge are just a few of the distinctive jobs in the San Francisco Bay Area. But it's a safe bet that few of the men and women in these jobs chose them at an early age. Most are thrilled to be in the positions they forged for themselves, but their paths were not, by any means, straightforward.

Most of the happiest career clients that I've worked with aren't doing anything remotely related to what they had hoped to do as a child. They are the ones who determined, after a lot of work and exploration, what the most exciting possibilities would be for them.

Self-Discipline

When you're confronted with an assortment of barriers in the search, you are also forced to become somewhat more disciplined in your efforts to overcome them. In addition, the very act of exploring your decision-making process takes some degree of self-discipline.

On the other hand, with barriers in front of you, you'll be able to experience the new type of decision-making strategy called positive uncertainty (Gelatt 1989). Basically, this type of strategy comes down to a simple issue. You will experience more and different possibilities than someone who is not overcoming barriers. You will learn to expect the unexpected. People who need to confront barriers learn how to use their imagination and make choices that lead to new experiences. You'll not only have more adventures, it is likely you'll have a more satisfying career. People who have to confront different barriers must also confront their own convictions about their career path. Others often don't have to do this, and therefore end up in careers that may not be as satisfying as those that are held by people who are jumping over barriers.

The people with the barriers are the seekers. They are the ones who are forced to utilize their imagination and to make new interpretations of information. They need to maintain their self-discipline while they do this. They need to continue to create and to not impulsively take a position. As you confront your barriers, try to see them as instigators of change. Try to let the barriers help you become more creative in this search and in the others to come. There can be some power in learning how to be comfortable with uncertainty. The barriers help you to keep your mind and your options open.

PART 4 | Staying on Track

10 | Feeling Overloaded

*That day, giving a loose to my soul, I spent on
the unimportant wood.*

—Robert Frost

Beware of Burnout

Stop. Before proceeding any further, it's important to think for a
moment about activities that will help you feel simultaneously more
organized and less stimulated. You need to learn to tighten your
strategy, filter out extraneous information, and care for your mental
and physical well-being. These skills will help you to avoid burnout
and be much more creative in your search.

Burnout is the depletion of your physical and mental resources.
You've probably used the term colloquially at work or school when
you felt you just didn't have the energy to take on another task.
While the concept isn't really new to you, you may not realize that
burnout is a serious problem.

Burnout carries a complex constellation of diagnostic signs; it's
more than just being exhausted. Symptoms include fatigue and

mental exhaustion, to be sure, but also include a quickness to anger, sleeplessness, suspicion, a "thin-skinned" attitude, and a feeling of disengagement. Among service workers, there is a numbness, a lack of concern, or disconnection from the clients who need assistance. There's little commitment to helping. How many times have you felt that a service worker just didn't care about the quality of his or her work? How often did you feel as if you didn't count or amount to much because a service worker didn't tend to your needs?

Louise was a physician who specialized in geriatric medicine at a well-established HMO in Arizona. She loved to work with older people, and had taken course work in gerontology for this reason. She was diligent, but not very efficient. She thought that it was more prudent to honestly serve her patients. She often stayed behind after work to complete the charts that she couldn't finish during the day.

Her HMO had a management change and created a policy mandating that physicians spend six minutes per patient, maximum. Louise thought that this policy might work for some patients, especially younger ones, but hers needed more time and service because they were usually sicker than younger patients. They also needed more time getting into and out of the clinic. They desired a lot more explanation about their treatments than younger patients. In addition, some patients had support from family members or ambulatory assistants who also desired information. This too required more time. Louise protested the time limits to the deaf ears of the HMO board. She was instructed to incorporate the wishes of the new management into her practice or, she was warned, she could move on.

Louise tried to live with the regimen dictated to her. She found that she was staying even later than before, was more exhausted, and worried, and began to be dismissive of patient concerns. By aiming for the unrealistic goal of simultaneously meeting the opposing needs of patients and the HMO, Louise was burning out. She disconnected emotionally from the patients, was sharp and critical with her colleagues, and was suspicious of even well-intended associates like her nursing staff.

Burnout strikes like this. It begins slowly, but the symptoms accumulate over time. It's brought about by excessive striving to achieve unattainable goals. You might reason that burnout is caused by the expectations that other people have for you, and that's certainly true. But the people who burn out tend to be those individuals who put high expectations on themselves. In the service and people helping professions, it has been compared to "compassion fatigue," the exhaustion that workers experience when they are worn down by emotionally caring for others.

There is even evidence that burnout is lethal. Consider the ruling of a Japanese court from the Nagging District, which ruled that an employee committed suicide because he was exhausted from working eighty-hour weeks. Hence, the employee's family was judged as deserving of compensation from the government. (Under Japanese law, the family of a deceased worker can collect compensation if the worker died from a job-related accident.) It will be interesting to watch whether or not there will be many more cases like this to follow.

The Burnout Factor in the Job Search

The job search is tailor-made for burnout. It's a process that takes a lot of effort, but gratification is delayed. You may feel that your choices are constricted because you have limited funds available to support your lifestyle. Your finances can feel beyond your control, keeping you on the edge of panic.

You may also feel that your upward mobility is constricted because you don't have appropriate education or skills to move ahead. There can be an inconsistency between your expectations of what you're going to get and the reality of what you're going to get. You are going to feel, more often than not, a sense of unfairness. Why do some people with even fewer skills than you seem to be given better opportunities than you?

In addition, there are now so many different activities that can be a part of the search that if you try all of them at once, you are very likely going to get frustrated. It will feel like there are just not enough hours in the day to complete even among the most urgent activities. If you are routinely turned down by the people you hope will hire you, then feelings of underappreciation and lack of power and charisma set in. You'll feel a loss of personal and professional community.

If you're finding yourself somewhat depressed and tired by the search, treat the symptoms seriously. Pay attention to these three warning signs, which are taken from Christina Maslach's *Burnout Inventory* (Maslach and Jackson 1981).

First is emotional exhaustion. This is manifested in frequent fatigue and the desire to tune out, take days off, sleep, or escape in some way to rest. Your emotional resources feel depleted, and you can't give any more to the search. You feel the need to withdraw from people at the time you need them most.

Second is depersonalization, or numbing out. This is what happens when you can't take in any more information. You feel like you

want to decompress, and the more people try to help you, the more
you are unable to hear them and what they have to offer. You don't
have positive feelings or respect for your network of supporters. In
fact, you may start to belittle them, treating them like objects as you
make jokes about them. In short, you've become apathetic to the
search process. You began with a vocational "high," and now you
just want it to be over.

Third, you notice that your personal accomplishments are wan-
ing. You feel like you must be making progress, but your outcomes
are not reflective of your effort. You work hard, but nothing seems to
be getting done. As your accomplishments abate, your frustration
over the search intensifies. The quality of your work deteriorates as
well. You aren't as careful as you should be with job applications,
résumés, and cover letters. You may send out material that is sloppy
and not representative of you. At some point you wonder whether
this is worth all the effort you're investing. It feels so hopeless.

Exercise 10-1   Are You Burning Out?

This job-search burnout checklist can help to determine whether or
not you are burning out. For each of the symptoms listed below,
check whether they apply to you.

_____ I dread having to send out another résumé and cover letter.

_____ I feel exhausted from the search and in need of a vacation.

_____ I notice that I don't pay attention to information sources the
way that I used to.

_____ I get angry when people try to give me advice.

_____ I seem to waste a lot of my time.

_____ I have too much to do and no time to do it.

_____ I disagree with most of the advice people give me.

_____ I can't tell what's right or wrong with my search anymore.

_____ I seem to get sick more often than I used to.

_____ My search is adversely affecting my sleep.

_____ I don't get emotionally prepared for my interviews.

_____ I tune out and daydream frequently.

_____ I don't research a company prior to my interview.

_____ I exercise less than I used to.

_____ I feel my search for a new job is a never-ending story.

_____ There isn't much that gives me pleasure.

_____ I feel I haven't achieved anything in a long time.

_____ I have long conversations about anything other than my search.

_____ I feel like escaping by reading or watching television.

_____ I just don't seem to care anymore about this whole search.

If you checked off more than five of these items, then you are showing signs of burning out. If you checked off ten or more, you are burned out and need to address the issue right away. Wherever you are on the checklist, it's vital to prevent burnout or remedy it during your search. Here's how.

Ten Tips to Beat Burnout

First, be aware of burnout and learn to recognize the symptoms. Items you marked on the checklist can help to pinpoint your areas of concern. Determine whether emotional exhaustion, depersonalization, or poor personal accomplishment is your problem. Maybe it's a combination of two or all three. Try to be specific about what is eating at you. Breaking burnout will allow you to produce more and better materials as a part of your search. It also keeps you from "hitting the wall," to use a marathon runner's metaphor.

Second, create a thought each day that will help you. Then decide how you're going to complete certain reachable goals and how you will acknowledge yourself. The chapter on goal setting can give you more guidance. Be sure to refrain from creating unattainable situations. Choose tasks each day that are doable and move you forward in the search. If you need to make a revision in your résumé, even if it takes only a few minutes, do it and remember that you did it. You attained something. When you put off too many activities, you start feeling less efficient and the lack of closure looms large. Over time, even simple unfinished activities seem more important than they really are.

Be sure that you establish your priorities daily. Keep lists of your most important and immediate needs and be sure to acknowledge your own accomplishments. Keep yourself realistic about what you can and cannot accomplish, even under the best of circumstances.

Third, as you look for work, accept compromises. If you're a little rigid about this, learn to be more flexible. If you hope to be a fashion model with six-pack abs, you can't have all of the pizza and beer that you want. If you want to be able to spend a lot of time with your family, don't pursue a job as a long-haul truck driver. If you want a job with little stress or responsibility, realize that you probably can't expect a six-figure income. If you want to have extra space in your home, you can't clutter it with objects that you don't use. Also, at this time in your work life, you don't need to be a hero. Burning yourself out with heroic attempts at search projects will be of no use to anyone. If you find that you need to be someone's hero, then engage in heroic tasks in areas other than the job search.

Fourth, find simple, clever ways to empower yourself. You probably have a personal identification number (PIN) for a phone card or a password on your e-mail. Change the password or PIN every two weeks or so to reflect a small goal you have for yourself. Joyce did this regularly and it made her feel that she was accomplishing something because she was being creative in her search. She used passwords like "focus," "connect," and "model" to serve as a regular affirmation of what she wanted to accomplish. It kept her motivated, creative, and humorous.

Fifth, increase your feelings of efficiency. You don't have to work harder to work smarter. For example, it's smart to keep your desk clear. If there's material on your desk that you haven't gotten to after a week, throw it away (not the bills, of course) or file it out of sight. If it's there today and it will be there next week, it likely will exemplify your own inefficiency. You'll feel like there's too much on your plate. Clean it up. A clear desk at the end of your day will give you a feeling of closure and order. It will also eliminate both paper and project buildup. When the paper builds, you feel as if you have too much to do, and then your worries about your own inefficiency return with gusto. Also figure out how much time each of your job-search activities will take. The underestimation of your search load is a great stress enhancer. If you think that you can do more than you can, you'll feel disappointed and frustrated when you haven't finished what you set out to do.

Make sure that you don't suffer from paper weight. Handle all papers only once. File what you'll use later and toss what is useless. Make sure you have files for current issues and others for material to review at a later time. Put date stamps on your files. Every month, review the date stamps and toss the material that is clearly stale.

Above all, make sure that your paper files are manageable, that your system is understandable to you over time, and that you can put as much material as possible onto your computer disks or drives.

Sixth, guard against tasks that are less goal oriented. For example, limit your telephone time. Let your answering machine or voice mail system pick up all your phone messages. Turn the speaker off, so you will not even monitor the calls. Answering the phone is a huge interrupter and makes your search day chaotic. If the news is bad, you'll be upset. If the caller is contacting you for a chat, you'll waste more time than is good for you.

If you can't get someone off the phone after you are done talking, don't respond to what the caller is saying. If you feel that's too rude, then allow for long silences when the caller completes a sentence. Don't ask questions, and eventually you'll extinguish the caller's interest in any further conversation. Give yourself permission to say "no" when you have to. Saying "yes" too much of the time will cause you to lose your focus. You can become more efficient not by going faster and faster, but by engaging in fewer activities. Make yourself your own priority, at least for the duration of your search. Keep the commitments that you have made to yourself. Be your best friend. You don't break your promises to a best friend.

Consider eliminating subscriptions to periodicals that are too distracting. Many people don't ever get to their professional literature, but they carry this material with them regularly and then complain that they have too much to do. The ever-expanding pile of unread material makes you feel that you aren't keeping up. The same can be said for reading the daily news. How are you using the daily paper? Would it be better for you to use the Internet to read only the most important articles? William found that he didn't need a paper at all. He simply read the headlines of the paper at newsstands on his way to and from home. He found that he didn't really need as much information from the local daily as he thought.

Seventh, reduce the number of outside stressors in your life. You may not be able to do this easily, but it's critical to focus on handling those things that are manageable. If you are in the midst of a personal family crisis or the breakup of a relationship, postpone your job search if at all possible. The same is true if you are in the middle of a health crisis. Be aware of your timing and the stressors of your life and try to do the search when you can focus. Try to begin each day with calmness and equanimity. Consider a short spiritual sentence or two for yourself. The writings of the Zen master Thich Nhat Hanh (1987) exemplify how simple words to begin the day can provide an antidote to the stresses of the job search.

Chronic stress will compromise your health, so keeping the stressors away will help to keep you in a good physical and mental space during the search. If you have trouble keeping the stressors out of your life, then try to find some ways to underreact to them. Traffic jams are always going to occur—you just can't predict when—so they're stressful. But you can think of them as an opportunity. Get some interesting tapes or tapes of language learning that you play only during these kinds of times. That way you'll turn a negative experience into one that is more positive.

There is also a simple truism to confronting stress. That is, keep on smiling. Open your lips and breathe easily Your friendly smile actually increases blood flow while releasing endorphins.

Eighth, be efficient with mindless busywork and delegate some of it out. This is especially true if you're at home during the search. You may love to clean your house, but during the search, it takes away time and focus. If you can get some help with time-consuming but mundane activities, do it, unless the mundane activities are those that you enjoy. Try to group the mindless activities together, in order to make them seem less distracting and keep you efficient. Try to eliminate phrases like "I'm happy to do it." You may be trying to win or satisfy someone else's needs while you're harming yourself. Give yourself permission to ask for help, especially from those you are closest to. And when you ask for help, guidance, or assistance, do it with a positive, uncomplaining attitude.

Ninth, if you are still having some difficulty with burnout, then maybe you need to get away from the search for a bit. It is quite all right to take some time off from the search, as long as you plan for it and put it into your schedule. However, you don't want time out, which lowers productivity, to put more stress on you. If that is the case, then you should take smaller rest periods in terms of hours (rather than days) off.

Tenth, always keep your goals in mind and stay focused.

Urgency Overload

We live in a frantic time, a nanosecond world. Everyone wants information immediately. It seems everyone is "wired" through pagers, cell phones, and fax machines. Some preteens even have sophisticated communication devices and access to 800 numbers so they can call home from anywhere.

Urgency is everywhere, and everyone appears to buy into it in order to remain competitive. Stock market strategists use market timing formulas to predict abrupt increases or declines in the value of securities. Some money managers track the different worth of a currency selling in two different places at the same time. Within seconds, they buy the currency at the cheaper price and sell it at the higher price, hoping to claim a profit.

But the urgency has left us overstimulated. Commutes to work are not times to reflect and listen to music anymore; they are times to communicate and make more deals. Janice reported that while sailing, she saw an ocean kayaker talking to his office on his cell phone while trying to relax among the dolphins. Commuters on rapid transit complain about the noise pollution they experience because so many riders are using their cell phones to generate business while they are commuting.

In the job search, urgency overload surrounds you. You feel you must provide information immediately or else fail to compete. This is partly true, but the real problem is that urgency overload makes you less efficient. This isn't because you stress out or burn out, although it's true that can happen. It's due to the fact that responding immediately can waste time. Why? Your objectives will lose importance because you'll be unable to prioritize search tasks. You'll manage daily events haphazardly. As you fall behind in your search schedule, you'll set overly ambitious but unreachable goals, which will reignite burnout. There are two ways of avoiding this: Prioritize your activities and value your time.

Prioritizing Can Help

Engage in meaningful activities. When you go to work, you have a schedule. You leave your home at a certain time, arrive at work, do your tasks, leave, and return home. You have a routine that is familiar and comfortable. In the job search, you have no routine— and that gives you the freedom to do what you want. That's fine, as long as you use the time appropriately. The problem is that most people don't. They take trips, enjoy leisure, meet friends, and do some of the social things that they had neglected. They enjoy the lack of structure, at least for a while. Remember how it was on holiday vacations from school? Suddenly you didn't have to deal with someone else's schedule. The problem is that after a while you have to create your own schedule. Josh is a case in point.

Josh had no regrets when he lost his real estate job. He had been disenchanted with the work for a while, so when his manager told him he was going to rent his desk space to another, Josh was okay with it. For several weeks after leaving his office routine, Josh busied himself with a variety of projects. He finished the cabin he was building out of town and put it up for sale. He helped his brother with the family olive business, and he spent time with his wife and three children. He had some savings and felt solvent.

Soon, however, Josh found that he was getting nothing done. He was sleeping late. He stopped going to his gym four times a week to work out, and he started to quarrel more frequently with his wife. His friends found that he demanded too much of their time. Josh never seemed to find time to hunt for work. He kept telling his wife not to worry, but she did worry because their savings were beginning to run low.

Josh had lost the ability to prioritize for himself. His life had become a maze of different activities; he had lost his sense of time. There was only "now" and "not now." This was frustrating for everyone, including Josh. He was neither valuing his time nor prioritizing his activities. He needed to learn to prioritize again, which seems like a simple endeavor but in fact takes a great deal of effort.

In the job search, there are two types of activities: those that are immediate, and those that are important. Sometimes an activity can be immediate but not terribly important, or it can be important but not immediate. The most pressing activities are those that are both important and immediate. For example, paying your bills is an important activity. At the beginning of the month, it's not an immediate activity. But if you put off paying your bills, suddenly it becomes an immediate and important activity.

The job search has some important long-term activities, such as putting together a support network and practicing your interviewing skills. There are also some immediate activities, such as responding to letters or phone calls, and getting back to an employer with an answer to a job offer. You should rate your activities in this fashion and create a schedule in which those activities that are immediate and important are always completed first.

Ironically, the activities that people often engage in first are those that are unimportant and not immediate. For example, people open the mail right after they pick it up rather than opening it when they have nothing more important to do. The mail causes a stir, and you lose some control. The situation is even worse with fax machines. As convenient as these may be, they can lead to inefficiency if each new, unanticipated fax elicits a whirling dervish of activity. People respond in an immediate but chaotic way. If they were to read the faxes at the same time every day, they could begin to prioritize their responses like they prioritize their time.

Exercise 10-2   Learning to Prioritize

Begin your prioritizing by listing your career search activities; evaluate their importance and immediacy. Rate those that are important and immediate with a one. Rate those that are important but not immediate with a two. Activities that are less important but immediate, rate with a three, and those that are unimportant and not immediate, rate with a four.

After prioritizing, act on those activities that are rated with ones and twos. Cross off the activity from the list after it's completed. Do your prioritizing every day, preferably in the morning. Eventually all of your activities will become ones and you'll complete them accordingly. You'll find that managing and prioritizing your activities is beneficial to your sense of control.

Value Your Time

Experience how precious your time is. When the late Senator Paul Tsongas was diagnosed with cancer, he decided to change his career path. He also withdrew his presidential candidacy. He noted in doing so that he had never met anyone who, on their deathbed, regretted not spending more time at the office.

You have less available time than ever. While you feel that you're overloaded, you're also characterizing your overload in terms of time. At the National Institute for Occupational Safety and Health (NIOSH) 1999 meeting on Work, Stress, and Health '99, new terms like "time poverty" and "time famine" were bandied bout. There is more urgency and more information than ever.

New technology does not seem to be giving you more free time—it may even be giving you less. Technology keeps you connected to the office, even when you're commuting, spending a quiet night at home, or lounging at the beach. Ironically, it may make you feel more out of control. A number of clients have told me that they "jump" or twitch when they hear the office cell phone ring or pager buzz.

You can replace your job and your money, but you can never replace your time. It's gone forever. Good career change is dependent upon your use of time. Do the right things at the right time. Be in the right place at the right time. That's empowering.

Your time is worth money. Count the hours you put into your job search and evaluate them as real currency. If your predicted annual salary is $12,500, your hourly wage is $6.40. If you waste an hour each day in your job search, in a month that costs you $130.25 and in a year it costs you $1563.00. If your predicted annual salary is $50,000 your hourly rate is $25.63. A wasted hour in a day of your job search costs you $538.23 per month and $6253.21 in a year.

How can you save time? Be a practical manager. Complete projects one at a time. Stay away from the crisis mentality. Balance yourself. Don't take on more than you should, or less than you should. Whatever you take on, be good at it so you finish it. You will not feel as much stress if you work long hours but are good at and enjoy what you're doing. Don't assume time-consuming responsibilities that may take twice as long to complete as anticipated. Try to stay away from those that make you feel unproductive or unrecognized and those that make you feel out of control.

Put limits on outside distractions. Use "Do Not Disturb" signs. Don't spend too much time on unproductive phone activity or meetings without purpose. Keep control over your visitors. Work to stop procrastination. If you find that you're procrastinating, break up your activities into small time slots. Ask yourself how you're going to spend your next five minutes, one minute, or twenty seconds. Break up time into measurable components and evaluate what you're doing. In addition, find ways to reward yourself for the work you're doing, unless you find that it has its own internal or psychic rewards.

Routine and trivial activities serve as a comfortable escape, and are best avoided. If the prioritizing activity described above does not work for you, or if you want to try another method to give greater structure to your day and find those lost periods of time, then make a schedule that looks like the daily planner you might have used at work. The planner can help you find the valuable moments that you may have lost by not managing your time.

For each day of the week, write down the activities that you do each hour. Look at the results each day. Can you find extra time? Can you see where your schedule needs to be better structured? Are there places where you can prevent duplication and streamline your activities?

Value the time you spend contemplating the future. If you are unemployed, spend time each day doing a few of those activities that you always wanted to do. Engage in any activity that will save you time in the future.

Information Overload

As already described, advances in information technology have resulted in an explosion of available information, which affects every aspect of the job search. You have phenomenal quantities of information at the click of your mouse, but this doesn't necessarily make the job search easier. It feels more frantic. There are so many strategies for engaging in the search today that it's difficult to know how to select one or more. In addition, after selecting a strategy or two, it's difficult to use them efficiently.

Select Your Strategies Judiciously

To avoid overload, it's important to develop a well-articulated strategy that works for you. Developing your career search demands that you try the newest strategies, but if you're not selective and try to use every single one you hear of, you'll become inefficient and tired. If you try only one strategy, and it's not particularly successful, chances are that you'll relinquish the search after a month or two because you won't be receiving any positive feedback to keep you going.

So how should you proceed? Be ready to add strategies. While one particular strategy may not be right for you, adding on strategies will increase the longevity of the search. To do this, you'll need to stay organized. If you add on too many new strategies, you will become exhausted and begin to burn out.

The best approach for narrowing the field is to determine which kind of information is best obtained at which resources. Engineers, for example, use the Internet regularly to advertise positions. They want responses by e-mail and fax and don't want to be bothered with contacts made other ways. Lawyers, on the other hand, rarely get recruited this way. Law firms advertise in legal papers and use legally focused executive recruiters. Some firms hire from the ranks of contract attorneys who have assisted on a case. Other lawyers recruit by using their professional and law school alumni networks. So the strategy you use should correspond with the methods of recruitment in your field.

Use Your Strategies Efficiently

The best approach is to put together a search that uses all the relevant information and technology in a format suitable for your specific needs. There are many strategies for engaging in your search. The method that most career counselors and assorted experts promote is one in which you assess your interests, personality characteristics, skills, and values, and define yourself as a package or product. After appropriate research, you can then match your skills with the work available. Keeping that in mind, you market yourself through the hidden job market of friends and acquaintances. You hustle for informational interviews, use new information to create new leads, and practice your interviewing and presentation skills. By hook or by crook, you introduce yourself to people with the power to hire you. Once you establish contact, you then convince them that they have the opportunity of a lifetime to enhance their company's riches by hiring you.

In addition to this generic strategy, there are a number of other useful techniques:

- Use the Internet. You can use the Net these days to partake of a host of activities, including assessment, marketing, and introduction. There are now literally hundreds of generic career and self-assessment Web sites (see Appendix) that are easily accessible. You can also research organizations through their Web sites and find out what they do, what they manufacture, and what types of jobs are currently available.

  Through many different sites, you can post your résumé on the Web and hope for the best. You can also type in key words and receive lists of jobs available by city, state, and nation. The Internet promises a lot and sounds like it will make your job search easier, but prepare yourself for frustration: The net is not consistently user-friendly for job searchers.

  After Bob received his mental health counseling degree, he searched the Internet. He typed in the word "counselor" on careermosaic.com and received hundreds of listings. But, to his chagrin, these included mostly sales counselors from organizations like The Good Guys and not positions in mental health counseling. He also received entirely different job postings with the words "attorney," "barrister," and "lawyer." Bob found that the Net could be very slow and he ran into traffic jams frequently. From time to time he was disconnected. He found much of the experience to be terribly annoying..

  If you choose to use the Net, be aware that many others are also searching this way because it appears to be so easy. You will need to stay well organized and use the "bookmark" function on your computer effectively. You should probably save all of your e-mail, at least for a while. Remember that the sheer number of job-related sites makes it difficult to navigate. In the end, you will still need to have good telephone skills, good interviewing skills, and the ability to ask intelligent questions.

- Research information on new jobs from different government agencies. The Department of Labor has a Web site (see Appendix), and there are also state and local sites. If you choose to use the Internet, be sure to check these out. In addition, there are some old gumshoe career-search methods that are effective in tracking down these jobs. You can take civil service exams for positions at the municipal, county, state, and federal personnel offices. Although most of these opportunities are continuously available, job searchers seem to rarely use them.

- You can do a mass mailing to employers with a carefully crafted résumé and cover letter. Depending on how many employers you hope to reach, this can be an expensive technique. It also demands that you do pretty sophisticated research to ensure that the right people receive your credentials. If you choose to do a mass mailing, be sure that the companies you choose are in fact ones that you would like to work for and ones that would clearly want you. Also, check out whether you could send this same letter and résumé over the Internet for no cost.

- Answering ads—whether on the Internet, in the newspaper, in trade publications, or in the job listings of professional associations—is also useful and can be effective. Some people go directly to union halls and other facilities where employers come to gather a workforce for the day, week, or month. College students go to their campus career centers. These activities can be time consuming, but they do get you moving and they do help you to meet people. Reading classifieds, particularly job descriptions, can keep you in touch with current word usage and technical language in different industries. You can later use the words in your résumé.

- Dropping in on private local personnel offices, executive recruiters, and the state unemployment office is another technique. While much of the time you will find people are not interested in you, it is possible to meet someone, even a client of the service who has just the kind of information that would be useful to you. You can also go to a company's personnel or general offices directly. This allows you to put faces to names and shows a certain amount of persistence. It is time consuming, so you must determine whether this is a good use of your time.

- Be a joiner. Join a job club. Volunteer. Use professional associations to assess, market, and introduce yourself. Whatever methods you use, create a written plan for yourself, like a business plan. Use it to evaluate your effectiveness and efficiency. Creating a plan with more than one of the strategies will keep you going; trying to use all of them will waste your time.

Caring for Yourself during the Search

While most of the activities in this book focus upon basic career strategies to emotionally empower you, there are activities that you can engage in that will help your search even though they do not seem to be directly related to career issues. They all have to do with experiencing a healthy balance in your life.

Exercise Vigorously and Regularly

Put this into a schedule of important and immediate activities. Exercise rids you of fatigue, worry, aggressiveness, frustration, and anger, while giving you extra energy. It keeps your outer physique strong and your internal juices flowing properly. Exercise lets your neural chemical system work the way it should and helps to reduce the "background noise" that develops during the day. If you have sleepless nights, morning exercise can rejuvenate you.

Exercise with friends. When you arrange your routine this way, you'll definitely show up. It's a good, healthy way to interact with people; you help them while they help you. Use some of the time to share your obsessions and worries about the search. A long walk, mountain hike, or bike ride can be combined with a picnic and used this way. You can save money at lunch by meeting a friend for a business lunch walk. The very worst thing that you can do is to obsess and worry alone.

If you feel that you can't possibly give up any time from your search in order to pump iron or kick up your heart rate, then try working exercise into you daily life. Climb stairs rather than taking the elevator. Bike to places that you need to go. You're probably not dressing for work each day, so enjoy the freedom of dressing in clothes that are comfortable for long walks or bicycling. Try walking or biking to the store or taking your dog on extra-long walks. You can also get to know your partner better by taking a few swing dance lessons. Activities like gardening and cleaning can get your heart rate up and increase your flexibility.

Richard was let go from his position as a security guard at a large downtown office building. He was proud of his work. But when his office building was sold, the new owners and new management team wanted to use another security service. Richard was devastated. He started his job search unmotivated and without much energy. He ate too much and gained thirty pounds. He became so depressed that he decided to end his life with a creative suicide. He would run until he keeled over from a heart attack. So he began running. He ran for a quarter mile the first few days of the week. He was surprised that he was still alive at the end of the week. He hadn't done anything with his search, since he thought he would be dead. After two weeks he was still alive and running a mile three times a week. He noticed, to his surprise, that he was feeling a lot happier. He was amazed at the amount of energy he had, and he discovered that he wanted to live. He began to put a job search together now that he was feeling so good. He continued to run but he found that he enjoyed it more with people he had met during his outings. He had new friends and new energy for the search.

This story is dramatic, but don't do something as unhealthy as Richard did. A vigorous exercise program should be developed in consultation with a health-care professional.

Store Your Ideas and Free Your Brain

Buy a small recorder or notebook to keep track of ideas and tasks. You can't remember everything, so don't try to. If you know information is recorded, then your brain is freed to engage in the other important components of the search. If you wake up at night with great ideas for your search, record them. If you obsess about a job interview, record the obsession. Even if something is keeping you up at night, you'll be amazed at how simplistic it seems in the morning. If you want to hear how well you answer interview questions, record the answers.

Sleep Well

You will find that with good sleep, your search will be substantially less painful—it may even be invigorating. Because sleep is the time when your immune system renews itself, sleep deprivation can damage your immune system. It also makes you feel impulsive and irritable. Learn to shut down your mind. Engage in quieting activities like reading fiction or poetry about an hour before you turn in.

When turning in, refrain from the news, talk shows, and violent programming, all of which will agitate you. Don't channel surf with a television remote control. Learn to live without an alarm clock. If your body is awakening naturally, you will have an instant assessment that you are getting proper sleep.

Try to refrain from eating right before bed. If you do happen to nibble on something, then make sure it's low in fat. Fat takes longer to digest and can lead to your experiencing weird dreams and fitful nights. Remember, the jokes about cherry pies and bad dreams may not have been so untrue after all.

If none of these techniques help, there is good evidence that a milligram of melatonin taken a half hour to an hour before going to bed can help elicit sleep. As you age, you become somewhat deficient in your production of melatonin; sleep deprivation is one result.

Don't Diet

The word "diet" conjures up all kinds of terrible images of deprivation. So don't do it. Instead, eat in a health-conscious, mindful way. You live in a country with abundant resources, good information about nutrition, and poor dietary practices. Despite all we know about the biochemistry of eating, we are an overweight and under-exercised nation. Try to follow the old adage, "Eat breakfast like a king, lunch like a prince, and dinner like a pauper." Eating right will improve your energy level and keep you forward thinking and positive. It's also one of the few activities that you have complete control over. If you can't control anything else, you can at least control your food and the quality, quantity, and timeliness of your food intake.

Learn what a reasonable portion of food looks like. Many people eat what is put in front of them without being sensitive to how much they are ingesting. Be aware of what a four-ounce and six-ounce piece of fish, chicken, or meat looks like. Create a system of portion control for yourself. You should also pay attention to how different foods affect your brain. While drinks loaded with caffeine, sugar, or aspartame give you a good jolt, they may also make you feel jumpy, upset, and mildly depressed. Everyone experiences different side effects, so monitor the effects foods have on you rather than relying on the experiences of others.

There are some good resources in this area. Try to get a copy of *Stealth Health* by Evelyn Tribole (1998) for some interesting new ideas about your diet and wellness. There are also Web sites that can help;

check out the Government Consumer Information Catalogue—Food and Nutrition (see Appendix).

Beware of Addictions

Watch out for any behaviors that are already getting or might get out of control. People become addicted to alcohol, substances, and behaviors because they are unable to fulfill essential needs. Addictions create very predictable sensations that make people feel good momentarily. They quite often eradicate pain and other unpleasant experiences. Addictions can also appear to bolster your sense of power and self-worth so you have feelings of control or achievement. In the job search you have large chunks of time available; without some well-developed organization, you can easily fall prey to the power of addictions. The added lack of self-esteem and feelings of helplessness and hopelessness make you particularly vulnerable. In the absence of social support and networking experiences, you may find that your addiction becomes your friend. The unfortunate reality is that the addictions exacerbate your search problems and dissolve your attempts at daily or organizational structure.

While you are probably familiar with drug and alcohol addiction, you may not be aware of some new addictions around you. Work addiction, for example, is a very powerful addiction. For some of you who have lost work, it may be tempting to escape into job tasks. Work addiction is a magnificent addiction because society is so willing to let us engage in it. The signs of work addiction have been organized into ten broad categories by Bryan Robinson (1989). He says that work addicts are:

1. In a hurry and need to stay busy

2. Obsessive in their need to control, do work themselves, and not ask for help

3. Perfectionists

4. Difficult in relationships

5. Binge workers

6. Unable to relax and have fun

7. So mentally preoccupied that they experience mental brownouts

8. Impatient and irritable

9. Lacking in self-esteem

10. Neglectful of their mental and physical health

Job searching can be addictive if you have these types of characteristics. There are other potential addictions that arise with the job search. One of these is related to the Internet, chat rooms, and the like. Jillian is a good example. She was most upset that she couldn't seem to get away from her Internet addiction. She had started using the Net during her search and sent out most of her resumes that way. She got responses on the Net and soon began to look forward to those responses. Each day began with checking her e-mail; she continued to check throughout the day. That kept her busy enough. Her behavior got out of hand when she began to wake up during the night to use the bathroom and then would go back online to check her mail. If she had mail, she would then stay up and respond to it, making it difficult for her to go back to sleep. She stopped sleeping well and felt exhausted and discouraged a lot of the time. The Internet was turning out to be frustrating, and she could not extricate herself from it. Mental health professionals are becoming more sensitive to work addiction and Internet addiction. Should you find that a work-related addiction is consuming you, check out a referral from your county mental health services department. In the meantime, try to work in a more balanced manner. Put moderation into your life agenda and practice some of the relaxation exercises suggested below.

Keep Yourself Quiet

There will be times during the search when you feel some degree of performance anxiety. It will usually come right before an important interview. To ensure that you won't be agitated, it's a good idea to learn the quieting reflex. This simple technique, developed by Herbert Benson at the Harvard Medical School, was suggested to me by Erik Peper at San Francisco State University. Basically, it involves teaching your body a relaxing response to a stressful event. Performers, public speakers, and individuals with performance anxiety have been helped immensely with the technique. I have made some variations on it for my clients. The technique I use has the following components:

a. quickly smile

b. sparkle or flash your eyes from left to right

c. drop your shoulders

d. take a diaphragmatic breath

e. imagine cool air coming down your right arm and your left arm

I have found that learning this technique well creates a relaxed response to stressful situations like the job interview.

Relax

There are a number of techniques that work. Transcendental meditation (TM), general meditation, yoga, deep muscle relaxation, and Benson's relaxation response (1975) are certainly useful. But you can learn a fast and simple method here. One of the simplest ways is to lie in a comfortable position. Tense and relax each of your muscle groups from your nose and forehead to your toes. Tighten and hold the tension for five seconds and then release it for ten seconds before moving on to another muscle group. When you're through and very relaxed, scan your body and focus on any places where tension remains. People often anchor tension in specific parts of the body, and eliminating the tension in these areas can help.

Another easy way of relaxing is through deep breathing. Sit in a comfortable chair and put both of your hands on your diaphragm. After relaxing with the deep muscle procedure just mentioned, lean back in the chair and breathe so that you feel your stomach distending. Your hands should move out rather than in. You will breathe less in your chest and more in what feels like your stomach. This diaphragmatic breathing is a very relaxed form of breathing. In fact, it's one of the first methods of inhaling that we naturally use to help us to relax prior to a stressful experience. After you begin comfortably breathing diaphragmatically, allow your eyes to close. As they do, travel backwards in time until you see yourself at a happy and comfortable place. Don't worry how far back you go, just take yourself back to a time that was significant in its comfort. Allowing your eyes to slowly rise up toward your forehead can help you see a better picture of yourself in your history. Then, as you visualize yourself, allow yourself to move into the memory, almost like entering a movie. Now, become that child that is you. Allow your child to take you on a tour of your earliest experiences, exploring images, dreams, and feelings. And as you release your resistance to this activity, let your child take you wherever you want. The activity allows you to remember and feel your developmental history.

Finally, throughout your search, it's useful to let go of some of your extraneous preoccupations and become more mindful of the issues and activities that are a part of the search process. This mindfulness can go hand in hand with another stress reduction/ relaxation technique called body scanning. It keeps you aware of your body as you focus your attention on the different areas of tension that exist within you. It is similar to other meditation-relaxation exercises and serves as a powerful stress reducer.

The exercise is simple and straightforward. Lie down on your back in a warm and comfortable place; a cushioned mat would be a nice choice. Close your eyes and become sensitive to the rising and falling of your midsection as you breathe diaphragmatically. Shift your awareness to the different spots where your body touches the mat, including your elbows, heels, head, back, and hamstrings. Then feel the entirety of the skin that envelops your body. When you are focused and ready, become aware of your toes, first your right and then your left. Feel the breathing go in and out of your toes; as you experience this, move to your arches, heels, ankles, calves, knees, thighs, pelvic region, stomach, chest, right and left upper arms, elbows, wrists, and fingers. As you feel the breathing, notice the tension in each of the areas and stay with that part of the body until the tension disappears or is significantly reduced. It will feel almost like your body is on a billowy cloud. Finish by feeling your shoulders, neck, and head, especially your cheeks, jaws, and forehead. And don't forget to include the back of your head. As you finish, imagine the air from your body exiting through an imaginary blowhole in the very top of your head. With this image, your body scan is complete. You will feel relaxed, comfortable, focused, and more empowered because you are more mindful and in control.

Take Yourself (Not Too) Seriously

Find the ironic humor that is a part of the search. You don't have to constantly show your pain and distress to be taken seriously. At pain clinics, patients are encouraged to keep their pain to themselves. Otherwise they develop a "pain" personality. Avoid the pain personality—don't discuss your unhappiness too frequently.

Be a Joy to Be Around

The more joyful you are, the more people will gravitate to you. The more they gravitate to you, the more they will want to help. If you get advice from people, don't tell them how you've tried their suggestion and it failed. Learn to listen without judging. Appreciate the ideas and contributions of others. If you need to complain, do it with just one person. It's best to pick someone who you pay to listen to your complaints; that way you won't burn out your support group. People in the job search are often egocentric and self-absorbed. Try to focus upon the interests of others to draw you away from that tendency.

Try Something Risky but Fun

There are elements of your search that are probably so horrible that they can be humorous in a sad sort of way. You know how a basset hound looks. It appears to be so troubled that it's funny. Take some of the more gruesome experiences you are having in your search and turn them into a three- to five-minute stand-up comedy club routine for yourself. You may find that this alleviates your stress while it amuses you. If you feel like taking a big risk, go to a local comedy club on an open mike night and try the routine. You never know what new opportunities this will bring to you. Who in the audience might help you? Could it be that the routine will also help your stage fright during future interviews? That's the beauty of a creative search technique. You never quite know what you are going to get. In your journal, enumerate the five most horrendous experiences in your search so far.

Don't Whine

Be clear and honest about what you are capable of doing. Whining is not going to help you solve your problem. If you whine a lot, you will get used to it and may even start doing it in interviews. You need to remain cordial and positive.

Keep Your Relationships Spirited and Intact

This is among the last suggestions here, but it could be the first. As you focus upon yourself, you may have a tendency to forget about the people who are the most important to you. Today professional firms and corporations are heeding the advice of experts and trying to get employees to plan a life with their families. Exhausting yourself and destroying your personal relationships is debilitating. There's no need for it, when prioritizing activities with your family is such a simple way to keep your most important support service intact.

Humor Is Necessary for Health

Give yourself a strong daily dose of it. Ever since the publication of Norman Cousins' *Anatomy of an Illness*, we've been aware of the health benefits of humor. Laughter increases your heart rate, stimulates your circulation, and helps to improve your muscle tone. It also helps to release endorphins and acts like a pain reliever. You will even discover that it keeps you alert and aids in memory.

Make Your Job-Search Office a Sanctuary

Add materials to it that show you count. Pictures, plaques, and letters are good places to start. Your office should be a room that cuddles you and makes you feel good. You need a place that reminds you that you're a valuable person who makes a difference in the world.

Be Sure to Play

Play activities can be spirited and can give you a sense of freedom. According to Diane Ackerman's new book *Deep Play* (1999), play activity is our brain's favorite way of learning. She also believes that play allows us to feel that we are whole people. Play creates a new way of thinking about life, with rules and order that are different from the rest of our job search and our everyday rhythms and expectations.

These suggestions are all ways to begin to changing your life patterns while you engage in your search. You probably won't try all of them, but hopefully you will find them intriguing. They will do more for your search—and for your continuing health—than you might think.

11 | I Still Can't Get a Job . . . So What Do I Do Now?

Don't worry about me—I have breathed the vivifying air of failure many times.

—Samuel Beckett

Take a Step Back

This is a time for reflection and evaluation. If you haven't gotten any job offers (or at least nibbles) from employers since you've started reading this book, then you need to do something different. Likewise, if you still feel some degree of emotional blockage, you need to take a more directed approach to free yourself up. Don't succumb to the unfortunate temptation to take anything that's available just to get a job or return to work.

A few years ago, professor Peggy Smith, my colleague at San Francisco State University, described mental illness by paraphrasing something that Einstein had said, years earlier. "Mental illness exists when you try the same set of ineffective behaviors over and over to solve a problem, being fully aware that none of them work. And you continue to try to solve the problem that way regardless." I added to her idea the notion that mental health, then, reflects the capacity to make measured changes in your approach when necessary. To be radically concise, I think that you can probably define mental health in one word: flexibility.

So if you have found that nothing that you are doing has worked very well, then you need to be flexible and make some changes—possibly even some pretty drastic ones. There is a lot of uncomfortable uncertainty in the work world. So, if you've spent a relatively short time engaged in your job search, you probably still don't have a clear idea about what might befall you.

Let's begin with a simple, straightforward approach. If you find that you're not getting answers about your search that are helpful and move you forward, then maybe you're asking the wrong questions. Or, maybe there aren't clear answers to your particular questions. Depending upon your field, even career experts don't have all of the answers.

Early in the book, I put forth eight career transition rules. Let's use them to get a handle on your situation. How well have you been able to follow them? Did you find them helpful or annoying? Try to make sure you have answers to the following questions.

Rule #1

Have you accepted the instability in the career world around you? Are you able to refrain from blaming yourself for your predicament? How well are you handling the uncertainty of the search?

Expect a significant degree of personal and work-related uncertainty throughout this process. But don't obsess about the uncertainty—it's a gargantuan waste of your time. And while you are recontemplating the instability and uncertainty of the job market, don't try to find external reasons why your search is failing. You need to draw away from issues that force you to ask questions like, "Why is this happening to me?" Instead, take an approach to your life changes that is akin to asking, "What am I going to do to handle this or make it better?" In times of both expansion and recession in the United States economy, I have worked with people who have been able to capture truly wonderful positions for themselves. Your creation of a suitable career path is not blocked by external sources. They may hinder you or cost you some time, money, and aggravation, but they are not the reasons for your difficult search.

Look around you. Mergers and acquisitions, a project-driven economy, low unemployment rates but high layoffs, outsourcing activities, and part-time employment are facts. They characterize the uncertainty of today's work world. But, in spite of these uncertain times, people are getting work. There are signs all over the place saying, "We will hire you." In certain areas like the Silicon Valley in California, firms can't fill openings. There are not enough available, qualified workers for certain jobs.

Sure, that may not be the case in your place or job arena, but there are jobs available. Why are they not available in your field? Maybe they are under a different name or title. Or maybe your fears of rejection keep you from making an attempt at application. If your fears are inhibiting you, then confront your fears, now, before moving any further along your career trajectory. Try rereading the chapter about fear and anxiety.

What should you do to locate positions that seem difficult to find? I would begin by looking at competing companies in your field, as well as companies that are competing with each other for market share. Regardless of your field, awareness of the competition can help you to determine how qualified you really are. I notice that whenever I am at a flea market or a sidewalk art show, vendors and street artists are always checking out what the others are doing. They're making themselves continuously aware of a changing marketplace, knowing that demand for their goods can change overnight.

This current level of business competition and instability has generated fabulous new opportunities for creative job intervention. Read some of the stories in newspapers and trade journals about companies that compete with each other. If you recall what your former company did, explore what others are doing that is similar. It is possible to go to a competing company and tell them that you have some knowledge that they might be interested in. If you can determine that you know how a particular facility operates, then try to get a "promotional" interview. Try out for a new company without the company necessarily knowing that you're trying out.

There are lots of places where you see this happening. Political consultants often go to the highest bidder. Some can put together a campaign for a person or an issue and then later switch issues or allegiances. In the California Faculty Association (CFA), one of the largest professorial unions in the United States, there are currently labor representatives who worked at an earlier time for the rival United Professors of California. These officials were out of a job when the CFA took over the contract bargaining for the California State University faculty. Instead of looking for jobs in other parts of the labor sector, many of them applied to work for the new union. They were well aware that the newly massive collective bargaining responsibilities would necessitate more staff. And, because they had been rivals, the old combatants were aware of what each side was up to. They had already demonstrated a sound track record. They had good contacts. Then they had to eat a little crow and apply for work. Many of these "turncoats" are still successful employees of the CFA.

Rule #2

Are you using the people around you? Do you stay in touch with people, especially those who can help you?

A cardinal rule of the search is that this is a group effort, a team sport. If you're trying to do it by yourself, you know that it's lonely, frustrating, and depressing. Although I have emphasized that real success in this business will be greatly enhanced by having a strong support network, most of the people I have had as career-counseling clients do not keep up these contacts. For some, no amount of encouragement seems to change their behavior. They tend to use me as their sole source of support. But I am only one person with one set of information, and I have my own biases, prejudices, and judgments.

You not only need to enlist group support, you need to make commitments to these supporters, like with weight-loss or smoking-cessation programs. There is no strength in your independence. It's a sad day indeed when you have burned out the people who can help you the most—at least with emotional support—by not giving them some relief. I've seen far too many relationships break up because the job changer's sole source of support was their life partner.

Rule #3

Are you using the resources around you? You can go back and reexamine a checklist of your outside resources. Are you "out there" being visible and present? Or are you holed up, hunkered down, and awaiting your demise?

By listening to what has been said already, evaluate yourself here. Have you gone to any meetings, schools, churches, synagogues, or other spiritual retreats? What about professional meetings, the chamber of commerce, the unemployment office? Like advertising on radio, television, or the Internet, you need to go, over and over again.

Take on a more cyclical approach, if you haven't already. People don't place an advertisement once. You don't hear a commercial jingle on the radio once. You hear it over and over, until it sinks in. And you know that more than one billboard, even a well-placed one, is used to promote a product. Yes, it is difficult and embarrassing, but you need to suck it up and be in places where there are resources and where you can meet with people for both support and information.

When you're out of work, you also have the time to take on a volunteer position, whether it is with a local PTSA, civic organization, political campaign office, charitable foundation, or sports team. Consider not just joining but being a leader. Educational and service organizations are always eager for people to support them this way.

When my children were little, I was amazed at how many new referrals would come to me because of the network I established in one highly visible position, as a soccer dad. By serving on a soccer membership committee or social committee, I was able to meet or be in contact with almost everyone in the league. Inevitably that would lead to, "So, what is it that you do?"

Finally, have you put some effort into seeking out the virtual classroom idea? Are there learning opportunities that you could take advantage of, but have yet to attempt? Even if you don't enroll in any classes, you should at least try to explore what is available.

Rule #4

Are you using your imagination? How truly creative have you been?

Are you still barking up the same tree, or have you expanded your notion of where you can go from here? If the positions that you're pursuing are the same type that you left, then you haven't put enough energy into the more creative sides of your personality. My own students, seeking to enter the counseling field, address this issue all the time.

The counseling field is becoming very competitive, and it demands a lot of creativity and flexibility in your thoughts about how you're going to help people. Potential counselors continue to enter our program (one of the largest in California), and the field in general without hesitation. As competitive as the field is, the vast majority of our graduates have developed satisfying counseling careers by using the portfolio approach. They may have an anchor job and then see five to eight clients on a part-time basis.

Plan B

As a bridge between rules four and five, if you have not already done so, choose a "plan B"—an alternative to what you're trying to achieve for yourself. The plan should be used in emergencies. I like to think of plan B as a short-term solution. To me it is like having a radiator leak in your car, but no extra money to fix the leak. A stopgap measure would be to buy an inexpensive container of liquid "Stop Leak" at an auto parts store. This solution can buy you a bit of time, but it is not a permanent solution. It is only plan B.

Plan B can make you feel somewhat more empowered than you feel right now. It is a good practice to create one for any minor or major crisis that is affecting your direction or path. Plan B involves the following activities:

- Brainstorming short-term possibilities (plan B) with others
- Retooling or reeducating yourself through adult or continuing education
- Checking market possibilities
- Developing a new marketing campaign
- Reviewing plan B with the original brainstorming group
- Implementing plan B
- Setting limits to plan B

Henrietta had been an interior designer for thirteen years when her design company merged with another. She was let go without any severance package and only four weeks' pay. The design market was competitive, and while she knew she was going to stay in it, she needed some time to market herself to others or to consider opening up her own shop. She knew that it could take a year for her to get this work.

When Henrietta and I worked together, she decided that her best plan B would be to take a thirty-day crash course in real estate sales, pass the exams for a license, and use her knowledge of interiors to help her segue into the higher-end real estate market in the San Francisco Bay Area. She lived and worked in the Silicon Valley, so she thought that was a good place to focus her efforts. She also felt this would be a chance to meet potential interior design clients. She could help them with design questions and refer them to other designers in the area. That information would eventually help her decide whether or not she should go back into interior design as a solo practitioner or with another firm.

This is an excellent example of a plan B. It is certainly not her first choice, but it does use her artistic, selling, marketing, and client-centered skills. It keeps her in contact with her field of specialization. It can be done quickly and is a good stopgap measure to keep her empowered while she decides how to reenter the interior design field. She found that some of the new information from the real estate classes could be used in both real estate and in interior design.

I have had other clients attend a thirty-day bartending class to learn this trade so that they could work at night while they searched for other jobs during the day. The plan B kept them highly active and connected to other people who could eventually be a part of their client base in a different job.

Rule #5

Are you rethinking your employment goals?

If you're out of work or contemplating change, then focus upon the CHANGE. Keep it in the forefront and remain aware that it is demanding and time consuming. This period is best used to consider alternatives to what you can do with your life's work. Pay heed to current events. By following some of the exercises in the book and developing your divergent thinking, you should have come up with twenty different potential career paths for yourself. If that is not the case, then go back to the earliest chapters and practice generating those kinds of ideas. We are at a wonderful time in our nation's vocational history, where we are witness to an explosion in new industries. Where can you play a role here? If you can't come up with ideas, then you need a trifle more effort and perhaps a class or two in continuing education to expand the possibilities.

Have you tried new ways of getting yourself known?

There are new ways of publicizing and advertising yourself. Perhaps the new model for today is to offer something for free initially; then when people become dependent on it, it has some worth and can be sold. Some Internet providers allow you to try a new game, but after a while you have to pay to join up. Hotmail began as a free e-mail service. But with every e-mail message that was sent out, Hotmail also sent along a little ad. So, if you had an e-mail account with Hotmail, you were, perhaps unknowingly, one of its salespeople. Hotmail spent very little money on advertising, but in a short period of time it had thirty million users. It has been sold to Microsoft for over $400 million. These marketing schemes could serve as models for your own new strategy.

Finally, if you want to look at creative, although sometimes out-rageous, marketing schemes, look at your current phone bill. Whether it's a wired or wireless bill, it is truly amazing what you have been convinced that you need.

While taking a discerning look at your employment goals, look again at your goal setting and time management throughout the search. Are you sure of your priorities? Is that reflected in your behavior and time management?

You want to be quite clear that you understand your goals and your objectives and that you are planning your minutes, days, and hours with these in mind. Make sure that you have created some kind of basic structure for your search. Write that structure out on the computer or on butcher paper if you have to.

Be conscious of how you use your unstructured time. If you find that it's used mostly for daydreaming and obsessing, then it's probably not being used very wisely. That's not to say that you can never daydream and obsess—just put limits on it and see it as an escape behavior. There are much more luxurious escape behaviors that are not so wasteful.

When I was writing my dissertation in graduate school, I found that during some of the more demanding and psychometrically sophisticated parts, I had a difficult time concentrating. I wanted to escape from the activity that I occasionally found aversive. What I did rather than daydream was to play solitaire. I would reinforce my own productive behavior by giving myself ten minutes each hour to play solitaire. By doing that I didn't feel like a victim, didn't obsess, and returned to my work feeling somewhat less foggy and more refreshed.

If you find that managing your time is difficult and not related to your goals, tell yourself each morning, noon, and night not to worry about the small stuff. Then remind yourself that everything unrelated to your search is small stuff.

Rule #6

Have you become panicky?

If that is a problem, what effect is the panic having? Is it spur-ring you forward or stifling your creative efforts? Most people who experience panic have a very difficult time hearing anything that is positive about themselves or the search. If you're in a panic now, or if you have experienced moments of panic during the search, you need to try two things. First, don't give negative and sarcastic responses to those who are trying to help you. If you do that even once, you'll turn off potentially important resources.

Second, if you're in the midst of panic, engage only in simple tasks that are easily achievable. And make sure that you do them. If you can go into a simple task with a beginning, middle, and end, it will give you the feeling of accomplishment and a sense of closure on at least one activity. You will gain nothing from overstimulating yourself with a lot of disorganized behavior. But that is just what people in a panic do.

Try to determine the nature of your panic. If it is related to not meeting specific expectations that you have set for yourself, then it might be most useful to change the expectations that you hold. If you have expectations for accomplishing a particular number of subgoals in a limited amount of time, it could be that you have just underestimated how long everything is going to take. Simply change the expectations.

Keep in mind that your feelings of panic can be challenged. You can increase your relaxation exercise program, engage in more vigorous physical activity, create more positive images of yourself, or meditate. This is not simple pop psychology. These methods really do work, if you employ them as a part of your search efforts.

Rule #7

Are you minimizing your stress level? Do you feel a sense of personal or vocational shame that you can't seem to get it together to get the job that you want?

Feelings of shame and humiliation are often one of the most demanding parts of the search. It is the part that keeps you fearful, anxious, depressed, obsessive, and of course, stressed out. But its biggest threat to your search is that it keeps you from telling more and more people that you need some help. Your embarrassment shuts you down. Sure, the process is difficult, but you need to be able to take something positive from it. Keep the excitement of possibilities at the forefront.

As a psychologist, I have come to know that virtually everyone has problems; some people just prefer to talk about them privately with a psychologist rather than with friends, family, or other cohorts. I suppose that's good for me because it's how I make a living. But I think that a lot of personal and career-related issues could be solved more easily if people would let go of their shame and try to talk to friends, colleagues, and relatives.

Look at another question in this category. Are you avoiding negative self-talk? All the internal dialogue you have with yourself should be reassuring and encouraging, not self-deprecating. This is not easy to do, but it can profoundly affect your approach. Be sure you don't travel into monotonous negativity. The best way to do that is to keep your internal dialogue directed toward positive thoughts and assessments about yourself. By referring to yourself as "dumb and dumber," you're going to end up "dumb and getting dumber." Purge the "stupid," "idiot," "failure" words from your vocabulary. It is most important at the difficult times of your search.

Using other types of global assessments—like telling yourself that nothing is working—are also not going to help you. If you're talking to yourself this way, then ask better questions. Start by listing all the parts of the job search that have failed. Once you've done this, then try to engage in behavior that is diametrically opposed to these activities. If you know what doesn't work, then the opposite of that may work. And whenever possible, avoid repeating activities that you know are going to fail.

After an initial period of excitement, have your activities and motivation slowed down, leveled off, or stopped?

This is exactly what happens with most job seekers. They are at first shocked that they'll have to engage in or develop a search plan. But after a few visits with me or another counselor, they are excited by the prospects of change and are envisioning new opportunities. Counselors have new ideas, are good motivators, and are certainly a source of support. But after a month or so, activity seems to wane among the seekers. The enthusiasm is gone and the fears and stress of the search settle in.

Sometimes the job-seeking client gets angry at the counselor because the search turned out to be more difficult than expected. The counselor was supposed to make it easier, but it doesn't seem to be happening that way. One of the things that has probably happened is that the job seeker was excited about trying something different, but tended to put most of their effort into finding a position that was similar to the one they had held previously. The initial excitement and newness faded quickly and they went back to pursuing that which was most familiar. It's dreadfully discouraging to lose hope, and that is exactly what happens here.

The search is a lot of hard work with a lot of disappointments. But it is here that you need to find different ways of enlisting your support network. Note how I, as a counselor or career psychologist, was not enough support for my own clients. And as much as I reminded them that they needed more support than simply mine, they had a hard time believing that they needed more than I had to offer.

Rule #8

Are you sure that this is the best time for you to be in a job search? You might ask this same question with a slightly different frame. Have you let go completely of your former job? Sometimes people need time and space away from their former relationships or work roles prior to beginning a new venture. It's possible you need to gain some distance.

Don't romanticize your old job. It's in the past. If you are engaging in dreamy reveries about your old workplace, then maybe you haven't moved on emotionally. Since people tend to only remember the good things, at the moment try to recall some that were not so good. Most workers have more than a few gripes about their old job. You undoubtedly had a few yourself. Remembering them can help you move on.

Do you know what is coming easily to you and what isn't? If you feel that nothing is working, you also need to rethink the nature of the search. What parts of it are you good at? What parts of it seem too demanding? I am never convinced that "nothing" is working in a job search. Frankly, quite a number of things are usually "working," you just haven't received a job offer. For example, maybe you've done an excellent job at self-appraisal, but you don't sparkle at interviewing. Thus you are proficient at knowing what you want, you just have trouble getting people to appreciate you. If this is the case, you'll need to either practice and refine what you're doing or try a different tactic altogether. You may need to meet with some of your support network to develop a new strategy. It's not that your job search isn't working—it's just that you need to improve some specific job-search skills.

You could also be someone who is just not marketing yourself appropriately. You know what you want and you interview well, but you can't seem to get people to respond to your marketing and advertising plan. It's like you have a great product that nobody wants to try. What would you do as a salesperson if your fabulous product just wouldn't sell?

Maybe your product could have different uses. Maybe it could be adapted to environments that have yet to be considered. Remember napalm? It started out as a weed killer. Can you believe what it ended up being famous for? How do you get your car windows clean? Click and Clack of *Car Talk* on PBS recommend using old

newspapers to wash your car windows. Now, I can't recall any news-
print company selling its product as car-window-wash material.

In a similar vein, try to consider yourself as adaptable and useful to many organizations. Try to find how your particular set of
skills and interests can fit into arenas that you've never considered
before. Take some of what you have learned about yourself and people in general during the search and add it to your campaign.

As your search evolves, ask yourself what part of the search
campaign you need to improve. Identify weak links. Questions can
take on a simple format like, "Where can I better manage my time?"
"What new people can I meet?"

The above questions are all designed to help you keep a simple,
practical framework in mind as you pursue the search. You have to
find a place within you to keep the faith in yourself and in the activities that are a part of the search. Some of this is simply that "you've
got to believe." In our country, members of religious organizations
are unflinching in their religious faith, even in the sight of terrible
tragedies. Whether it is storms, bombings, shootings, riots, or dis-
eases like AIDS and HIV, people maintain their faith. They will comment that there is some purpose to what is happening and that we
just may not be able to understand what it is.

I suppose that in some way you can liken these tragic experiences to the job search. With all of the difficulty around you during
your search, you need to believe that a greater good will come of it.
Something good usually does! In all of my years of counseling people
through the job-change process, I believe that over 80 percent of the
job changers actually ended up with something that was *better* suited
for them. This could have been in salary, benefits, or greater happiness and fulfillment. Whatever the final result, it was better than
what they had before. That may not feel so good to you right now in
the midst of turmoil, but try to keep it in mind.

A Few Final Thoughts

Throughout the book, I've tried to focus upon you, the job seeker,
with a series of ideas and remedies to help you with the job search.
With all of this, try to keep the search in perspective. Here are a few
final thoughts.

Your search is an experience. You can make it just as pleasant or
as unpleasant as you want. That is your choice. I've worked with
many people who found that their search was in fact a very uplifting
experience, a chance for new discovery and an opportunity for life
change. Others have been beaten down and depressed by it. Still

others have become enraged during it. The emotional experience you have in your search is up to you.

I've also worked with people who were fully employed and thought by everyone to be very successful, but who were dreadfully unhappy. I have known others in what you might perceive as average jobs who felt completely fulfilled by what they were doing in both work and leisure. Again, it's up to you.

I believe that there is an opportunity with a job search to have a major impact on your life and your thinking. You have the choice to be mindful and conscious of what you are doing. You have the opportunity to be present with yourself and your thoughts. How you experience your job search or even your job is contingent on the perspective you choose. If, even in this most demanding time, you can experience peacefulness and opportunity and empowerment, then you have created for yourself the chance to be truly outstanding in this search, the next one, and the rest of your life.

Resources

Ackerman, D. 1999. *Deep Play*. New York: Random House.

Bandura, A. 1977. Self-Efficacy: Toward a Unifying Theory of Behavioral Change. *Psychology Review* 84:191–215.

Benson, H. 1975. *The Relaxation Response*. New York: Morrow.

Betz, N. 1992. Counseling Uses of Career Self-Efficacy Theory. *The Career Development Quarterly* 41:22–26.

Bolles, R. N. 1999. What Do You Have to Offer the World? *San Francisco Examiner*, March 21, J–3.

Bowlby, J. 1980. *Loss, Sadness, and Depression*. New York: Basic Books.

Butler, J., and R. Baumeister. 1998. The Trouble with Friendly Faces: Skilled Performance with a Supportive Attitude. *Journal of Personality and Social Psychology* 75:1213–1230.

Cottle, T. 1992. When You Stop You Die. *Commonweal*, June 19, 16.

Gelatt, H. B. 1989. Positive Uncertainty: A New Decision-Making Framework for Counseling. *Journal of Counseling Psychology* 36: 252–256.

Goleman, D. 1995. *Emotional Intelligence*. New York: Ballantine.

Hanh, T. N. 1987. *Being Peace*. Berkeley, Calif.: Parallax Press.

Holmes, T. H., and R. H. Rahe. 1967. The Social Readjustment Rating Scale. *Journal of Psychosomatic Research* 11:213–218.

Jepson, D. A. 1993. Career as Story. Unpublished paper presented at the American Counseling Association Convention, Atlanta.

Krumboltz, J. D. 1991. *Manual for the Career Beliefs Inventory.* Palo Alto, Calif.: Consulting Psychologists Press.

Kübler-Ross, E. 1969. *On Death and Dying.* New York: Ballantine.

Kwatinetz, D. 1998. What's Your Real Job? *Newsweek,* October 12, 16.

Maslach, C., and S. Jackson. 1981. *The Maslach Burnout Inventory.* Palo Alto, Calif.: Consulting Psychologists Press.

Maslow, A. H. 1954. *Toward a Psychology of Being.* New York: Van Nostrand Reinhold.

Miller, W., and M. Seligman. 1976. Learned Helplessness, Depression, and the Perception of Reinforcement. *Behavior Research and Therapy* 14:7–17.

Mroczek, D., and C.M. Kolarz. 1998. The Effect of Age on Positive and Negative Affect: A Developmental Perspective on Happiness. *Journal of Personality and Social Psychology* 75:1333–1349.

Robinson, B. 1989. *Work Addiction.* Deerfield Beach, Fl.: Health Communications.

Sinton, P. 1999. A Nose for Business. *San Francisco Chronicle,* March 31, B1-3.

Tolchin, S. 1996. *The Angry American.* Boulder, Colo.: Westview Press/HarperCollins.

Tribole, E. 1998. *Stealth Health.* New York: Viking-Penguin.

Workman, B. 1999. Stanford Scientist's Second Life Making Violins. *San Francisco Chronicle,* April 1, A19.

Appendix: Web Sites

Career Search

www.careermosaic.com
www.careercentral.com
www.careerpath.com
www.monster.com

Career Coaches

www.coachfederation.org
www.mentorcoach.com (for a free newsletter)

Distance Learning

www.OnlineLearning.net (UCLA Extension)

Female Entrepreneurs

www.independentmeans.com

Government Jobs

www.dol.gov

Nutrition and Health

www.pueblo.gsa.gov/food.htm

Sites for Seniors

www.seniornet.org
www.thirdage.com
www.aarp.org
www.senior.com

Venture Capital

Venture Capital Resource Library: www.vfinance.com
National Venture Capital Association: www.nvca.com
Small Business Administration: www.sba.gov

More New Harbinger Titles

MAKING HOPE HAPPEN

A powerful program shows you how to break old self-defeating habits, overcome roadblocks, and find new routes to your goals.
Item HOPE $14.95

BEING, BELONGING, DOING

Thoughtful self-discovery exercises help you reevaluate priorities and explore practical ways of keeping the crucial components of your life integrated and in balance.   *Item BBD$10.95*

FACING 30

Yes, there is life after 29. This wry and enlightening book takes on the big career and personal issues and helps to ease women into their thirties with their humor and hope intact.   *Item F30 $12.95*

WORKING ANGER

A step-by-step program designed to help anyone who has had trouble dealing with their own anger or other people's anger at work.
Item WA $12.95

LIVING WITHOUT PROCRASTINATION

Provides effective techniques for unlearning counter-productive habits, changing paralyzing beliefs and attitudes, developing task-directed thinking, and attaining a new sense of purposefulness.   *Item LWP $12.95*

DON'T TAKE IT PERSONALLY

Shows you how to depersonalize your responses to rejection, establish boundaries that protect you from hurt, and develop a new sense of self-acceptance and self-confidence.   *Item DOTA $12.95*

Call **toll-free 1-800-748-6273** to order. Have your Visa or Mastercard number ready. Or send a check for the titles you want to New Harbinger Publications, 5674 Shattuck Avenue, Oakland, CA 94609. Include $3.80 for the first book and 75¢ for each additional book to cover shipping and handling. (California residents please include appropriate sales tax.) Allow four to six weeks for delivery.

Prices subject to change without notice.

Some Other New Harbinger Self-Help Titles